The Complete Idiot's Reference Card

Ten Smart Ways to Invest in Mutual Funds

1. **Zero in on your investment goals.** Understand what you want to accomplish before you get involved with mutual funds. Are you saving for your child's future college education or your retirement? Are you looking for a temporary place to park your cash so you can earn more than a bank account?

2. **Understand your tolerance for risk before you invest.** Determine whether you are an aggressive, moderate, conservative, or least-risk investor. Then, you can make the right investment decision.

3. **Invest in mutual funds for the long term.** You need to invest through thick and thin. Because you can lose when you invest in mutual funds, you need time to make back any losses. Invest for a minimum of five years.

4. **Pay yourself first. Invest regularly.** That way, you'll buy more shares of your fund when the price is down. Over the long term, you build your wealth.

5. **Reinvest any income you get from your fund to buy more shares.** Your profits will pile up over the years.

6. **Diversify. Own different types of mutual funds, such as stock, bond, and money funds.** One type of mutual fund will zig while the other zags. Losses in one fund can be offset by gains in another.

7. **Compare fund fees, charges, and commissions before you invest.** Make your money work for you, not your stockbroker. Check the cost of several funds before you plunk down your cash.

8. **Investigate before you invest. Do your homework.** Compare the performance, risks, investment objectives, and costs of several funds before you invest. That way, you're sure to find the best deal.

9. **Open an IRA retirement savings account.** You'll invest for the long haul, and your profits will grow tax-deferred until you retire.

10. **Make sure you've taken care of your insurance needs before you invest in mutual funds**. Do you have adequate life insurance? Do you have disability insurance coverage to protect your family in the event of an untimely death? If not, consider obtaining life and disability insurance coverage first. Then, start a mutual fund investment program.

Five Ways to Mutual Fund Profits

1. **Invest in no-load mutual funds.** These funds charge no commissions, so 100 percent of your money is invested in the fund of your choice.

2. **Invest in common stock mutual funds for long-term growth.** Over the past 30 years, the average diversified common stock fund grew at an 11 percent annual rate.

3. **Take advantage of mutual fund families that have a wide variety of funds to pick**. As your financial condition or needs change, you can find the fund that's right for you.

4. **Invest early and often.** Don't procrastinate. If you're investing annually, make your investment at the beginning of each year. Investing monthly? Do it at the start of each month. That way, your money will grow faster and longer over the years.

5. **Invest to beat the tax man.** If you avoid paying Uncle Sam taxes on your investment earnings, you have more money in your pocket. Consider tax-free bond and money funds if you pay at least 28 percent of your income to the IRS.

Mutual Fund Risk/Reward Chart

Investor Risk Level/Objective	Type of Fund	Risk/Reward
	Stock Funds	
Speculative	Precious metals	Highest/Big gains
Speculative	Most sector	Higher/Big gains
Aggressive	Aggressive growth	High/Maximum capital growth
Aggressive	International growth	High/Maximum capital growth
Aggressive	Small company	High/Maximum capital growth
Aggressive	Growth	High/Long-term growth
Moderate	Growth and income	Moderate/Growth plus income
Moderate	Equity income	Low-moderate/Income plus growth
Conservative	Income	Lower/Long-term income
Conservative	Utility	Lower/Long-term income
Conservative	Balanced	Lower/Income plus growth
	Bond Funds	
Aggressive	High-yield	High/High income
Aggressive	Long-term government	High/Income
Aggressive	Long-term tax-free	High/Income
Aggressive	International	High/Income
Moderate	Intermediate-term	Moderate/Income
Moderate	Intermediate tax-free	Moderate/Income
Conservative	Short-term	Lower/Income and less risk
Conservative	Short-term tax-free	Lower/Income and less risk
	Other Funds	
Safety-minded	Money market	Lowest/Income and least risk

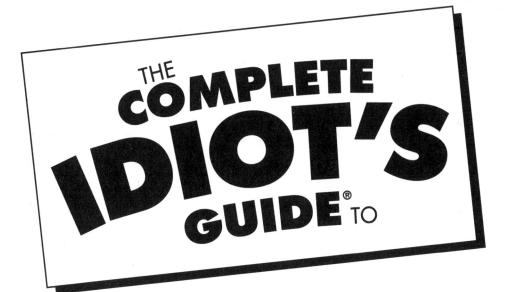

Making Money
with Mutual Funds
Second Edition

by Alan Lavine and Gail Liberman

alpha
books

A Division of Macmillan General Reference
A Simon & Schuster Macmillan Company
1633 Broadway, New York, NY 10019

Praise for the first edition of the Complete Idiot's Guide to Making Money with Mutual Funds:

"I want everyone to go out and buy this book!"
—Jim Barry, host of PBS-TV's Financial Freedom

"Good advice."
—Myron Kandel, CNN Moneyline and CNNfn

"A book worth reading. Al and Gail are two of the most knowledgeable experts on mutual funds."
—Charles DeRose, host of the Charles DeRose Financial Advisor Show, United Stations Radio Network

"*The Complete Idiot's Guide to Making Money With Mutual Funds* ranks as one of my favorite mutual fund books."
—Gerald Perritt, Ph.D., author of *Mutual Fund Almanac*

"This book's light style eases the burden of learning about mutual funds for beginners, and offers ideas useful even for families with lots of mutual fund know-how."
—*Mutual Funds* magazine

"This friendly guide gives readers the information and advice they need and want, in an easy-to-understand, easy-to-enjoy format. In a lighthearted, witty, and humorous style, it shows readers how to read a prospectus, where to find no-load funds and more."
—Amazon.com

"A great help in making informed investment decisions."
—Marla Brill, Fundsinteractive.com

"Great book."
—Tony Sagami of Investorsquare.com

"Idiot and expert alike can benefit from what is without argument the most comprehensive yet fun book about mutual funds."
—Robert Powell, editor-in-chief, *Mutual Fund Market News*

To Gail Liberman's late grandparents: Ruth Gold, who taught her how to read, and Jacob Gold, who taught her how to save

©1998 Alan Lavine and Gail Liberman

Macmillan Publishing books may be purchased for business or sales promotional use. For information please write: Special Markets Department, Macmillan Publishing USA, 1633 Broadway, New York, NY 10019.

International Standard Book Number: 0-02-862413-0
Library of Congress Catalog Card Number: 98-85700

00 99 98   8 7 6 5 4 3 2 1

Interpretation of the printing code: the rightmost number of the first series of numbers is the year of the book's printing; the rightmost number of the second series of numbers is the number of the book's printing. For example, a printing code of 98-1 shows that the first printing occurred in 1998.

Printed in the United States of America

Note: This publication contains the opinions and ideas of its author. It is intended to provide helpful and informative material on the subject matter covered. It is sold with the understanding that the authors and publisher are not engaged in rendering professional services in the book. If the reader requires personal assistance or advice, a competent professional should be consulted.

The authors and publisher specifically disclaim any responsibility for any liability, loss, injury, or risk, personal or otherwise, which is incurred as a consequence, directly or indirectly, of the use and application of any of the contents of this book.

ALPHA DEVELOPMENT TEAM

Publisher
Kathy Nebenhaus

Editorial Director
Gary M. Krebs

Managing Editor
Bob Shuman

Marketing Brand Manager
Felice Primeau

Senior Editor
Nancy Mikhail

Development Editors
Phil Kitchel
Jennifer Perillo
Amy Zavatto

Editorial Assistant
Maureen Horn

PRODUCTION TEAM

Production Editor
Donna K. Wright

Copy Editor
Kris Simmons

Cover Designer
Mike Freeland

Photo Editor
Richard H. Fox

Illustrator
Jody P. Schaeffer

Designer
Glenn Larsen

Indexer
Ginny Bess

Layout/Proofreading
Angela Calvert
Lisa Stumpf

Contents at a Glance

Contents

xi

Foreword

We're in the midst of a mutual fund revolution and, as with any revolution, there will be winners and losers. The winners will be those investors who take the time to learn about the opportunities—and the pitfalls—of mutual fund investing. Make no mistake about it, investing wisely and well in mutual funds is becoming more challenging with each passing year. Why? First, because investors have more choice. (New mutual funds are being introduced at a rate of more than one a day!) While more choice may seem like a good thing, it also creates more confusion. Second, investors are being bombarded with all sorts of advice on mutual fund investing, much of it biased. It's no wonder that so many investors end up investing their money inappropriately—either they pick the wrong funds, or they don't diversify their mutual fund investments adequately.

Alan Lavine and Gail Liberman have once again come to the rescue. Their new edition of *The Complete Idiot's Guide to Making Money with Mutual Funds* will not only guide you through the mutual fund investing maze, but it will also help you become an excellent fund investor.

Alan and Gail are uniquely qualified to be your mutual fund advisors. I have known them for many years and have always been impressed with their ability to transform the complexities of the mutual fund revolution into easy-to-understand strategies that investors of all financial means can profit from. You will soon become one of the many, many readers who have learned to take control of their fund investments and, hence, their financial future by following Alan's and Gail's expert and sensible guidance.

Many people are intimidated about investing in mutual funds. Let's face it, there are a lot of people in the financial services industry who would like you to believe that investing is complicated and the average Joe and Jane are simply incapable of making sensible investment decisions. Well, in this book you'll find out how straightforward sound fund investing can be. Beginning with their "10 Commandments of Mutual Fund Investing," Alan and Gail lead you step-by-step through the process of understanding the various kinds of mutual funds to selecting the right funds to meet your investment objectives to evaluating your fund holdings quickly and easily.

I particularly like their straightforward approach to putting together a diversified mutual fund portfolio. This is an area where many investors fall short. They don't pay sufficient attention to investment allocation because, frankly, the strategies aren't easy to explain and understand. But Alan and Gail have a gift for translating complicated—yet essential—investment concepts into language that everyone can use.

Whether you're new to mutual funds or are already an experienced fund investor, this up-to-date edition of *The Complete Idiot's Guide to Making Money with Mutual Funds* will help you make the most of your fund investments so that you can achieve your financial dreams—sooner rather than later.

—Jonathan D. Pond

Mutual Fund Commentator, Public Television's *Nightly Business Report*

In addition to his work as a mutual fund commentator, Jonathan Pond has hosted three public television specials on investing and personal financial planning.

Introduction

You've heard about mutual funds. Maybe you've read about them. Or you might know someone who has invested in them. Getting started is easier said than done, however. If you invest your hard-earned savings based on what your friends, neighbors, or that ultra-friendly stock broker or insurance salesman down the street say is hot, you're sure to get stung. In fact, you probably have friends who already are crying in their beer over their ill-fated investment decisions.

We whole-heartedly can relate to your need to avoid these scenarios. We know first-hand—both as mutual fund investors and as husband-wife journalists. We spent a combined 34 years with our fingers on the pulse of both the mutual fund and banking industries. For your benefit, we've also combined our marital temperaments of conservatism (fear) and aggressiveness (speculation) to present to you the complete unbiased story of how you can both win and lose at mutual fund investing. It is by assessing the pros and cons of the investments that you can determine what's right for you.

With this updated second edition of *The Complete Idiot's Guide to Making Money with Mutual Funds*, you easily can locate all the information you need—both before and long after you take your first venture into mutual funds. And once we help you determine whether mutual fund investing is right for you, we'll present you with quick and safe ways of managing your stash.

For your benefit, we've taken all the jargon out of investing and spelled things out in plain English so that learning to invest is as easy as learning to ride a bike. Consider this book our gift to you so that you can reap the most benefit possible out of your hard-earned money for both yourself and family. It's just a matter of doing a little homework, learning exactly how mutual funds work, and making your own decisions based only on sound financial planning and a little research—not on the word of somebody else looking to make a buck.

This book is a starting point. It will help you:

➤ Learn how mutual funds work and what they invest in

➤ Understand the stock and bond markets

➤ Find the mutual fund investment that's best for you

➤ Avoid losses

➤ Build your wealth long-term

➤ Invest for your child's college education

➤ Invest for retirement

> ➤ Manage your investments

> ➤ Save on taxes

> ➤ Deal with a bear market and much more.

How to Use This Book

The Complete Idiot's Guide to Making Money with Mutual Funds zeros in on all the crucial facts you need to know to invest in mutual funds. The important details about mutual funds are covered in five parts.

Part 1, "Meet the Mutual Funds," explains how mutual funds work. This section nails down the dos and don'ts of mutual fund investments and shows you how to develop a savings plan. You'll learn all about stocks and bonds, as well as the pluses and minuses of mutual fund investing. You'll also get a rundown of the different types of mutual funds and learn how to tell whether a fund is a winner or loser.

Part 2, "Getting Started," helps you discover exactly what types of investing you can handle without hitting the Maalox bottle. Then, you'll learn how to locate funds that are right for you. You'll also find out where to get mutual funds and how much you'll pay for them. You'll discover how to track down the best fund deals. You'll learn about the resources available to help you pick your mutual funds.

Part 3, "Zoning In on the Picks," gets to the nitty-gritty. You'll learn how money funds work and exactly how safe they are. You'll learn about the different types of bond funds available to investors and the risks they carry. Chapter 14, "Building Your Wealth with Stock Funds," looks at all the types of stock funds—aggressive, small company, growth, growth and income, and international—and what they invest in. You'll also learn about stock funds for special situations.

Part 4, "Quick and Easy Investment Plans," gives you time-saving tools to manage your money like a pro. This section reviews several easy-to-use investment strategies to build your wealth. You'll learn how to invest regularly so that you automatically buy fund shares at low prices. If you prefer to take your profits and run, you'll discover how to buy low and sell high. You'll learn how to diversify your portfolio to get the best returns with the least risk. You'll also find out a low-risk way to invest your retirement savings in mutual funds and beat the performance of the old bank account.

Part 5, "Mutual Fund Investing for Special Situations," reviews important issues you need to know when you invest in mutual funds. You'll learn how to cope with a bear market in Chapter 21, "Loaded for Bear: What to Do When the Stock Market Falls Out of Bed." In Chapter 22, "Taxes: To Pay or Not to Pay?," you'll learn the most painless ways to pay the tax man on your mutual fund profits. Chapter 23, "Saving for Important Life

Goals," shows how to determine the amount of money you'll need for your child's college education and your retirement. Because it's expected that many of us will live to see age 90, you need to know how to make your hard-earned money last!

Extras

We built a launch pad for you to get started with mutual funds. To make it as simple as flipping your car's ignition switch, *The Complete Idiot's Guide to Making Money with Mutual Funds* is chock full of tips to ensure that you have a successful trip into the world of mutual funds. Look for these elements in the book to point you in the right direction.

News You Can Use

This is your instant access to important news that can help you save and invest. You learn extra little details to make even better investment decisions.

Money Matters

Watch these potholes on the road to successful mutual fund investing! These tips tell you what to avoid so you can save money in the long run.

Technobabble

Want to speak the same language as the investment pros? No problem. It's all highlighted for you as a quick reference in these little boxes.

Hot Tip!

Hot tips help you invest. We cut through the red tape and tell you the wisest moves. You'll learn quickly the most profitable route to take on your mutual fund journey.

Acknowledgments

We'd like to thank the following people who helped us along the way. Special thanks to Jennifer Perillo, editor with Alpha Books, not only for making this book possible, but also for always taking time out of her busy schedule to respond!

We also would like to thank our editors at various publications for their support throughout the years. Robert K. Heady, founder of *Bank Rate Monitor*, brought us together in more ways than one. Also, a word of gratitude to the *Boston Herald* for running Alan Lavine's column for 16 years and giving him a forum to develop his mutual fund expertise. Special thanks to Mary Helen Gillespie, of the *Boston Herald*, who, as our wedding present, gave us our first husband-wife newspaper column together!

Thanks also go to Ted Bunker, *Boston Herald*, business editor; Evan Simonoff, editor of *Financial Planning Magazine*; Tom Siedell, editor of *Your Money*; John Wasik, editor of *Consumers Digest*; Susan Postlewaite, managing editor of the Miami, Fort Lauderdale, and Palm Beach *Daily Business Review*; and Charles DeRose, host of the "Financial Advisor" syndicated radio program.

Also, Robert Powell, editor-in-chief of *Dalbar Inc.*, for getting us off on the right foot with our first edition; Rick Telberg, editor of *Accounting Today*; Peter Philipps, managing editor of *NAPFA Advisor*; Joseph Thoma, former editor of Scripps-Howard's *FiftyPlus Lifestyles*; and Christy Heady, America Online's MoneyWhiz.

Gail Liberman would like to acknowledge all the folks at the Associated Press, UPI, the *Asbury Park Press*, and the *Courier Post* in New Jersey for launching her career. She'd also like to thank her husband, Alan Lavine, for his undying support and continuous education on the subject of mutual funds.

We'd also like to thank Alan Lavine's Mom, Doris Lavine, and Gail Liberman's parents, Si and Dorothy Liberman, for all their support.

Special Thanks to the Technical Reviewer

The Complete Idiot's Guide to Making Money with Mutual Funds, Second Edition, was reviewed by an expert who not only checked the historical accuracy of what you'll learn in this book, but also provided valuable insight to help ensure that this book tells you everything you need to know about successful mutual fund investing. Our special thanks are extended to Tony Sagami.

Part 1
Meet the Mutual Funds

Once you read this part of the book, you'll be richer than you are right now. After all, you've got to have money before you can invest in mutual funds, right?

In this part, you discover ways to come up with money you didn't know you had. You'll also learn what it means to become an investor.

You'll discover the advantages and disadvantages of mutual funds. There is a tremendous variety of mutual funds to choose right now. When you know what options are out there, you can zero in on the funds that are right for you.

Chapter 1

The Ten Commandments of Mutual Fund Investing

In This Chapter

➤ How mutual funds work

➤ Who runs the funds?

➤ How mutual funds are regulated

➤ Ten rules to live by

Let's face it. You have good reason to pick up this book. Everybody's buzzing about mutual funds these days.

One of every three American families now owns a mutual fund (or funds). More are discovering mutual funds through pension plans, which are offered by an increasing number of companies. Even life insurance companies offer sexy insurance policies that invest in mutual funds! Needless to say, a lot of people are becoming more familiar with these little investment chaps.

There's a good reason for this mad rush to mutual funds. The past five years have been a great time to invest: In fact, had you invested in certain mutual funds five years ago, chances are you would have more than doubled your money by now. With more than 6,800 mutual funds to pick from (8,000 to 9,000 if you add in their variations), investing in just one mutual fund can be a mind-boggling task. If you're like most people, you keep the bulk of your money in bank savings accounts because you're afraid you'll make the wrong move.

Fear no more. Whether you're just beginning to invest in mutual funds or you've already taken the plunge, a new world of investing is about to unfold. Once you know the ropes, mutual funds can be your ticket to a whole variety of money-making opportunities. This chapter introduces you to the world of mutual fund investing.

Welcome to the World of Investing

When you were younger, you probably had a piggy bank. You filled it up and took the next big step: You carted it to the bank and opened a savings account. You knew your savings account was safe. You couldn't lose money. Every once in a while (assuming you left your money in there), you'd notice it was growing in value.

With your savings account, you couldn't lose any money because it was federally insured. Interest rates on savings weren't bad. Up until the mid-1980s, they used to be 5.25 percent to 5.50 percent. Today, if you keep your money in a bank savings account, you get peanuts. Rates average about 2 percent. After taxes and inflation, what you're earning in your tried-and-true passbook savings account is zilch!

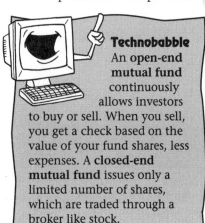

Technobabble
An **open-end mutual fund** continuously allows investors to buy or sell. When you sell, you get a check based on the value of your fund shares, less expenses. A **closed-end mutual fund** issues only a limited number of shares, which are traded through a broker like stock.

If you want to make more money, investing is about the only way to go. When you enter the world of investing, you're giving yourself a promotion. You're taking a more active role in building your wealth, and you stand to make more as a result. By putting your money in a mutual fund, you're also giving up some of the safety and security of your piggy bank and savings account. If you learn what makes mutual funds tick, however, you can make educated investment decisions that help your nest egg grow.

What Is a Mutual Fund and How Does It Work?

Think of a mutual fund as an investment company that pools the money of people just like you for one common reason, to make more. Not all pots of money are alike. It's up to you to select the right mutual fund for you based on your own needs.

Technobabble
The **investment advisor** is an organization hired by the mutual fund company to manage a mutual fund's investments. A **portfolio manager** is the professional who actually manages the fund.

With a mutual fund, you buy a portion of a variety of investments, including stocks and bonds. (We'll explain more about stocks and bonds in Chapter 3, "Investing: Your Options, Your Risks, Your Rewards.") Exactly how much money you make or lose in your mutual fund can change daily, as you'll learn in later chapters. It all depends on how much of the fund you own and how well your mix of investments performs. As Chapter 3 explains, owning a lot of different investments helps to protect you against losing money. If one investment in your mutual fund does poorly, you have a number of others to cushion the blow.

Now who in the heck has the time to do all this stock and bond picking? Not many of us, that's for sure. With a mutual fund, you're paying a team of professionals to be on your side. Each investment advisor of the fund or the portfolio manager has his or her own method of picking stocks and bonds. (We'll talk more about the professionals who run mutual funds later in this chapter.)

There are two types of mutual funds. The most common, which this book primarily discusses, are *open-end funds*. Open-end funds operate as a door. Money flows directly into the fund when investors buy and goes directly out when they sell. The other type is *closed-end funds*, which technically are not mutual funds. You'll learn about those in Chapter 16, "How Ya Doing?"

With a mutual fund, the big pool of money we talked about previously is managed by a company, which is frequently the organization that started the fund. This management company either serves as or hires the fund's *investment advisor*. The advisor employs a *portfolio manager* and his or her research staff to select investments for the mutual fund.

Technobabble
A **prospectus** is a legal disclosure document that spells out information you need to know to make investment decisions on a mutual fund or other security.

A **profile fund** is a simplified prospectus that briefly explains what you need to know about a mutual fund before you invest.

Mutual funds are subject to strict federal regulations. If you call an investment company, it is required to send you certain disclosures before you invest. It may choose to send you either a three- to six-page document, known as a *fund profile*, or its longer, more cumbersome parent—the *prospectus*. Regardless, no matter who you buy your mutual fund from, a prospectus must be sent to you upon confirmation of the sale.

We strongly urge you to ask for a prospectus up front. That's because it spells out in more detail the investment objectives of the fund, risks, fees, and other important information you really shouldn't be without before you fork over your hard-earned cash. You'll learn more about what's in these documents and what you should look for in Chapter 9, "Seeking a Second Opinion."

Generally, mutual funds continuously offer new shares to the public. (A share is a unit of ownership in the fund.) They also are required legally to buy back

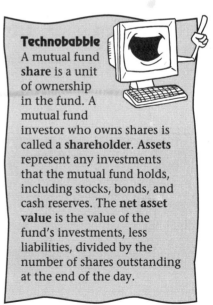

Technobabble
A **mutual fund share** is a unit of ownership in the fund. A mutual fund investor who owns shares is called a **shareholder**. **Assets** represent any investments that the mutual fund holds, including stocks, bonds, and cash reserves. The **net asset value** is the value of the fund's investments, less liabilities, divided by the number of shares outstanding at the end of the day.

outstanding shares at the shareholder's request. When you sell shares in a fund, you receive a check based on its share price or net asset value (less any sales charges, if applicable). The *net asset value* is the value of the fund's investments, less liabilities, divided by the number of shares outstanding at the end of the day.

Introducing the Cast of a Mutual Fund

Like any company, the mutual fund management company is an organization run by a number of people. You want to understand how it works because you've entrusted it with your hard-earned cash. Although mutual funds are set up under state law, usually as corporations, they differ from other companies.

First, a mutual fund is legally entitled to hire a company to handle the bulk of its services. It typically hires the investment advisor (also known as an investment advisory firm) to manage your mutual fund. It also may make arrangements to have the fund sold through a brokerage firm.

The following sections review the cast of characters who make a mutual fund work.

The Investment Advisor

The investment advisor is one person, or in some cases, a group of the key people, in a mutual fund, including the portfolio managers and staff. You've probably seen some portfolio managers on TV's *Wall Street Week*, spotted their quotes in magazines, or read some of their books. These people select, buy, and sell investments based on the fund's investment objective. The investment advisor is paid an annual fee based on a percentage of the value of the fund's cash and investments, or assets.

The Board of Directors

A mutual fund has a board of directors to make major policy decisions and oversee management. These are important people. The directors steer the fund's course, determining investment objectives and hiring help. The directors keep tabs on investment performance, as well as that of investment advisors and others who work for the fund.

Technobabble
The **invest-ment objective** describes what your mutual fund hopes to accomplish.

The Shareholder

Mutual fund investors are known as shareholders. When you invest in a mutual fund, you actually buy a share or portion of a mutual fund. Each share has a price tag. If a fund sells for $10 a share and you invest $1,000, you're the proud owner of 100 shares of the fund. Mutual funds, like many other companies, are democratic. Because you own shares in the fund, you have voting rights. As part owner, a shareholder gets to vote in the election of the board of directors. The shareholder also must approve many operational changes within the fund, including accounting procedures and the *investment objective.*

Custodians and Transfer Agents

As you can imagine, the millions of mutual fund transactions executed each year require a gargantuan behind-the-scenes record-keeping effort. The securities a mutual fund invests in are kept under lock and key by an appointed custodian, usually a bank. The custodian may respond only to instructions from fund officers responsible for dealing with the custodian. The custodian safeguards the fund's assets, makes payments for the fund's securities, and receives payments when securities are sold.

Fund *transfer agents* maintain shareholder account records, including purchases, sales, and account balances. They also authorize the payments made by the custodian, prepare and mail account statements, maintain a customer service department to respond to account inquiries, and provide federal income tax information, shareholder notices, and confirmation statements.

The Underwriter

The *underwriter* is an organization with a staff of salespeople who either administer sales directly to the public or meet with the brokerage firms to convince them to sell the fund. Brokers sell fund shares to the public and collect a commission for the sale. Chapter 8, "Secrets of Mutual Fund Shopping," provides more detail about what you pay for a mutual fund and who sells them.

Mutual Funds Make It Easy to Invest

Boy, a lot of important people and ingredients make a mutual fund. The end result, however, is that mutual funds provide one of the simplest ways to invest, especially if you count yourself among us working stiffs and lack time and training to manage money like the Wall Street big boys.

News You Can Use

There is now more money in mutual funds in bank, thrift, and credit union deposits combined. At the end of 1997, banks and thrifts had $4.044 trillion in deposits, whereas mutual funds had nearly $4.5 trillion in assets, according to Fed and Investment Company Institute data.

Chapter 4, "Mutual Funds for Everyone," shows you how to pick the right funds, as well as strategies to get the best returns from your investments.

Technobabble
Returns, also called **total returns**, are the percentages of gains or losses on your investments, including the reinvestment of income.

Hot Tip!
Many mutual funds became sweeter investments in 1998 thanks to the new Taxpayer Relief Act of 1997, which cut taxes on investment capital gains. You'll learn more about this in Chapter 22, "Taxes: To Pay or Not to Pay?."

Hot Tip!
There are close to 7,000 mutual funds, but not all are alike. Depending on your particular needs, you can find a mutual fund that's right for you. In Chapter 3 and Chapter 5, learn more about the different types of mutual funds.

Investing in mutual funds is not rocket science. With a little understanding of the subject, you can do it yourself. All you need are three to six well-managed funds with good long-term track records. If you invest regularly for 10 or 20 years, history tells us you should do just fine. Trust us. It's really not that difficult. Stick with some of the outstanding funds and fund groups mentioned in this book, and you might become a lot wealthier over the years.

What if you're convinced you can't do it? As we always say, it's better to pay someone to help you invest in mutual funds than to not invest at all. If you must, you can opt to hire a financial professional. Wait a minute! That doesn't give you carte blanche to close this book right here. After all, you're the only one who's equipped to make certain that you're getting good advice for your own money. Either way, it is important to have a good understanding of mutual funds before you take the plunge.

If you need help picking funds in your brokerage account or your company pension plan, expect to pay about 1 percent of the money you invest. For that fee, you can generally find a professional to make sure that your batch of funds continues to do well. If some funds fizzle out, your investment pro should find you some better ones (we hope). Chapter 8 discusses where you can find professional help if you just can't do it yourself.

Here They Are: The 10 Commandments

Have we whetted your appetite? Good. Get ready to proceed. However, we don't want you to invest one penny in a mutual fund until you read and thoroughly digest these 10 critical rules of mutual fund investing:

1. **Always understand exactly what you're investing in.** You can lose a bundle if you pick the wrong kind of mutual fund. Read carefully the free literature that mutual fund companies provide.

2. **Don't rush out and buy the first mutual fund that looks good.** You first have to identify your investment goals, determine how much you need from your investment (see Chapter 2, "Mutual Funds: To Own or Not to Own?"), and figure out how much you're willing to risk losing (see Chapter 6, "Which Funds Are Right for You?").

3. **Don't try to make quick profits.** Always invest for the long term. You should plan to keep some of your mutual funds for an absolute minimum of 5 to 10 years.

4. **Mix up your investments.** You can cut your chances of losing money by putting your money in different types of investments. Chapter 6 shows you how.

5. **Have your investment money taken out of each paycheck automatically before you have a chance to spend it.** Mutual funds have automatic investment programs. Money is electronically withdrawn from your checking account and invested in the fund.

6. **Do your homework.** Once you determine how much money you need and by what time, as well as how much you can afford to lose, research the best investments to meet your goals. Most library business sections offer information on mutual funds.

7. **Avoid paying high commissions and fees for mutual funds.** Make your money work for you, not for your stockbroker. Read about this in Chapter 7, "The Cost of Investing."

8. **Make sure your mutual fund investment earns enough so that your nest egg at least keeps pace with rising prices.** Chapter 5 discusses this further.

9. **Know when to sell your mutual funds.** Chapter 16 explains ways to evaluate how a fund is doing. You'll learn when to get rid of a mutual fund that's a lemon.

10. **Invest to beat the tax man.** Take advantage of Individual Retirement Accounts (IRAs) and other tax shelters. Chapters 22 and 24, discuss how you can make tax-deductible contributions and watch your money grow tax-free until you retire.

> **Hot Tip!**
> You can buy mutual funds either directly from the mutual fund company or from stockbrokers or financial planners licensed to sell them. People who sell mutual funds are called registered representatives (or reps for short). They are registered and regulated by the U.S. Securities & Exchange Commission. Chapter 7 explains how much you pay in each case.

The Least You Need to Know

➤ With a mutual fund, investors pool their money with one common goal, to make more.

➤ A mutual fund's investment decisions are made by the portfolio manager, or a team of managers, who is an investment advisor hired by the mutual fund.

➤ When you invest in a mutual fund, you own shares of the fund, which gives you certain voting rights.

➤ Invest for the long term. Don't try to make quick profits in mutual funds.

Mutual Funds: To Own or Not to Own?

Do you need extra cash in time for your next rent payment? Are you a teenager who wants to start saving for college? Maybe you are a retiree who wants to increase your limited income over the next five years.

Regardless of who you are, it never hurts anybody to raise a little extra cash for the cause—and nobody wants to lose his or her shirt in the markets, right?

We hear ya—on both counts. In this chapter, you'll learn how to figure out how much money you need and by what time. As Thomas A. Edison would testify if he were here today, making a plan is Step 1 toward getting where you want to go. That's what this chapter is all about.

Is Father Time on Your Side?

Your age has a lot to do with how you save. Unless you're a Rockefeller, 20- and 30-year-olds typically don't have as much money to invest as people who have been working for 20 years. Nevertheless, younger investors do have an important advantage when it comes to investing. They have more time for their money to grow. Big-ticket events such as retirement and children's education are further away, so it's all right for younger people to put away a little less money on a regular basis. Plus, they have all those years to watch their money grow.

If you're in your 40s and you're just getting into mutual funds, you have a shorter period to save for retirement, so you might need to save more. Get into your 60s, and it might be more important to keep what you already have to meet your everyday living expenses.

How does all this relate to mutual funds?

Probably the most critical factor in figuring out how (or whether) to invest in mutual funds is determining when you need your money. It also influences which mutual funds you choose. You will learn in the following chapters the advantages of investing in mutual funds and what funds are right for your situation.

One thing is for sure: Depending on your needs, mutual fund investing should be a long-term affair. History has shown repeatedly that over the long term (say, 20 years), most mutual funds perform substantially better than bank savings accounts or CDs. History also has proven that the longer you have to invest in a mutual fund, the slimmer your chance of losing money. That's why it's important to get a fix on your investment goals and how long you have to invest.

Setting Your Goals

If you're like most Americans, this part of the exercise will astound you. When you see on paper the money you're going to need throughout your life, there's a good chance you'll want to hop right on a space shuttle and move to another planet!

Don't get discouraged. Fortunately, mutual funds and other types of investments are here to help you achieve your goals. The sooner you start planning, the better off you'll be. As astounded as you are at the staggering costs most people encounter in their lifetimes, you'll be just as surprised when you see how quickly your money can grow.

Why Do I Need to Invest?

First, find a comfortable chair. Then, sit down with a pad and pencil and jot down all the reasons you'll need more money in the future.

To organize your thoughts, first zero in on every money emergency you might have. Cars, unfortunately, need to be repaired. Teeth need to be fixed. No doubt, you've got out-of-town guests that need to be taken out to dinner. What about emergency trips or medical emergencies? And don't forget the dentist and eye doctor. You've got to have a cash reserve of three to six months of your income to meet emergencies. This money should be in a secure place where you can tap it right away.

Next, list your short-term goals. Most people buy a car every five years. That's going to cost you some big bucks. The way new car prices are rising, in a few years the average new car will cost $22,000 to $28,000. What if you've been dreaming about buying a house in five or six years? You might need $20,000 to $25,000 for a down payment. You'll also need money—$2,000 plus—to furnish it.

Once you cover emergencies and the stuff you need, it's time to focus on longer-term needs. If you're going to send a child to college in 18 years, expect to pay a whopping $30,000 to $40,000 a year by the time Junior's ready. Looking to retire? If you're making $35,000 annually now, you'll need about $500,000 earning 7 percent interest annually to make the same amount, discounting the impact of inflation.

Next, think about those little luxuries. Sure, you don't absolutely need it, but wouldn't it be nice to keep a yacht and a winter home in Florida?

Now that you've written down your financial necessities and desires and ranked them in order of importance, attach a price tag to each. Figure out how much each item is likely to cost.

Finally, look at the time frame you have to invest for each of your goals. For example, if you've just had a baby, chances are you have 18 years before your child will be ready for college. That's 18 years you have to come up with the cash. On the other hand, if you're driving an old clunker, you might have to shell out that $20,000 for a new car in one year. That's not much time at all!

> **Hot Tip!**
> Chapter 13, "Choosing the Right Bond Fund," Chapter 14, "Building Your Wealth with Stock Funds," and Chapter 15, "Mutual Funds for Special Situations," will help you find the right mutual funds to help you meet long-term needs. Chapter 23, "Saving for Important Life Goals" goes into more depth in helping you figure exactly how much you'll need for college and retirement.

Once you have your financial plan mapped out, you can start socking away your cash. You can take advantage of mutual funds to invest in tax-advantaged savings plans for your child, such as the Uniform Gifts to Minors Act (discussed further in Chapter 22 and Chapter 23), and retirement plans, such as IRAs, SEPs, the new Roth IRA, or Keoghs (discussed further in Chapter 23).

Investment Goals Worksheet

Goal	Amount You Need	When You Need It
Cash reserves		
Retirement		
Child's college education		
Second home down payment		
Travel		
Estate		
Other		

This worksheet can help you set your investment goals.

In Chapter 11, "Money Funds: Better Than a Bank Account?," you'll learn all about money market mutual funds. These less risky mutual fund investments come with a checkbook. If you've already saved six months of income, you might be ready to try some new investments. In Chapter 6, "Which Funds Are Right for You?," you'll also learn how to determine your risk tolerance, which is how much money you can stomach losing in any given year. Then, you'll be able to put both pieces of information together to make the right kinds of mutual fund investments.

Starting a Savings Plan

You want to invest in mutual funds to meet your goals. "But I have no money," you balk. Regardless of whether you have money to invest, it always pays to squeeze as much as you possibly can out of your budget for investing.

This needn't be as painful as it sounds. We're willing to bet you have more cash than you think sitting right under your nose. To figure out exactly where you stand, first list and then add up your monthly income from your paycheck, savings, and other sources. Then, get your checkbook register and list all your monthly expenses. Subtract your expenses from your income to determine the amount of cash you have available to invest monthly.

Finding Money to Invest

Monthly Income

Paycheck (after taxes)	_____
Other	_____
Total Income:	_____

Monthly Spending

Rent or mortgage	_____
Utilities	_____
Groceries	_____
Entertainment	_____
Vacations	_____
Car payments	_____
Car repairs	_____
Gas	_____
Car insurance	_____
Health insurance	_____
Life insurance	_____
Disability insurance	_____
Child care	_____
Child support or alimony	_____
Gifts	_____
Educational expenses	_____
Pet expenses	_____
Newspapers and magazines	_____
Hobbies	_____
Miscellaneous expenses	_____
Savings	_____
Credit cards and loans	_____
Total Expenses:	_____

**Monthly Cash
(Income - Expenses)** _____

Use this worksheet to get a better handle on the cash you have available for investing and to see whether you are spending too much in some areas.

15

Money-Saving Tips

Whether the money you have left for investing is a large sum or a big fat zero, it's time to set up a spending (and savings) plan for next year—including, without fail, money to invest!

Even before you look for big ways to cut your expenses, we bet you can save $20 a month on little items, such as the gum, candy, and coffee you buy every day. If you put that $20 into a bank account that pays 5 percent, you earn an extra $3,100 of savings in 10 years. Imagine how that money will grow if you invest in a mutual fund!

Technobabble
Your **goals** are all your future desires. A **spending plan** is a strategy to help cut wasteful spending so you can invest.

Hot Tip!
If you want some bright ideas about how to cut the fat out of the family budget, send a stamped, self-addressed envelope to the Consumer Federation of America, P.O. Box 12099, Washington, DC 20005-0999, for a free copy of *66 Ways to Save*.

You can pick up back issues of *The Tightwad Gazette* for $1 each by calling 207-524-7962. You can also check out books by Amy Dacyczyn: *The Tightwad Gazette*, *The Tightwad Gazette II*, and *The Tightwad Gazette III*, all published by Villard Books, New York.

Here are some big money-saving ideas that are easy to implement right away, yet needn't ruin your life:

➤ Make certain you are on the lowest-cost utility plans possible.

➤ Where possible, use halogen or fluorescent bulbs to dramatically cut your electric bills.

➤ Consider putting water savers on your faucets and a timer on your water heater.

➤ Find out the peak hours for utility costs, and consciously avoid phone and electric use during those periods.

➤ Use coupons at grocery stores and restaurants.

➤ Bring your lunch to work more often.

➤ Avoid office vending machines. Don't buy your coffee.

➤ Eat at lower-cost restaurants.

➤ Alter routes so that you purposely bypass your favorite stores or food stops.

➤ If possible, buy in bulk. Consider joining a warehouse such as Costco, Price Club, or Sam's Club.

➤ Go to matinees rather than full-cost shows.

➤ Review your medical, auto, and home insurance regularly to make certain you are getting the best value for your money.

➤ Pay off your credit-card debts. You might be paying as much as 15 percent to 21 percent interest on credit-card bills. Paying those off provides a better return than you'll get on many mutual funds.

➤ Choose inexpensive vacations. Rather than go to Aruba, you can find a nice resort close to home. You can still have a good time and save a bundle.

News You Can Use

Looking for ways to reduce your credit-card bills? You can get information on low-rate credit cards for a small fee from the following companies:

Bank Rate Monitor, Box 088888, North Palm Beach, FL 33408, 800-327-7717 (http://www.bankrate.com).

RAM Research Corp., P.O. Box 1700, Frederick, MD 21702, 800-344-7714 (http://www.cardtrak.com).

Manage Your Money like a Pro

You'd be surprised what a little savvy cash management can do for your long-term financial picture. Why not take some tips from professional money managers, whose job it is to use efficient cash-management tactics to make their money work for them?

This section describes a few ways to manage your cash like a pro. By following these guidelines, you can free as much as $150 a year for investing. That annual investment, earning just 5 percent, can grow over 20 years to an extra $4,960 for retirement—not a bad reward for no lifestyle cutbacks.

The key to cash management is to invest your money right away and pay your bills at the end of the month. You may already have an interest-bearing checking account, but you can also take advantage of higher interest rates and invest in a money market fund (discussed in Chapter 4, "Mutual Funds for Everyone," and Chapter 12, "Bonding: Investing with Bond Funds"). Then, follow this plan:

➤ Deposit all your checks as soon as you receive them; then you will earn interest right away if you have a NOW account.

➤ Avoid all bank fees. When you withdraw money from ATM machines other than your own bank's machines, for example, you pay as much as $1.50 on every transaction.

➤ Use your employer's payroll direct-deposit program. The money is electronically credited to your interest-bearing checking account and earns interest immediately. Some institutions also waive checking fees if you direct-deposit your paycheck.

➤ Along the same lines, if you automatically have money taken out of your interest-bearing checking account to pay life insurance or disability insurance premiums, do it at the end of the month. That way your money earns interest for a full month before you pay your life and health insurance bills.

➤ Avoid bank package accounts—unless you shop around and find an unusually good deal. With a package account, you usually get free or low-cost checking if you use other bank services (for example, invest in bank CDs and savings accounts or handle your mortgage and car loans with your bank). The problem, however, is that you might not need all those services. Plus, you're locked in. Not only are you restricted from looking for better deals at other banks, but once you get one of these package accounts, it's hard to get out. Banks, knowing this, find it easier to quietly raise fees and the thresholds for avoiding fees.

➤ If you want to save $10 to $20 a month in bank checking account fees, some institutions, such as USAA Bank (800-945-3803), offer nationally available no-fee checking, complete with ATM access. Also, many banks offer free accounts on the condition that you can live without overdraft protection, don't want your canceled checks or an ATM card, or will direct-deposit your paycheck or Social Security check.

➤ If you can join a credit union, do it. Credit unions typically pay higher rates on bank savings accounts, charge lower fees on checking accounts, and offer lower consumer loan rates than many banks. Call Credit Union National Association at 800-356-9655 for the number of your state credit union league, which can direct you to a credit union you might join.

➤ Shop for higher yields on your bank accounts. The average checking account pays a measly 1.5 percent. However, some banks pay as much as 4 percent to 5 percent on bank money market deposit accounts. To locate banks with higher yields, visit http://www.bankrate.com.

➤ Pay off those credit-card bills before you invest. It doesn't make sense to pay 15 percent in credit card interest when your investments don't earn as much. With the hundreds of dollars you save in interest payments, you can invest in some well-managed mutual funds.

➤ Charge smart. As long as you carry no outstanding balance on your Visa or MasterCard, for example, you get a 20 to 25-day grace period each month before the bill is due. Make your purchases at the beginning of the billing cycle (just after the monthly closing date). Then, you have 25 days before the credit card company bills you, plus 10 days or more before you have to pay the bill.

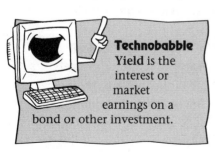

Technobabble
Yield is the interest or market earnings on a bond or other investment.

➤ Find a checking account with no minimum required balance. Suppose you're required to keep at least $700 in your checking account. That $700 is dead money earning no interest. Had you invested that money in a Treasury bond fund over the past five years, your money would have grown at an annual rate of about 7.50 percent. Your $700 could have been worth $1,005.

➤ Make sure your bank offers the services you need. "Free checking" might not be a good deal for you if you do not get your canceled checks at the end of the month or if you are required to perform all your transactions by mail, computer, or ATM. It's also possible your bank has no ATM access or has only one or two branches that aren't close to where you live.

➤ Avoid low-interest NOW accounts. You can earn about 1.5 percent on your checking account balances, and you may be required to maintain a specific balance in your account to earn interest. Chances are the return is so low after inflation and taxes that it's often not worth it. It's better to put the money into a higher-yielding Money Market Deposit Account that pays 5 percent or more.

➤ Watch the terms of your home equity loans or credit lines. Look for programs with no closing costs, no annual fees, and no fine print instructions that penalize you if you pay off the loan early. When the institution promises no closing costs, you want to be certain the appraisal is included. Watch out for programs that allow you to borrow more than 100 percent of the equity in your home. Not only is the IRS apt to prohibit you from deducting interest on more than 100 percent of your home's appraised value, but you'll probably also pay more for your loan.

➤ Make sure you're getting the best deal on your credit cards. Look for no-annual-fee deals that let you pay off monthly without accruing interest. Make sure you pay them off monthly! Ideally, you want to find a low rate too—just in case. Watch out, though, for credit cards with disappearing grace periods (those that allow just 20 days rather than the normal 25 to 30 days to pay off your balance). Also avoid credit cards that hit you with a whopping late fee if you're one day late.

Hopefully, we've demonstrated that you don't necessarily have to cut out all the fun in your life to come up with some extra cash. Often, with just a little brainstorming and tweaking here and there, you can cut expenses you really didn't need to be shelling out anyway. Yes, you can make money with mutual funds if you invest for the long term. Now that you've turned up a few more bucks you might not have known you had, you should be ready to compound this stash by investing in your favorite mutual funds, which we'll show you how to pick in the coming chapters!

The Least You Need to Know

➤ Always know how much money you need and by what deadline.

➤ Monitor your monthly income and expenses.

➤ Make adjustments to the way you spend to free extra cash for investing.

➤ Look for ways to cut everyday expenses to free money to invest.

Chapter 3

Investing: Your Options, Your Risks, Your Rewards

Are you getting ready to join the mutual fund club? Sixty-six million Americans own a mutual fund, according to the Investment Company Institute. Before you join this select fraternity, however, it's important to understand the investments that mutual funds make.

Mutual funds come in a variety of flavors. You wouldn't buy a car without checking the tires and looking under the hood. This chapter pops open the hood on mutual fund investments. It explains how mutual funds are invested and the advantages mutual funds have to offer you as a potential investor.

Stocks, Bonds, or Cash?

Congrats! In Chapter 2, "Mutual Funds: To Own or Not to Own?," you probably came up with money you didn't even know you had. Before you get excited and plunk down all that cash, you need to know about all the critters that can hang out in a mutual fund.

In Chapter 1, "The Ten Commandments of Mutual Fund Investing," we mentioned that you normally can buy stocks, bonds, or cash investments directly from a stockbroker. Stockbrokers have one word for all this stuff: *securities*. A mutual fund may invest in one type of security or a mix of different kinds of securities.

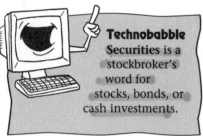

Technobabble
Securities is a stockbroker's word for stocks, bonds, or cash investments.

A mutual fund's value may rise or fall rapidly—or slowly—depending on the types of securities investments it makes. (The exception are money market mutual funds, which are designed to maintain a constant $1-per-share value.) The following sections describe the kinds of securities you'll find in a mutual fund and how each security affects how much money you make from your mutual fund investment.

Taking Stock

Stocks provide a way for a company to raise money. The company sells stock shares in exchange for money to use to grow the business—by buying new equipment or performing research and development, for example.

If you or your mutual fund own shares of a company's stock, you're a big shot. Not only are you part owner of that company, but also you might get to share in its earnings, which may be distributed to shareholders in the form of *dividends*. If the mutual fund owns shares of a particular dividend-paying stock, it pays these dividends to you, based on the number of mutual fund shares you own.

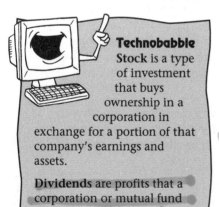

Technobabble
Stock is a type of investment that buys ownership in a corporation in exchange for a portion of that company's earnings and assets.

Dividends are profits that a corporation or mutual fund distributes to its owners.

If the company profits, it's good news. The share price of the stock can increase, which in turn, hikes the value of its shares. The company's board of directors may vote to increase the dividends they pay shareholders. Unfortunately, the opposite can also happen. If the company does poorly, the value of the stock may decline, and dividends may be cut or eliminated entirely.

Stocks are probably one of the riskiest investments for individuals and mutual funds. Stock funds may earn—or lose—a ton of money before you have a chance to blink your eye.

News You Can Use

The two major types of stocks are common and preferred. If you own preferred stock, you receive dividends before common stockholders do. You also get preferred treatment over common stockholders when it comes to getting your investment back if the company goes under. Preferred stocks tend to pay slightly higher dividends than common stock, but the share price usually doesn't rise as much. Most individual stockholders and mutual funds own common stock.

Bond Basics

A *bond* is an I.O.U. issued by a company or a city, county, state, or federal government or its agencies. When you buy a bond, you are lending money to the bond issuer. In exchange for the loan, the issuer promises to repay the money on a specific date, known as the *maturity date*. If you or your mutual fund own a bond, you, as lender, receive fixed periodic interest payments.

Bonds require a minimum investment of at least $1,000, which is also known as the *face value* or *principal*. After you buy your bond, you or your mutual fund can hold it to maturity and get the principal back, or you can sell it before maturity.

Bonds can be tricky to understand. There are three ways that describe how much interest income you will receive from a bond. It's important to understand them all so that you don't get mixed up later when you begin to invest in bond mutual funds:

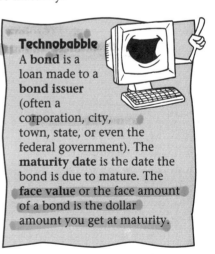

Technobabble
A **bond** is a loan made to a **bond issuer** (often a corporation, city, town, state, or even the federal government). The **maturity date** is the date the bond is due to mature. The **face value** or the face amount of a bond is the dollar amount you get at maturity.

➤ The *coupon rate*, which we call the *stated interest rate*, tells you the interest payment in dollars that you will receive from the bond as a percentage of the bond's face value.

Suppose, for example, you buy a newly issued bond for $1,000 and it has a coupon rate of 7 percent. That means you receive a total of $70 in interest income from the bond for the year. Year in and year out, you will collect $70 from the bond until it matures. Then, you get your $1,000 back.

Technobabble
The **current yield** of a bond is the annual interest you get on a bond, divided by the changeable market price (as opposed to the bond's face value). The **yield to maturity** is the annual rate, factoring interest compounding, that the bond pays if you hold it to maturity.

The **coupon rate** is how much interest you get based on an annual percentage of the bond's face value.

➤ Bonds have two yields. The *current yield* is based on the current market price of the bond, which can fluctuate based upon market conditions.

Suppose a bond with a face value of $1,000 declines in value to $900. It still earns $70 a year in interest income, based on the bond's stated interest rate. As a result, the current yield of the bond is $70 divided by $900, or 7.78 percent.

➤ You also have to consider a bond's *yield to maturity*. Bonds typically pay semiannual interest over a specific time period. That means the interest generally compounds twice a year until it matures. The yield to maturity of a bond is the yield you get if you hold it for the entire term, assuming compound interest.

News You Can Use

You may already be familiar with U.S. Savings Bonds. These bonds operate differently from most other bonds we're discussing here. U.S. Savings Bonds are sold at half the price marked on the face of the bond. However, unlike most traditional bonds, savings bonds have a variable rate, subject to change every six months. Plus, interest automatically is credited monthly, and you lose three months worth of interest if you cash out within five years. At this writing, savings bonds paid slightly more than 5 percent—less than both one-year Treasury-bills and 30-year Treasury bonds. But they could prove more attractive in the long-run if rates head up.

How Bonds Are Classified

Bonds issued by the United States government are backed by the full faith and credit of Uncle Sam. Corporate bonds are not. Once you go beyond Uncle Sam, you have to make sure you invest in financially strong companies. That's why it's important to look at bond credit ratings.

Certain companies, such as Standard & Poor's and Moody's, rate the financial strength of bond issuers, based on the ability of companies to repay principal and interest on time. The highest quality bonds are rated AAA. Bonds rated below single A stand a greater chance of failing to repay their debts during tough economic times. Unless you're a seasoned investor, you might want to stay clear of investing in bonds with lower ratings—or mutual funds that invest in them.

Other Bond Risks

When you buy bonds or invest in bond funds, you not only have to look at the issuer's financial strengths, but you also must deal with changing bond prices. Chapter 12, "Bonding: Investing with Bond Funds," and Chapter 13, "Choosing the Right Bond Fund," discuss the risks and ratings of bonds in more detail, but it is important to note that you can get into trouble even with the highest-quality bonds if you're not careful. Interest rates and bond prices move in opposite directions, so it's not always a time for rejoicing if interest rates head up. It means that your bonds are losing value if their coupon rates (stated interest rates) are less than the going rates.

Put yourself in a bond buyer's shoes. If you could buy a newly issued bond paying a stated interest rate of 7.5 percent by investing $1,000, you certainly wouldn't offer Joe Biddle the same $1,000 for his bond paying a stated rate of 6.5 percent, would you? Unless you can buy the bond for less money, it's simply not worth putting up your hard-earned cash for a lower yield. That's exactly how the big bond traders think. Moreover, the longer the term (time to maturity) of the bond, the riskier it appears to the bond investor and the less it is valued. Why? The longer the term, the greater the period an investor has to worry about the threat of rising interest rates.

If interest rates rise 1 percent, a 2-year Treasury note (which is just another word for a short-term bond) loses nearly 2 percent in value. By contrast, a 30-year Treasury bond loses about 12 percent in value. Chapter 14, "Building Your Wealth with Stock Funds," shows you exactly how much rate shifts can affect bond prices.

Believe it or not, bond investors also might get their principal back faster than they'd like. That's because issuers might have the right to call their bonds or return the bondholder's principal. Bonds get called when interest rates fall. The issuer then sells lower-yielding bonds and reduces its interest payments.

Most people invest in bond funds for income and safety. You are lending companies or Uncle Sam money when you invest in a bond or bond fund. In return you get interest income, plus your initial investment or principal is returned at maturity. By contrast, when you invest in stocks, you are the owner of a company and share in its profits. As a result, if a company is profitable its stock price rises. You don't get that kind of growth when you invest in bonds. Historically, stocks have grown at an annual rate of around 11 percent over the past 70 years. By contrast, bonds have grown at nearly 6 percent annually.

Kinds of Bonds a Fund May Own

You can typically find the following variety of bonds in your mutual fund if it invests in bonds:

➤ U.S. Treasury bonds, issued by Uncle Sam.

➤ U.S. government agency bonds, issued by agencies of the national government.

➤ Municipal bonds, issued by state and local governments.

➤ Corporate bonds, issued by companies.

➤ International bonds, issued by foreign corporations or governments.

Money Market or Cash

Cash or money market investments are short-term loans to banks, governments, or companies. Although they're considered the least risky types of securities, there's still a chance with a cash investment that you might not get back your principal, or original investment. One of the most common cash investments is a CD or time deposit, such as the type you might already have at your local bank. However, unlike most of us, mutual funds generally invest in these in amounts of $1 million or more.

Going It Alone

The good news is that any of the securities just discussed has the potential to earn more (and in some cases, much more!) than your old faithful savings account.

The bad news, as we warned you earlier, is that none of these securities is quite as low-risk as Federal Deposit Insurance Corp. (FDIC) insured savings accounts and CDs. You've probably heard the horror stories yourself. Joe Biddle's stockbroker has inside information on a company that makes 3D video games. "Buy the stock," the stockbroker whispers. "Double your money in a couple of days. Buy now and sell when everybody gets wind of this deal."

Aha! Joe empties his bank account and buys 500 shares at $10 a share for a total investment of $5,000. The next day he opens the newspaper. "Video Games Cause Creepy Slime Disease," the headline announces. Wham! The next day, everyone sells. The stock's price plunges to $5 a share. Worried that it soon could drop to zero, Joe also sells. His loss is $2,500, or half of his investment.

A similar situation could happen with a bond if Joe happens to invest in a weak company that falls on tough times. Suppose that Joe, based on his stockbroker's advice, invests $5,000 in a new bond issued by the same 3D video game company. Investors get wind of the fact that the company might have a tough time paying back interest and principal to the bondholders. Bondholders tie up the stockbroker's phone lines all day trying to sell their bonds. The price of the bonds drops, and Joe is worried it could get worse. Joe sells his bond for $4,000—$1,000 less than he paid for it.

The Mutual Fund Advantage

With so many people investing in mutual funds, you'd think there has to be a good reason, right? Actually, there are several.

The following sections show why mutual funds are so well-suited to almost everyone, and why they stack up so favorably when compared with other types of investments.

Technobabble
Diversified means funds are spread among a large number of different investments.

Mutual Funds Are Diversified

When you invest in a mutual fund, you needn't worry so much that you're investing in one dud. As mentioned earlier in this book, most funds own a large number of investments. In other words, they're *diversified*. If one investment owned by the fund performs poorly, there's still hope that the others might rally. At least, you're less likely to lose as much.

Federal laws give you some added protection. A diversified mutual fund is required to invest in at least 16 companies. The Securities & Exchange Commission (SEC) says that no more than 25 percent of a diversified mutual fund's assets are allowed to be in a single stock or bond issuer. Meanwhile, no more than 5 percent of the remaining 75 percent of the fund's assets can be in any one company. A mutual fund also can't own more than 10 percent of the outstanding voting stock of a company in which it invests. All these requirements contain an awful lot of numbers. But it sure can be great news if just one of your mutual fund's holdings happens to tank!

Suppose a fund owns 50 different stocks, including Computer Chip Inc. One day, there is terrible news about Computer Chip Inc., and the stock price drops 5 percent. That's a big loss for a stock! The other 49 stocks don't drop in price, however. In fact, some rise. At the end of the day, that Computer Chip Inc. loss didn't put much of a dent in the value of the fund. Whew!

Mutual funds also relieve you of a major workload. Who has time nowadays to play the stock market or find a company with a great credit record? Not only that, but by the time we peons hear about a great investment, it's generally too late to profit from it. The Wall Street pros sell us the hot tips and bank their whopping profits. Where does that leave us? In the hole.

Enter mutual funds....

You Get Your Own Investment Pro

With a mutual fund, you get your own highly trained hired gun (or guns) working full-time to ensure that you make money. The fund manager, or portfolio manager, has all the investment research at his or her fingertips and even visits companies before investing in them. This individual often earns a high salary plus a bonus at year's end if a fund performs better than similar funds. This gives the fund manager a high level of incentive to ensure that the fund does well. Some funds are managed by a team of portfolio managers.

You May Get Higher Returns

With a mutual fund, you have greater potential to grow your money over the long term than you do in a bank. After all, look at the securities that mutual funds invest in. Historically, stocks have earned 10 percent annually, bonds have earned more than 5 percent annually, and plain old CDs have earned about 3 percent annually. (Of course, we won't even discuss the piddling yields on savings accounts right now.) However, once again, the value of your mutual fund fluctuates with changing market conditions, so it's possible that you can also lose money with these investments.

Mutual Funds Pay You Back

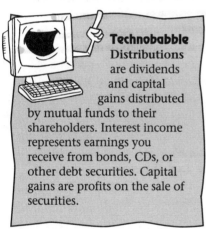

Technobabble
Distributions are dividends and capital gains distributed by mutual funds to their shareholders. Interest income represents earnings you receive from bonds, CDs, or other debt securities. Capital gains are profits on the sale of securities.

What a mutual fund earns on its investments is ultimately passed on to you as *distributions*. You can receive three types of distributions from a fund:

1. When the fund owns bonds, it earns interest income.

2. When a fund owns stocks, it earns dividends. The dividends are a share of company profits that are paid periodically to its shareholders.

3. When the fund sells either stock or bond investments at a profit, the profits are called capital gains.

You can receive your distributions in cash, or you can have your mutual fund reinvest the money to buy more shares in the fund.

You Get Your Money Whenever You Want It

You can buy and sell all or part of your mutual fund whenever you want. Just call the fund or your stockbroker toll-free and give your directions on a tape-recorded line. You generally can get your cash in a couple of days. (In fact, many funds even give you a book of checks when you purchase them.)

You Have a Fund Family

Many mutual fund families offer investors a wide variety of mutual funds. The funds may invest in different kinds of stocks, bonds, or cash equivalents based on different investment objectives. When one investment company owns a number of mutual funds, those funds are considered part of a fund family. The T. Rowe Price Group of Funds, Baltimore, for example, has more than 20 different stock and bond funds in its family of funds. Mutual fund families make investing easy. As your money situation or the market changes, you can switch from one fund to another.

Technobabble
A variety of funds available to investors from one investment management company may be known as a **fund family**.

You Can Go to the Supermarket

Don't want to limit your mutual investments to a single mutual fund family? Today, you can go to the "supermarket." We're not talking about the place you buy watermelons and potatoes. Rather, brokerages such as Charles Schwab and Fidelity, as well as banks, let you select from a number of mutual fund families through their special mutual fund "super-markets." The advantage is that although you might pay a little more for your fund (we'll get into the bad news—fees—in Chapter 7, "The Cost of Investing"), you get one single statement. You also can switch investments with one phone call to a broker.

Mutual Funds Are Easy to Reach

If you're investing within a fund family or through a broker, you can typically call toll-free and switch from one fund to another as investment conditions or your financial needs change. Generally, there is no charge.

Most fund families will also send you free how-to booklets to help you invest wisely. The material is educational, but don't forget that the fund families want your business. It always pays to do your own independent homework.

You Don't Have to Be Rich

As we told you earlier, you don't need beaucoup bucks to invest in a mutual fund. Although you might need several thousand dollars to invest in individual stocks and bonds, you can get started in a mutual fund with as little as $100. With most funds, however, you need $500 to $1,000. Minimums may be lower for IRA accounts. *This part has changed*

Money Matters
Unlike safer investments, such as CDs from banks, which are regulated by the Federal Deposit Insurance Corp., you're not guaranteed to receive your original investment back with a mutual fund. Before investing, it's critical to investigate the quality of a mutual fund's investments.

Mutual Funds Are Highly Regulated

Mutual funds are regulated by both the SEC and your own state's regulators. The funds are required to report their financial activities to these agencies. Meanwhile, mutual funds are also required to send shareholders financial reports. Often, reports are consolidated for a fund group or family. Therefore, if you own more than one mutual fund in a fund group or family, you won't necessarily need to keep track of a hundred different pieces of paper.

You Can Save for Your Retirement

Mutual funds are a great way to save for retirement. When you open your mutual fund account, you can set it up as an Individual Retirement Account (IRA). With this retirement plan, which you'll learn more about in Chapter 23, "Saving for Important Life Goals," not only do you get the benefits of mutual fund investment profits, but also you might get to deduct annual contributions from your income on your federal tax return. Meanwhile, you pay no taxes on your earnings until you retire.

You can also invest in the new Roth IRA, which is also discussed in Chapter 23. You might think of a Roth IRA as an upside-down version of the IRA. You pay taxes on your annual contributions. However, at retirement, you get to take money out of your Roth IRA tax-free.

Mutual funds also work similarly in other retirement plans. Self-employed individuals can use mutual funds in their Simplified Employee Pension Plans (SEPs) or Keogh plans. Companies may set up 401(k) investment plans for their employees. Your 401(k) retirement plan contribution, which often is matched by an employer, is taken off the top of your salary. With a 401(k) plan, you might be able to lower the income tax you pay on your wages and the earnings grow tax-deferred. We'll go into more detail in Chapter 24, "Care and Feeding of Your 401(k)."

You can have as many mutual funds as you want in your retirement account, and you can switch back and forth between those funds. You must keep your money in your retirement account mutual funds, however. If you move it into mutual funds outside the account, the IRS may consider it a withdrawal from your retirement plan and sock you with taxes on the amount withdrawn.

You Get Automatic Investment and Withdrawals

You know how you can have your paycheck automatically deposited in your checking account? You can do the same with your mutual fund. As little as $50 a month can be automatically withdrawn from your checking account and invested in your mutual fund. If you're retired and need income, you also can arrange to receive monthly checks from your mutual fund, in addition to having your mutual fund automatically reinvest distributions to buy more shares in your fund. You can also arrange to invest the distributions of one fund automatically into another fund, provided that it is in the same family.

The Least You Need to Know

➤ The kinds of securities a mutual fund invests in affects the value of the mutual fund.

➤ Mutual funds invest in stocks, bonds, or cash equivalents. Some invest in all three. They are professionally managed and well diversified.

➤ Unlike a typical FDIC-insured account, there's always a chance you can lose much of your original investment in a mutual fund.

➤ With stocks, you own a piece of a company. You can quickly make a lot of money, but you also can lose big.

➤ Bonds are like loans to companies or governments.

Mutual Funds for Everyone

As someone once said, there's a mutual fund for all seasons. To zero in on the right fund or funds for you, you first need to know which categories to examine. Would you like a fund that takes risks in the hopes of big gains? Do you want a fund that invests in small companies or a fund that invests in large companies? Do you want a fund that invests overseas?

Funds specifically aimed at the more squeamish investor enable you to earn a decent return on investment with little risk. Part 3, "Zoning In on the Picks," discusses in more detail the different types of mutual funds and the investments they make. In this chapter, you'll get acquainted with the different ways mutual funds are classified.

What Flavor Is Your Fund?

Now that you know about all the stocks, bonds, and cash investments that make up mutual funds, critters roaming around inside mutual funds, you're ready to get to the real meat of the matter—the funds themselves. As we mentioned before, there are more mutual funds than you can shake a stick at. Before you can determine which mutual funds are right for you (more about that later in Part 2, "Getting Started"), you need to review the menu.

News You Can Use

Different types of funds pay different types of distributions, so your need for regular income is an important key to determining what type of fund you select. (See Chapter 3, "Investing: Your Options, Your Risks, Your Rewards," for a discussion of the different kinds of distributions.)

For example, stock fund distributions may come from capital gains and dividends. A bond fund distribution also may come from capital gains as well as interest income. Some funds, such as income funds, own both stocks and bonds. They may pay distributions from all three sources: dividends, capital gains, and interest income.

Mutual funds might invest in stocks of one particular type of company. Some specialize, for example, in small new companies. There also are funds for middle-size companies and some for larger companies. Certain funds invest in companies based in one particular type of industry, such as utilities or technology. Still others invest in companies that mine gold bullion. Some funds invest in the stocks or bonds of companies overseas.

Whenever you're considering a mutual fund, it's important first to pin down a mutual fund's investment objective. Fund objectives tell you exactly what the fund manager hopes to accomplish with your money. Often the fund objective is smack dab in the fund's name, but to double-check, always locate the fund objective, which tells the fund's main goal or goals, in the fund's prospectus. You can also double-check things with the salesperson for the fund.

It's only by learning about a fund's investment objective that you can determine whether it matches your own.

Look for These Clues

Now, put on your Sherlock Holmes hat and get out your magnifying glass. You're going to learn a couple of clues to help you decipher what's in a mutual fund.

Please note that the high, low, and average total returns of the fund groups discussed in this chapter are based on the Morningstar Mutual Fund Performance Report. The average annual returns discussed are based on the 10-year performance ending in 1997.

Clue No. 1: Growth

If you see the word *growth* in the name or investment objective of a mutual fund, chances are that fund invests largely in stocks. By growth, we mean that the fund is designed to register big increases in the share price. You may be in for a roller-coaster ride with growth funds because their share price can go up and down.

Based on historical performance, investors tend to make great profits with growth funds over the long term, but they also risk losing the most. Funds with the word *growth* in the fund objective are apt to fall into one of the following categories:

Technobabble
Growth means long-term appreciation in value as a result of increases in share price. **Aggressive growth** means that the fund makes more speculative investments for short-term profits. Funds that invest for growth own companies that are growing their earnings at a fast clip.

➤ *Aggressive-growth funds*, also known as *capital appreciation funds*, are among the most speculative funds. The fund manager often seeks to make quick gains. Although these funds have the potential to give you large returns on your investment, they also can rack up the heaviest losses.

For example, aggressive stock funds as a group delivered an average annual total return of 14.8 percent over the past 10 years, reaching a high of 54.5 percent in one year, but also hitting a low of –8.7 percent in another. Examples of aggressive-growth funds include AIM Equity-Aggressive Growth Fund, IDS Strategy Aggressive Equity Fund, and USAA Mutual Aggressive Growth.

Technobabble
Small company stocks are stocks of relatively new companies that are traded on the NASDAQ stock exchange, which, by the time you read this book, was supposed to be merging with the American Stock Exchange.

➤ *Small company stock funds* also are aggressive investments. These funds invest in younger companies whose stocks are traded over the counter. Small companies plow profits back into the company to grow their businesses and eventually become larger outfits. This is what you bank on as an investor.

Typically, fewer shares of a small company stock are traded. As a result, small company stock prices can be volatile. Heavy buying or selling of a small company's stock can send it soaring or plunging at a moment's notice. Over the past 10 years, small company stock funds as a group have delivered an average annual total return of 16.6 percent, with the high reaching 50.3 percent and the low, –9.5 percent. Examples of small company stock funds include Acorn Fund, Third Avenue Small Cap Value Fund, and the Oakmark Small Cap Fund.

News You Can Use

Stock fund portfolio managers use different strategies that they hope will make their shareholders richer. They use two basic investment styles to select stocks.

Stock funds that buy on value tend to invest in overlooked stocks that appear as if they could increase in price. The funds gain when the companies register unexpected profits and other investors start buying the stock in droves.

By contrast, fund managers who invest for growth want to own companies whose earnings are growing rapidly, often at more than 25 to 30 percent or more a year.

Does it matter which style a fund manager uses? Over 10-year periods, there has been little difference in the returns on funds that invest for growth or value. However, over a shorter period (three months to three years, for example), it is possible for one investment style to outperform the other. You can hedge your bets by owning stock funds that invest for growth and value, or you can stick with one style and invest regularly for the long term.

➤ *Growth funds*, which are a tad less risky than aggressive-growth funds, invest in the stocks of companies that have been around a while and should be profitable for years to come. These funds have the potential to appreciate in value, but they also can suffer big losses. Over the past 10 years, long-term growth funds as a group have delivered an average 16.0 percent annual total return, with the high reaching 36.7 percent and the low, –4.8 percent. Examples of growth funds are T. Rowe Price Growth Stock Fund, Strong Growth Fund, and Twentieth Century Growth.

➤ *Specialty funds*, also known as *sector funds*, invest in the stock of one specific industry. These funds generally are among the riskiest because the fund manager puts all the eggs in one basket. Not all specialty funds are alike. Some are riskier than others. It is also possible to find some specialty funds, such as utility stock funds, that are considered relatively low in risk.

Utility stock funds invest in businesses such as electric utilities, telephones, or telecommunications. They tend to have high yields because the firms whose stocks they own pay out most of their profits in dividends, which is a nice benefit for retirees living on a fixed income. These stocks perform relatively well during an economic recession. (After all, everyone uses electricity, even in a recession.) Over the past 10 years, utility stock funds had an average annual total return of 13.8 percent. The high was 31.3 percent and the low was –8.3 percent. Examples of utility stock funds include ABT Utility Income Fund, Fidelity Utilities Income, and Prudential Utility Fund.

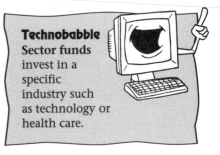

Technobabble
Sector funds invest in a specific industry such as technology or health care.

Other specialty funds include those that limit their investments to chemicals, financial services, health care, real estate, technology, and so forth. These funds can be high-risk gambits. Investors can earn whopping returns on investment—or they can lose their shirts if they invest at the wrong time. For example, the average technology stock fund delivered a 17.1 percent annual return rate over the past 10 years, with a high of 46.0 percent and a low of –5.1 percent for an entire year. Examples of specialty funds are the Evergreen Global Real Estate, Fidelity Select Biotechnology, and Invesco Strategic Financial Services.

News You Can Use

Looking to find your mutual fund's rating by Morningstar Mutual Funds, published by Morningstar Inc., Chicago? Good luck! Morningstar's rating categories differ from the categories both we and the rest of the industry use. Its rating categories are based on both investment style and what's known as *market capitalization* of the stocks the fund holds. Market capitalization is the total value of a stock traded on the stock exchange based on the share price and the total number of shares outstanding. Large company stocks, for example, typically have market capitalizations of $1 billion. Small company stocks have market capitalizations of under $500 million.

Looking for a growth and income fund? You'll probably have to hunt under Morningstar's categories of large-cap value funds, large-cap growth funds, or large-cap blend funds, which invest for both growth and value. Other categories Morningstar uses include mid-cap value, mid-cap growth, small-cap value, and small-cap growth, as well as blends of each of those.

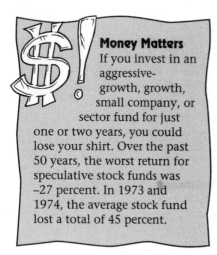

Money Matters
If you invest in an aggressive-growth, growth, small company, or sector fund for just one or two years, you could lose your shirt. Over the past 50 years, the worst return for speculative stock funds was –27 percent. In 1973 and 1974, the average stock fund lost a total of 45 percent.

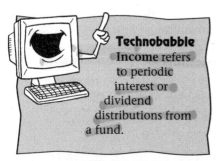

Technobabble
Income refers to periodic interest or dividend distributions from a fund.

Gold and precious metals are another popular type of specialty fund. Gold and precious metals, such as platinum and silver, tend to soar in value when the prices for necessities zoom. For that reason, some investors routinely keep a little money in gold funds. Recall that in the late 1970s, around when the price of oil shot up 40 percent, the price of gold also hit $800 an ounce. Mutual funds that invested in gold mining stocks gained a whopping 100 percent. Gold funds, however, are volatile investments and can lose big when the prices of goods and services stagnate or fall. Over the past 10 years, gold funds as a group experienced an average annual total return of –3.4 percent, with a high of 85 percent and a low of –42.5 percent. Examples of gold funds include U.S. World Gold Fund, Lexington Gold Fund, and IDS Precious Metals.

Clue No. 2: Income

The word *income* in the name or investment objective of the fund means the fund pays periodic dividends. These funds tend to be less risky than growth or aggressive-growth funds because the periodic income helps make up for any future potential declines.

If you invest in an income fund, however, be prepared for lower overall returns long-term than you might get with a growth or aggressive-growth fund. You normally do not get the increase in share price and thus the increase in the value of the investment that you would get from investing in aggressive-growth or growth stock funds. Funds with the word *income* somewhere in the investment objective probably fall into one of these categories:

➤ *Growth and income funds* own primarily stocks of well-established companies that pay out a lot of dividends to their shareholders. They strive first for growth or long-term gains over income. These funds can pay off handsomely, and they are less risky than aggressive stock funds. For example, over the past 10 years, growth and income funds as a group experienced a 15.7 percent annual total return, with a high of 36.7 percent and a low of –4.8 percent. Examples of growth and income funds are Scudder Growth and Income Fund, Neuberger & Berman Guardian Fund, and Babson Value Fund.

➤ *Equity income funds*, which also invest in stocks, are similar to growth and income funds, but they tend to favor income a bit more than growth. As a result, they can be less risky than other types of stock funds. For example, over the past 10 years, equity income funds have delivered an average annual total return of 14.2 percent, with a high of 26.6 percent and a low of –6.2 percent. Examples of equity income funds include Franklin Equity Income, Vanguard Equity Income, and Oppenheimer Equity Income.

➤ Income funds invest in higher-yielding stocks plus bonds. You get income first along with some growth. These funds usually invest in utility, telephone, and *blue-chip stocks* (stocks issued by well-established companies that typically pay a lot of dividends). Investors do not get as much growth out of income funds as they do by investing in growth or growth and income funds. Over the past 10 years, income funds had an average annual total return of 12.6 percent, with a high of 26.6 percent and a low of –6.2 percent.

➤ Examples of income funds are Vanguard Wellesley Income Fund, Income Fund of America, and Pioneer Income Fund.

News You Can Use

Some stock funds pay little, if anything, in the way of distributions. Small company stock funds, for example, don't distribute much dividend income to shareholders at all. Why? These funds invest in smaller companies that are busy pumping all their profits back into their businesses. However, a fund that invests in small company stocks may sell the stocks at a gain and may produce capital gains.

At the opposite end of the spectrum are funds that trade stocks frequently, such as most aggressive stock funds. An aggressive growth fund may pay a lot of distributions that come from both stock dividends and capital gains.

Mutual funds are required to distribute 98 percent of their earnings from dividends, interest, and capital gains to their shareholders. But they don't necessarily all do it at the same time. Most funds distribute income from interest monthly and income from stock dividends every three months. Capital gains are distributed once a year, usually in December. (You can find out when a fund pays distributions by reading the fund's prospectus, which you learn more about in Chapter 8, "Secrets of Mutual Fund Shopping.")

When you open an account with a fund, you have a choice. You can elect to receive the distributions from the fund by check, automatically deposit the distributions into a fund family's money fund, or reinvest the distributions into new shares of your existing fund. If you don't need the income, it's generally best to reinvest.

Another Type of Income Fund

Don't be surprised if your mutual fund salesperson calls a fund a *fixed-income fund* even though you can't necessarily find those exact words in the fund's investment objective. Fixed-income fund is another term for a *bond fund*. Bond funds are considered among the least risky mutual funds because bondholders have first priority for payoff if a company goes under.

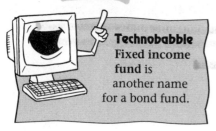

Technobabble
Fixed income fund is another name for a bond fund.

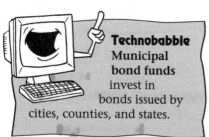

Technobabble
Municipal bond funds invest in bonds issued by cities, counties, and states.

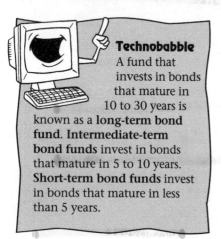

Technobabble
A fund that invests in bonds that mature in 10 to 30 years is known as a **long-term bond fund**. Intermediate-term bond funds invest in bonds that mature in 5 to 10 years. **Short-term bond funds** invest in bonds that mature in less than 5 years.

However, as we discuss in Chapter 12, "Bonding: Investing with Bond Funds," and Chapter 13, "Choosing the Right Bond Fund," these funds can rise and fall in value as interest rates fluctuate. Inflation also can erode the purchasing power of the money.

Until now in this chapter, we've explored primarily stock funds. Of course, there are a dizzying array of bond mutual funds to sift through as well. Recall that bond funds may invest all or part of their money in issues of corporations, foreign governments, U.S. Treasury securities, or U.S. government agencies. Municipal bond funds pay income that is free from federal, and, in some cases, state taxes.

Bond funds also are identified by the types of bond investments they make. For example, if the fund invests in bonds of Uncle Sam or affiliated agencies, the bond fund usually has the words *government securities* in its title.

Some bond funds are also identified by their bonds' terms. A fund that invests in bonds that mature in 10 to 30 years is known as a *long-term bond fund*. *Intermediate-term bond funds* invest in bonds that mature in 5 to 10 years. *Short-term bond funds* invest in bonds that mature in less than 5 years.

The longer the bond fund's term, the greater your chances of losing money if interest rates rise (see Chapter 3). Of course, on the up side, when interest rates fall, bond prices rise. There are a slew of bond categories to consider. Chapters 12 and 13 take a closer look at bond funds that may be right for you based on your income needs and tolerance for risk. Chapter 13 also takes a closer look at why long-term bond funds show greater changes in price when interest rates change. Bond funds also generally fit into two broad groups—taxable and tax-free.

Taxable Bond Funds

Think of it: high yields and low risk. An investor's dream….. That's what a number of mutual fund companies and promoters would have you believe about their funds. Unfortunately, in the mutual fund world, these two investment objectives don't, as a rule, go hand in hand. Taxable bond funds are a good example of this.

Some corporate bond funds invest in high-quality corporate bonds issued by companies rated double AA and triple AAA by Standard and Poor's and Moody's. (You'll learn more about bond ratings in Chapter 13.) Others, called *high-yield bond funds,* invest in bonds of companies with lower credit ratings. High-yield bond funds, as you've probably already deducted, have higher yields than other bond funds.

Some funds invest a small percentage of the assets in nonrated bonds. The outfits that issue these bonds are not rated for credit worthiness by Standard & Poor's and Moody's. That does not mean the bonds are bad deals. Some corporations choose not to have their bonds rated. So the fund manager has to evaluate the financial strength of the company.

Essentially, here's the deal. A bond has to pay more interest if it has a lower credit rating or no one would invest in it. Suppose you had the choice. You could buy a bond issued by Scurvy Inc., which is B-rated, or you could invest in a Hope-to-Succeed Corp. bond, rated AAA. If they both have the same current yield, Hope-to-Succeed Corp. clearly is sure to be the better choice.

Government mortgage bond funds, which invest in bonds issued or guaranteed by U.S. government agencies to help finance mortgages, pay higher yields than plain old Treasury-bond funds. These funds sport higher interest rates than 100 percent U.S. Treasury bond funds because the agencies technically are private, rather than a direct branch of the least risky bond issuer, the U.S. government. In other words, they're one notch higher on the risk ladder. Some funds invest in both U.S. Treasury bonds and U.S. government agency mortgage bonds.

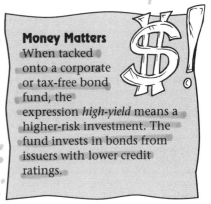

Technobabble **High-yield bond funds** invest in bonds of companies with lower credit ratings. They tend to have higher yields.

Money Matters When tacked onto a corporate or tax-free bond fund, the expression *high-yield* means a higher-risk investment. The fund invests in bonds from issuers with lower credit ratings.

Hot Tip! Is your mind boggled by all the bond funds available? Here's a good investment rule of thumb: The higher the interest rate, the riskier the investment.

In most cases, you won't get the capital appreciation from a bond fund that you get from a stock fund over the long term. These funds are designed to pay investors monthly income.

Tax-Free Bond Funds

As mentioned in Chapter 3, tax-free bond funds invest in municipal bonds, or bonds issued by states, cities, and counties and paid through taxes or project revenues. These are considered tax-free investments.

There are several types of tax-free bond funds available. Funds with the phrase *municipal bond* in their names typically invest in bonds throughout the United States. This enables the fund manager to find the best investments nationwide with the least risk. Interest income from these bonds is exempt from federal taxes, but not state taxes.

Investors residing in high-tax states such as New York, Massachusetts, California, and Pennsylvania also can invest in single-state municipal bond funds. As the name implies, these funds invest in the bonds of a single state, so residents of these states avoid paying both state and federal taxes on their interest income.

Hot Tip!
Insured municipal bond funds have been some of the best-performing tax-free bond funds over the past several years. These bonds are insured against default by insurance companies that specialize in municipal bonds.

As with taxable bonds, high-yielding tax-free municipal bond funds invest in lower-rated municipal bond issuers. Investors may get more interest income from high-yield municipal bond funds, but there also is a greater risk that they can lose if an issuer has problems paying back its principal and interest.

A word to the wise: Investors may find themselves paying some taxes on their municipal bond fund's earnings. Although the interest income isn't taxed, investors pay taxes on capital gains distributions. If a fund manager sells a bond at a profit, those profits must be passed on to the shareholders. Investors pay tax on long-term capital gains distributions from the sale of bonds held in the portfolio for more than 18 months. Short-term capital gains from the sale of bonds held for 18 months or less are taxed at the shareholder's income tax rate.

Balanced Funds

Balanced funds bridge the gap between stock funds and bond funds; that is, they split their investments relatively equally between stocks and bonds. Most of these funds invest 60 percent in blue-chip stocks and 40 percent in U.S. government or high-quality corporate bonds. Some funds, however, may invest 10 percent to 15 percent of their money in small company or foreign stocks.

Balanced funds are less risky than stock funds but a little riskier than certain bond funds. For example, balanced funds have experienced an average annual return of 12.6 percent over the past 10 years, with a high of 26.3 percent and a low of –2.8 percent. You might not necessarily find the word *balanced* in the title of these types of funds, so you'll have to check the fund's investment objective. Examples of balanced funds include the Dodge & Cox Balance Fund, Fidelity Puritan Fund, CGM Mutual Fund, and American Balanced Fund.

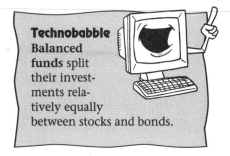

Technobabble **Balanced funds** split their investments relatively equally between stocks and bonds.

International Funds

International funds invest in stocks or bonds worldwide. You can pick from a wide variety of international funds: international growth, growth and income, and small company stock funds. Some funds invest in a specific region of the world, such as Europe, Asia, or Latin America. Some funds invest in a single country. Some funds invest worldwide, excluding the U.S. Those funds that invest in both the U.S. and foreign countries are known as global funds or world funds.

The more countries a fund invests in, the less risky it is. That's because the financial markets of different countries don't always move the same way. When the Japanese market drops in value, for example, the European markets may be moving higher. As a result, losses in one country may be offset by gains in another. Over the past 10 years, foreign funds have grown at an average annual rate of 8.8 percent, with the high being 36.5 percent and the low, –11.6 percent.

Regional funds or single-country funds are riskier than diversified international funds because all your eggs are in one basket. Your fortune may rise and fall within one country or area of the world. If there is a political uprising in the Far East, for example, the Asian stock markets may tumble. If one country, such as Japan, falls on economic tough times, Japan fund investors can lose investment value. Regional or single-country fund investing can be a boom-or-bust proposition. Over the past 10 years, for example, the funds that invested in the countries of the Pacific Basin had an average annual return of 4.6 percent—but the high was a whopping 75 percent and the low was –27 percent.

Technobabble **Single-country mutual funds** invest in one country's financial markets. A **regional fund** invests in the financial markets of a region of the world, such as Europe. **International funds** invest all over the world except the U.S. **Global funds** invest in the U.S. and the rest of the world.

On the bond side, some funds invest in corporate and government bonds worldwide. These funds are the least risky of the international bond fund group. People who invest in international bond funds should not expect to earn a whopping amount more than they would by investing here at home. Bond funds that invest worldwide, for example, had an average annual total return of 7.2 percent over the past 10 years. By contrast, on average, U.S. bond funds gained 8.5 percent over the same period. However, by investing in international bond funds, you get diversification. A U.S. bond fund may zig, and a bond fund that invests worldwide may zag. For example, in 1987, on average, T-bond funds lost almost 1 percent in value for the year. By contrast, on average, world bond funds gained 16 percent that year.

For Even Less Risky Returns...

As we told you in Chapter 3, money market funds invest mostly in money market or cash equivalent investments—typically short-term government and company debt and CDs. These tend to be lower yielding and have lower total returns, but they are less risky than the other types of funds described earlier in this chapter. Several types of money funds are available:

➤ *Government-only money funds* invest in Treasury bills and short-term U.S. government debt. These are the least risky money funds because the investments are backed by Uncle Sam.

➤ *General-purpose money funds* invest in bank CDs, short-term corporation I.O.U.s (called commercial paper), and other short-term debt. Because their investments are not backed by the U.S. government, these funds pay higher yields.

➤ *Tax-free money funds* invest in short-term municipal obligations, and single-state money funds are both federal and state tax-free.

Hot Funds

Some of the hottest newer types of funds in the industry are index funds. An *index fund* invests in the stocks that make up a specific published index, used to measure market performance. The most common indexes are the S&P 500, the Russell 2000, or the Lehman Brothers Bond Index.

These index funds can have different investment objectives. Don't get sold on them just because of their hot performance—until you've examined whether they actually meet your investment objectives.

Hot Tip!
The Mutual Fund Education Alliance offers a 60-page investor's kit that explains the basics of mutual fund investing for $15.00. For the kit, write The Mutual Fund Education Alliance, Dept. 0148, P.O. Box 419263, Kansas City, MO 64193-0148. For additional information, you may visit its Web site at http://www.mfea.com.

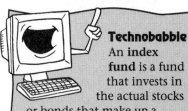

Technobabble
An **index fund** is a fund that invests in the actual stocks or bonds that make up a specific published index, typically used to measure an investment's market performance.

Tax-efficient funds use a variety of techniques designed to minimize taxes to shareholders.

Another hot new type of fund that investment companies are aggressively pushing lately are *tax-efficient funds*. These funds use a variety of techniques aimed at minimizing tax consequences, but again, they could have different investment objectives that may or may not meet yours. We'll get into tax-efficient funds more in Chapter 22, "Taxes: To Pay or Not to Pay?"

The Least You Need to Know

➤ Some mutual funds aim for growth in the value of your investment; others may aim for income from interest and dividends.

➤ Bond funds or fixed-income funds pay you income and may invest both here and abroad.

➤ You can invest in funds that own small, medium-size, or large company stocks.

➤ Balanced funds invest in both stock and bonds for more conservative investors.

Chapter 5

Is a Fund a Winner or Loser?

In This Chapter

➤ Betting on the right mutual fund

➤ Deciphering those performance figures

➤ Understanding total return

➤ Knowing what the averages are

Before you invest in a mutual fund, you need to act like a schoolteacher and give it a cool, objective evaluation. Once you know the ABCs of mutual funds, you can make a solid lifetime investment.

To evaluate a fund, you first have to know what to look for. Several measurements determine how well a fund has performed, how much it's likely to lose, and what you can expect to earn today.

You can get information about a fund's total return, yield, and measures of risk, which are discussed later in this chapter, from several sources of information, including the fund's prospectus, local newspaper mutual fund tables, or papers such as *The Wall Street Journal.* Then, once you finally invest, it's important to keep your eye on the ball. In this chapter, you'll learn all the important signals.

Check Out the Yield

There are a lot of numbers associated with mutual funds, and it's important to be sure you're comparing apples to apples. As discussed in Chapter 3, "Investing: Your Options, Your Risks, Your Rewards," a mutual fund pays distributions based on dividend income from stocks, interest income from bonds, and capital gains from the profitable sale of both.

The yield, expressed as a percentage of the fund's current net asset value or price per share, tells how much income you get from these sources. It measures the interest income, in the case of bonds, or dividend income, in the case of stock funds. This figure is particularly useful if you need steady money coming in—to pay monthly bills, for example. It allows you to compare the periodic income each fund generates.

Technobabble
The SEC yield—the required yield in disclosures and advertising—shows income from dividends and interest, less expenses, during a time period on a per-share basis.

The yield is expressed as an annual number; it represents a yield for a full 12 months. Suppose, for example, a fund paid 60 cents in dividends for the year and the fund's net asset value is $10. Sixty cents divided by 10 equals 6 percent.

The SEC requires funds to disclose their *SEC yield*, which is the income investors receive from dividends and interest, less expenses, during a particular time period on a per-share basis. This yield does not include any capital gains the fund has earned during the year. Bond mutual funds typically report 30-day SEC yields.

Even if you need regular income from a mutual fund, be sure to look at the fund's SEC yield and compare its total return with similar funds.

Check Out Operating Expenses—They Can Cost You

Fund expenses are taken out before the mutual fund distributes income or dividends. Like any company, the mutual fund must pay for the normal cost of doing business—including, for example, costs associated with the management of the fund, custody of the fund's assets, and servicing the fund's shareholders. These operating expenses are not paid directly by the investor. They are paid by the fund from its assets before distributions are made to the investor. The higher the operating expenses the fund has, the lower the amount of distributions to shareholders. Chapter 8, "Secrets of Mutual Fund Shopping," discusses mutual fund costs in greater detail.

The Whole Ball of Wax: Total Return

In a mutual fund, you don't just profit from distributions in the form of interest and dividends. You also stand to make money if the market price of your mutual fund rises. *Total return* figures in the whole kit and caboodle.

What good is it to invest in a high-yielding fund only to find that the market value of the investment has dropped? Total return measures how well the fund is doing overall. If a fund manager is making the right investments, buying the right securities, adjusting the fund's investments to avoid large losses, and letting the profits roll in, the fund will have a positive total return.

Simply put, total return represents the change in the fund's share price plus the amount of money generated from reinvested income and capital gains distributions. Divide this by the original share price to calculate your total return rate. (You don't need to worry about fund expenses when you calculate the total return. As mentioned previously, the mutual fund deducts expenses before paying you distributions. As a result, the fund's yield already reflects the expenses that were taken out.)

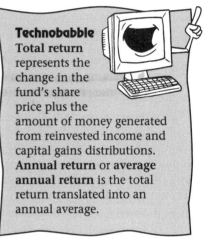

Technobabble
Total return represents the change in the fund's share price plus the amount of money generated from reinvested income and capital gains distributions. **Annual return** or **average annual return** is the total return translated into an annual average.

If all you know is that the total return of a fund over three years is 52 percent, you're stuck! That doesn't tell you the average annual return that most publications quote. You have to do some complicated algebra to come up with this number (which, by the way, is 15 percent).

We'll make life easier for you. Table 5.1 shows the annual average return based on the total return you've calculated. Simply look to the right for your total return under the column that represents the number of years you figured. Your annual return is to the left.

Table 5.1 Figuring the Average Annual Return

	Number of Years of Total Return		
Annual Return	*3*	*5*	*10*
5%	15.8%	27.6%	62.9%
6%	19.1%	33.8%	79.1%
7%	22.5%	40.3%	96.7%
8%	26.0%	46.9%	115.9%
9%	29.5%	53.9%	136.7%
10%	33.1%	61.1%	159.4%
11%	36.8%	68.5%	183.9%
12%	40.5%	76.2%	210.6%
13%	44.3%	84.2%	239.5%
14%	48.2%	92.5%	270.7%

continues

Table 5.1 Continued

	Number of Years of Total Return		
Annual Return	*3*	*5*	*10*
15%	52.1%	101.1%	304.6%
16%	56.1%	110.0%	341.1%
17%	60.2%	119.2%	380.7%
18%	64.3%	128.8%	423.4%
19%	68.5%	138.6%	469.5%
20%	72.8%	148.8%	519.2%

The annual return is the most frequently reported number on mutual funds. A number of mutual fund reporting services (discussed in Chapter 9, "Seeking a Second Opinion") list the annual average returns—so do your local newspapers.

Checking Out the Fund's Long-Term Batting Average

Got the hang of it? A good fund has a good long-term batting average, but over the short term, like a baseball player, the fund can have some off years. Perhaps a fund manager had a bad case of the hiccups in 1995. That doesn't necessarily mean you give up your Mickey Mantle or Hank Aaron of the mutual fund world. In Chapter 6, "Which Funds Are Right for You?," you will learn to pick the funds that are right for you based on your investment comfort level.

With all this talk about total returns and the growth in the share value of mutual fund investments, what could an investor expect to earn over the long term? Past performance is no indication of future returns, but history does give an indication of what you can expect. To help zero in on your mutual fund choices, here are average annual total returns on stocks, bonds, and cash investments over the past 70 years, according to Ibbotson Associates, a Chicago-based research firm:

➤ **Common stocks.** 10 percent annually over the past 70 years. In any given year, you had a good chance of earning between –11 percent and +21 percent.

➤ **Corporate bonds.** 5.5 percent annually over the past 70 years. In any given year, you had a good chance of making between –3 percent and +14 percent.

➤ **U.S. government bonds.** 5 percent annually over the past 70 years. In any given year, you had a good chance of making between –3.6 percent and +13.6 percent.

➤ **T-bills (cash).** 3.7 percent annually over the past 70 years. In any given year, you had a good chance of making between just under 1 percent or +7 percent.

How Risky Is It?

There are a couple of easy ways to figure out how risky a fund is. The more volatile a fund, the greater chance you'll see wide swings in total return and the share value of a fund. The swing in performance as measured by the fund's total return is known as *volatility*. In bad years, a volatile fund will lose a lot more money than other funds. However, in good years, you can see double-digit returns.

Technobabble
Volatility is how much a fund's price goes up and down.

Rate Your Stock Fund's Volatility

By looking at one simple number, you can tell how risky your stock fund is. The fund's *beta* tells you how much volatility, and therefore, risk, there is within the fund's portfolio in relation to the stock market average. Ask a fund service representative for the beta, or look it up in several reports discussed in Chapter 9.

This all might sound like Greek to you, but it's really simple. The lower the beta of your stock fund, the lower your risk. The beta measures stock fund performance in relation to the S&P 500, an index of 500 stocks, that is considered a standard measure of how the overall stock market performs. The S&P 500 has a beta of 1, so a mutual fund with a beta greater than 1 should both win more and lose more than the stock market average. By contrast, a fund with a beta of less than 1 won't gain as much as the S&P 500, but it also should lose less when the stock market heads south.

Technobabble
A stock fund's **beta** tells you how risky the fund tends to be in relation to the stock market. A fund with a low beta is less risky than the stock market in general.

A fund's beta may help you decide on the type of stock fund that fits your tolerance for risk. If you are investing for long-term growth, you want to be sure you have a fund with a beta that's more than 1. That way, you know that the fund can perform well in a rising stock market. You might want to avoid a fund with an excessively high beta. It may be a hot-performing fund, but it can also lose a lot of money.

Technobabble
The S&P 500, an index of 500 stocks, is considered a standard measure of how the overall stock market performs.

By contrast, even if you are a conservative stock fund investor, you don't want to invest in a stock fund that has a real low beta. Funds with betas below .5 may keep a lot of money in cash investments and bonds. These are very low-risk stock funds. Typically, funds with betas below .5 or .6 do well when the stock market declines in value. These funds register higher total returns compared with higher beta stock funds during bear markets when stocks drop. Consequently, you might not get the share value growth that you need to meet your financial goals over the long term.

Joe Biddle was considering two mutual funds for his retirement, which was 20 years away. One, the Grow Like Crazy stock fund, had a beta of 1.2. Another, the Steady As You Go stock fund, had a beta of .85. Although Joe wanted the Grow Like Crazy fund, his wife, Bertha, was a little nervous. Because the Grow Like Crazy fund had a beta of 1.2, if the stock market plunged, the fund could be down 20 percent more than the market. They finally decided on the Steady As You Go fund.

How Did a Fund Do in Bad Years?

Hot Tip!
The Morningstar Mutual Fund Report and the Value Line Mutual Fund Survey, which are available in public libraries, also evaluate a fund's risk. These reports look at how funds do in down markets, and then they rank the funds. These ratings automatically show how one fund stacks up against another.

If looking for betas is not your cup of tea, there's an easier way to gauge a stock fund's risk. Compare how a number of stock funds did in bad years, such as 1973, 1974, 1981, 1987, 1990, and 1994. Suppose you're seriously considering three stock funds and they've all performed about the same. Here's what to consider:

➤ Growth stock fund A has grown at an annual rate of 13.25 percent over the past 10 years, stock fund B gained 12.98 percent, and C was up 13.4 percent.

➤ Compare the funds' returns in 1987, 1990, and 1994. As you can see from Table 5.2, Fund B lost the least in the most recent bad years. It gained a little less than the others, but it wasn't far off the mark. Fund C gained the most, but it also seemed to lose the most in bad years.

Table 5.2   How Sample Funds Did in Bad Years

Fund	1987	1990	1994
A	–6.0%	–9.0%	–12.0%
B	–3.0%	–6.0%	–5.5%
C	–8.0%	–9.5%	–9.5%

The idea is to find the most consistently performing funds. So if you're comparing several funds that have similar returns, stick with the funds that did the best in down markets. That's an indication the fund manager navigates well. If you see funds that show wild swings in total return from year to year, he or she might be making big bets that pay off in some years, but not in others.

How to Gauge a Bond Fund's Risk

There are a couple of ways to tell whether a bond fund is too hot to handle. These measures, called *duration* and *average maturity*, can help you assess the riskiness of a bond fund. As discussed in Chapter 3, bond prices move in the opposite direction of interest rates. When interest rates rise, prices for bonds with lower rates fall. By contrast, when interest rates fall, prices for bonds with higher interest rates rise.

Duration measures how much your bond fund will increase or decrease in value with a 1 percent change in interest rates. A fund with a duration of 4, for example, drops about 4 percent in value if interest rates rise 1 percent, but it increases 4 percent in value if interest rates drop 1 percent. By contrast, a fund with a duration of 10 loses 10 percent in value if interest rates rise 1 percent but increases 10 percent in value if interest rates drop 1 percent.

There's another easy way to measure a bond fund's risk: Look at its *average maturity*. The lower the average maturity, the less money the fund loses when interest rates rise. The higher the average maturity, the more money the bond fund loses if rates increase. By contrast, the higher the average maturity, the more the bond fund will make if interest rates fall.

Bond mutual funds typically own a lot of different bonds that mature in different years. How do you tell the average maturity of the bonds owned by a bond fund? Ask the fund rep or check the prospectus or semiannual and annual reports.

Technobabble
Duration tells you what percentage the value of your bond fund will rise or fall with a 1 percent change in interest rates.

You can lose a lot of money in a bond fund that has a duration of 10 or more. These funds invest in long-term bonds. If interest rates rise 1 percent, the fund will lose 10 percent.

Technobabble
Average maturity is the average length of time that bonds in a mutual fund's portfolio mature.

Tips on Spotting a Winning Fund

Chapter 16, "How Ya Doing?" shows you how to evaluate a fund or several funds' performances after you already own them. You will learn when to dump the losers and keep the winners. As a rule of thumb, it's a good idea to monitor the performance of a fund or funds you're thinking of buying for a while—at least once every three months. See how the fund reacts when the stock market zooms or plunges. Then, compare it with similar funds. That way, you'll get a feel for how the fund performs over the investment cycle. Ideally, you want the fund that loses less in down markets and does great in up markets.

Once you own a fund, it's a tough cross to bear when the value drops. But assuming you've done your homework, it's generally best not to unload it just because it has lagged behind its peers for several months. Give it at least three years or more. The reason: Its important to see how the fund does during the investment cycle, which includes both good and bad economic times.

Unfortunately, there is no totally magic formula to evaluate a fund's performance. A well-managed fund may look like it's doing poorly compared with other funds during down times simply because the fund manager is actually smart. He or she might be using the down period to load up on cheap stocks. Then, when times improve, that fund, like most good funds, could rebound with a vengeance.

Small company stock funds, for example, have displayed some of their greatest performances in rising markets right after a recession. By contrast, when business is booming, it's the large company growth stock funds that tend to zoom. Overall, funds that invest for growth or value take turns outperforming each other about every 18 months, according to State Street Research, Boston.

The lesson to be learned: If you're investing in mutual funds, you need to do quite a bit of homework up front and then be patient—at least for a while. It may be the investment style rather than the fund itself that is temporarily out of favor.

As tempting as it might be, it doesn't usually pay to switch funds as soon as one type of fund starts doing better than another. If you play investment tic-tac-toe, you're only apt to make Uncle Sam and your mutual fund company richer. Not only might you be paying fees for the trades, but also you could be hit with taxes.

If you keep well-managed growth and value funds through thick and thin, you won't have to worry too much about the investment cycles. You can devote your energy to playing golf, softball, tennis, or shopping!

If you need growth from a stock fund, take these steps:

1. Compare a fund's total return over at least 3, 5, and 10 years.
2. Check a fund's beta to see how it will do compared to the overall stock market.
3. Look at how the fund did in bad years.

Your objective is to find the fund with the best total return, the lowest beta, and the least amount of losses in bad years.

Don't choose the funds with the hottest short-term track records. Last year's winners could be this year's laggards.

If you need income from a bond fund, take these steps:

1. Compare funds' SEC yields over the past few years. You want to invest in a bond fund that pays consistent income to its shareholders.
2. Compare the funds' total returns over at least 10 years. Earning high yields doesn't help you much if the value of your investment is declining.

3. Check out the funds' average maturities. Bond prices and interest rates move in opposite directions. So if interest rates rise, bond prices fall. The longer the maturity, the greater the decline.

4. Look at bond funds' durations. The numbers tell how much your fund will rise or fall if interest rates change 1 percent.

Your objective with bond funds is to get the highest yield with the least amount of risk. Don't chase after high-yield funds. High-yield funds own speculative investments in financially weaker companies. The companies have to pay higher yields to attract investors and compensate them for the risk. So remember, the higher the yield the greater the risk.

Whether you invest in stock or bond funds, it is also important to find out who is managing the fund and his or her track record. If a fund manager leaves, it could be a warning sign to get out. But don't jump ship right away. A new manager may breed new life into a fund.

The Least You Need To Know

➤ Look at the fund's total return before you buy.

➤ Check a stock fund's volatility rating or beta.

➤ See how a fund does in bad years.

➤ The higher the yield, the greater the risk when it comes to investing in bond funds.

Part 2
Getting Started

Now we're getting serious, folks. The most important part of mutual fund investing is featured in the coming chapters—before you fill out the application. You need to make sure you're picking the right funds.

Don't worry; you don't need an MBA to do this. All you need are a few tricks. Believe it or not, the key to mutual fund investing is not necessarily knowing any major secrets about the direction of interest rates or major industry trends. It's knowing yourself and then knowing what to look for based on your own unique nature.

We're not talking major brain surgery here, so just sit back in a comfortable chair and relax. Consider this the matchmaking part of the book. It will help you figure out your own personal investment profile and steer you in the direction of funds that may be right for you.

Which Funds Are Right for You?

Are you ready to invest? Get on your mark, get set.... Wait a minute. Stop the music!

Stock and bond prices sure bounce up and down a lot. Are you really ready to rock and roll? If you pick up the business section of your local newspaper any day of the week, you'll see what we mean. Sure, you might be inspired because of a newspaper or magazine report that some mutual fund investors are making big profits. Wow! ABC mutual fund gained 20 percent so far this year. Joe Biddle invested $1,000, and six months later, it's up to $1,200! Then again, none of us needs to get fried by investing our life savings in a hot stock fund, only to have it nose-dive over the following few weeks.

Over the past five years, you would have more than doubled your money in the average run-of-the-mill mutual fund. Today, stock prices are at record levels. Interest rates could rise, and there are serious economic problems in Asia. So don't expect to earn those whopping returns of the past.

Although you now have a clear picture of your savings goals and how to free the money to invest, that's not enough to get started.

Take it from one member of this team, a former diehard CD investor: You have to be sure you understand what you're getting into before you spend your hard-earned cash on anything that fails to move consistently in a northerly direction. That's why we're here, so read on.

What Are Ya in For?

Unfortunately, there are some pain-in-the-neck risks you must contend with when you invest in mutual funds—such as losing money. You also can make a killing, however. Your success as a mutual fund investor depends largely on how you handle the downside of this otherwise attractive investment.

Take John and Mary, who just retired to sunny West Palm Beach, Florida. They live on John's pension, Social Security, and some savings. Before John retired, he put the bulk of their life savings—$25,000—in a mutual fund.

Three months later, the value of his fund had plunged $3,000. Before John had time to regret his investment decision, he managed to crack his tooth on a cashew nut while eating dinner with Mary in a local Chinese restaurant. Because he had no dental insurance, he was forced to spend $3,000 for a bridge. He had to sell his mutual fund at precisely the wrong time. That's what we mean by risk—investing in a mutual fund when you really can't afford to lose.

Hot Tip!
Mutual funds are long-term investments. The longer you invest, the less chance you have of losing. Based on financial history, stocks never have lost money over any 20-year period, according to Ibbotson Associates, Chicago. However, if you invest for just one year, you could lose money close to one-third of the time.

Invest for five years and expect at least one bad year. This will give you a good idea why it's important to invest in stock funds for the long term.

What's risky for John and Mary, however, may not be risky for somebody else. Tad, a 35 year-old dentist, makes 100 grand a year. Tad is comfortable investing in mutual funds because he is aware that even though the $10,000 he invests today can drop in value over the short term, he also knows that mutual funds are great investments for the long term. Tad has a good job. He can afford to invest for 25 to 30 years and build a nest egg. He won't be upset if his $10,000 investment is worth $9,000 at the end of this year because there's a good chance it could be worth $12,000 at the end of the following year.

There are a few reasons a mutual fund can fall in value. We already discussed many of these in Chapter 3, "Investing: Your Options, Your Risks, Your Rewards." Mutual funds invest generally in stocks, bonds, or both. When tons of investors buy stocks, stock prices head up. If those same investors sell stocks, stock prices can take a dive. The value of a mutual fund that contains stocks changes according to what investors do. You should make sure that your investment decisions take into account anticipated market trends.

Believe it or not, there's also a risk that your investment can be *too* safe. If you stay in an FDIC-insured savings account, for example, your money might not grow fast enough to keep up with the prices of food and utilities. This is known as *inflation*. True, your bank account is federally insured. You can't lose any money if your friendly banker goes out of business.

Have you checked the interest banks pay on savings accounts, though? It's between 1 and 3 percent. What good is it if a few years down the road, you live on an investment that makes 100 bucks a week, but it costs $104 for groceries? You still have to reach into your pocketbook because you are $4 short. Suppose you're saving for your child's college education. The cost of college is rising about 6 percent a year, and you estimate you need $100,000 for 4 years of tuition at Home Town State College in 18 years. If you earn too little on your investment and it grows to only $85,000, you're in the hole. Where are you going to get the rest of the money?

Now, we don't want you to get overly upset about these Chicken Little stories. As mentioned at the beginning of the book, mutual fund managers are fully aware of these bugaboos and take steps to limit losses.

> **Hot Tip!**
> Over the past 20 years, stock mutual funds have been the best way to beat inflation. Bond mutual funds come in second.

Zeroing In on Your Comfort Level

Here's where we get into the real soul-searching part of mutual fund investing. It's time to find out more about the real you. You are real, right? By figuring out a few things about both yourself and your investing temperament, one of two things will happen—or perhaps even a little of both. You'll be able to decide what type of mutual funds are right for you. (Perhaps you will adjust the way you think about mutual funds in general. After all, it could well be time to make some changes in your investment personality if it's preventing you from making the kind of money you should make over the long term!)

By asking yourself a few basic questions, you'll develop a better idea of the risk you're willing to assume when investing in mutual funds. You'll learn whether you're a conservative investor or a risk-taker.

> **Technobabble**
> **Conservative investors** like less risky investments that lose little money. **Moderate investors** are willing to see the value of their mutual funds drop slightly in return for long-term profits. **Aggressive investors** want to earn big gains but also are willing to accept big losses.

"That's easy to figure out," you say. "I don't want to take any risk. I don't want to lose any money!" We fully understand. None of us wants to risk his or her hard-earned savings—not even the smartest investors among us. As we indicated earlier, "risk" means something a little bit different when it relates to mutual funds—or any other investment, for that matter. It involves evaluating how much money you're willing to lose in exchange for the potential for greater earnings long-term. If you keep your money under the mattress, you might think you're avoiding all risk. Just wait, though. In 30 years, that mattress stash might not even buy one loaf of bread!

Nevertheless, you don't want to invest in risky funds if you are a safety-minded investor. By the same token, if you like to invest aggressively, conservative funds aren't for you. Once you have this information in hand, you can explore the kinds of mutual funds that fit your risk profile. You'll also learn how to divide your investments.

Risk Acceptance Quiz

To help determine your risk tolerance, select (circle) the letter that best expresses your answers to the following questions:

1. How old are you?
   A. Over age 65 (1)
   B. Between age 55 and 65 (2)
   C. Between age 35 and 55 (3)
   D. Under age 35 (4)

2. How much are you willing to lose in mutual fund investments in any given year?
   A. 1 percent (1)
   B. 3 percent (2)
   C. 10 percent (3)
   D. 15 percent (4)

3. How important is regular income from your investments? (That is, do you need to use the interest and dividends from your investments to cover expenses now?)
   A. I absolutely need the income. (1)
   B. I could use the income from time to time. (2)
   C. I don't need the income now but may one day. (3)
   D. I would rather reinvest the income in new shares of the fund. (4)

4. How important is reinvesting your fund's dividends, interest, and capital gains in new shares for growth?
   A. I would rather get a check from my fund group. (1)
   B. It is somewhat important to reinvest. (2)
   C. It is important to reinvest. (3)
   D. It's very important to reinvest for long-term growth. (4)

5. How important is it to avoid losses and know your money is safe?

    A. Very important (1)

    B. Important (2)

    C. Somewhat important (3)

    D. Not important (4)

6. How important is it that your money grow faster than the prices you pay for the things you need?

    A. Not as important as getting regular income. (1)

    B. I want it to grow as fast as the cost of things I need. (2)

    C. I want it to grow more than the cost of things I need. (3)

    D. I want it to grow much faster than the cost of things. (4)

Add the numbers in parentheses to the right of each of your answers to determine your total risk-tolerance score:

➤ If your score is 10 or less, you are a *conservative investor*. This means that safety is as important as seeing your money grow in value over the years.

➤ If you score between 10 and 20, you are a *moderate investor*. You are willing to see your mutual funds decline in value a little bit in return for long-term growth.

➤ If you score 20 or more, you are an *aggressive investor*. You are willing to accept larger short-term losses than most people in return for substantial gains long term.

Most people who need income to pay their monthly bills are safety-minded investors. They can't afford to lose. Then again, there are those—often persons in a younger age group—who need to be investing in stock funds for growth, but simply are scaredy-cats. They want to hide in CDs, U.S. Treasury bills and money funds. If you're in this category, and have money you probably won't need for 10 years or so, you might want to reevaluate your financial personality. Your fear just might be holding you back.

After you take this test, look at your age and financial goals. Don't be afraid to invest—at least in a well-managed growth and income fund—money that you won't be needing any time soon. Still afraid? Chapters 17 through 20 provide some easy-to-use strategies so that you can reduce the risk of losing money.

Which Funds Are Right for You?

Now for your first class at the Culinary Institute of Mutual Funds. You have the ingredients lined up: how much risk you can stand, how much money you need by when, and the types of mutual funds from which to select. Now, you're going to mix it all together.

The general rule is the higher the yield in the case of bond funds, or the higher the total return in the case of stock funds, the more risky the mutual fund. (Unfortunately, even the most savvy investors can't necessarily have everything!) Investing for the long term is key to reaping any benefits from an aggressive or growth-oriented mutual fund. If you invest for a year or two, you can lose. Investors with just a couple of years to invest also need to protect what they have in less risky investments.

It's time to take what you've already learned about yourself and mutual funds and put it into a format to meet your needs. You'll see which funds are appropriate for which types of investors. You'll also discover how to split up your money among different types of funds to get the best return with the least amount of risk. You now know about how much heat you can stand. The time has come to select the funds that match your risk temperature. The quiz earlier in this chapter helped you determine whether you are an aggressive, moderate, or conservative investor. You know how much you can stomach losing in a year's time in return for the long-term profits. You also know whether anything short of an FDIC-insured investment makes you queasy.

What Are Your Options?

Let's take a minute to review the investments available. Think of investing in funds based on a pyramid of risk, such as the one illustrated here.

At the top are the riskiest funds, the funds that can lose or gain a lot of money over a short time. The riskiest funds often pay the highest returns. For instance, funds that invest in just one sector of an industry can gain 70 percent or lose 30 percent in any given year.

Next in line are aggressive growth funds and small company stock funds. You also can win or lose big with these. Although speculators often move in and out of aggressive growth and small company stock funds, these funds also are excellent long-term investments. Sock money into one of these babies for 20 years, and you could have a nice retirement nest egg.

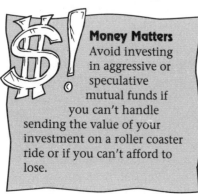

Money Matters
Avoid investing in aggressive or speculative mutual funds if you can't handle sending the value of your investment on a roller coaster ride or if you can't afford to lose.

Next in line are growth funds, which also are considered good investments for the long term. These funds tend to invest in larger, well-established companies, but they also can be risky. Moderate and conservative investors may invest at this level. Growth and income funds and balanced funds are sleep-at-night stock funds. You can get rich slowly and with relatively low risk with these funds.

Corporate bond funds are next on the pyramid. You'll earn higher yields, but typically, you won't get the kind of growth you get from stock funds. Funds that invest in Treasury bonds are less risky than their corporate counterparts because the bonds are backed against default by Uncle Sam.

At the bottom of the pyramid are the least risky funds—short-term bond funds and money market funds. If you have a short-term investment time span, it's best to stick with the lowest-risk funds.

Pyramid of Risk

How mutual fund risk stacks up.

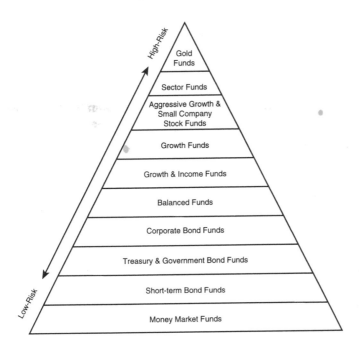

High-Risk
Low-Risk

Gold Funds

Sector Funds

Aggressive Growth & Small Company Stock Funds

Growth Funds

Growth & Income Funds

Balanced Funds

Corporate Bond Funds

Treasury & Government Bond Funds

Short-term Bond Funds

Money Market Funds

Matchmaker, Matchmaker, Make Me a Match

Investing in mutual funds is a long-term affair. If you pick out the right types of funds, you can stick with them for life. In our travels, we've talked to people who've been investing in the same funds for more than 10 years. They've made them part of their family. After all, these investors are trusting an investment company with their life savings. As long as their funds do better than 50 percent of similar funds, they just keep socking away the money to meet future goals.

Avoid a Fistful of Mistakes

Make yourself happy by picking the right funds. Unfortunately—and you've probably heard all too many of these horror stories—many mutual fund investors don't. Here are the mistakes many fund pickers make:

1. They chase after the hot funds. Once you read about a hot fund with a sizzling return in the newspaper or a personal finance magazine, it's usually too late to invest!

2. They invest to make a quick profit. If you do that, you could lose big. Mutual funds, on the whole, should be a long-term investment.

3. They chase after high yields. Remember, the higher the yield, the greater the risk. When comparing a short-, intermediate-, or long-term bond fund to its respective group averages, be suspicious if a fund outyields similar funds by a wide margin.

    Suppose the average long-term bond fund yields 7 percent, and you are looking at a specific long-term bond fund that yields more than 10 percent. The fund that yields over 10 percent must be high-risk. How else could the fund pay those yields?

4. They play it too safe. CDs and money funds are good short-term places to park your money. If you're socking away money for your retirement, however, stock funds historically have offered a better deal for the long term.

5. They pick unsuitable funds. If you need income and lower risk, you should not be investing in aggressive stock funds.

6. They pick a fund based on its name alone, rather than check the actual securities the fund buys. You can't always tell by the name of the fund.

7. They panic and sell when the market goes down.

8. They buy funds based on hot tips from their friends.

Getting a Good Fit

Just wear the wrong size shoes for a day and see how you feel. There's nothing worse for your lovely disposition. The same goes for mutual funds. Chapter 4, "Mutual Funds for Everyone," discusses the different kinds of funds in which you can invest. Now, try on a fund for size. Table 6.1 ranks stock and bond funds by their risk level, as well as the potential for the following types of rewards:

➤ Big gains refer to potential for high total returns because the objective of the fund is to speculate for the purpose of rapid and large increases in the share value of the fund.

➤ Maximum growth refers to the potential of producing the highest total returns from funds that invest most aggressively in stocks.

➤ Growth refers to higher-than-average total returns because the funds invest in stocks for long-term growth in the share value of the fund.

➤ Income refers to the potential ability of the fund to provide investors with regular interest or dividends.

➤ Low risk and least risk refer to the potential capability of the fund to preserve your principal.

Table 6.1 Getting Comfortable with a Fund

Investor Risk Level/Objective	Type of Fund	Risk/Reward
Stock Funds		
Speculative	Precious metals	Highest/Big gains
Speculative	Most sector	Higher/Big gains
Aggressive	Aggressive growth	High/Maximum capital growth
Aggressive	International growth	High/Maximum capital growth
Aggressive	Small company	High/Maximum capital growth
Aggressive	Growth	High/Longer-term growth
Moderate	Growth and income	Moderate/Growth plus income
Moderate	Equity income	Low-moderate/Income plus growth
Conservative	Income	Lower/Long-term income
Conservative	Utility	Lower/Long-term income
Conservative	Balanced	Lower/Income plus growth
Bond Funds		
Aggressive	High-yield	High/High income
Aggressive	Long-term government	High/Income
Aggressive	Long-term tax-free	High/Income
Aggressive	International	High/Income
Moderate	Intermediate-term	Moderate/Income
Moderate	Intermediate tax-free	Moderate/Income
Conservative	Short-term	Lower/Income and less risk
Conservative	Short-term tax-free	Lower/Income and less risk
Other Funds		
Safety-minded	Money market	Lowest/Income and least risk

Getting the Best Returns with the Least Risk

There is one more step to nailing down your mutual fund investments. Once you know your risk level, you can invest in different types of funds so that you can get the best possible return with the least risk.

Technobabble
When you **diversify** your mutual fund investments, you own different kinds of funds so that losses in one fund can be offset with gains in the others. Diversification is designed to give you the best returns with the least possible risk.

Hedging is selecting investments so that the losses in one or more investments are offset by gains in others and vice versa. To hedge, you look for investments that perform at odds with each other. When one is gaining value, the other is losing value, and vice versa.

Earlier in this book, we told you that the major advantage of mutual funds is that they diversify their investments. A mutual fund might, for example, buy stocks of several different companies. This way, if one stock performs poorly, the others still might perform well. Gurus say it could pay to take a similar strategy when you pick your mutual funds. They call this *diversification*.

Diversification means that if you divide your investments the right way, gains in one type of mutual fund can offset losses in other types of funds. One kind of fund may zig when the other zags.

Look at it this way. Suppose you're graphing the performance of a couple of mutual funds. Over several years, Fund A's performance looks just like an M. It goes up and it goes down. Fund B's performance looks like a W. It goes down, then up, then down, and back up again.

If you own just one of these funds, you're in for a wild ride. If you own them both, you get an entirely different picture. Losses in one fund are offset by gains in the other. You get a less bumpy ride. In the following figure, the gains and losses of A and B together give you C.

How diversification works to smooth out the bumps.

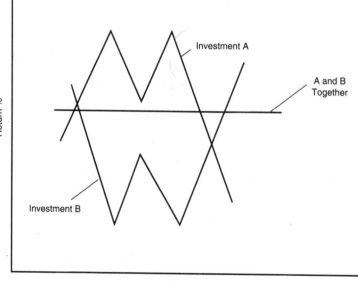

68

Slicing Up Your Investment Pie

How do you know how many of your available investment dollars to invest in each kind of mutual fund? One easy way to figure it out is to subtract your age from 100; the number you get is how much to invest in stocks. If you are 40 years old, 100–40 = 60. You should put 60 percent of your money in stocks and 40 percent in bonds and money funds.

Your stockbroker or financial planner also can help you find the best mix of funds. Many offer computer software that can analyze your goals and risk tolerance to come up with a mix of investments that's right for you. You can do it yourself by using the material that investment companies will send you upon request. You need to perform your own research, which we help you through in Chapter 9, "Seeking a Second Opinion."

The Main Ingredients

You need four ingredients to diversify your mutual fund recipe:

> ➤ **Stock funds.** Invest in stock funds for growth and inflation protection. Recall that stocks historically have earned 6 to 7 percent more than the rate of inflation.

> ➤ **Bond funds.** Invest in bond funds for income and to hedge against stock fund losses. Stock fund and bond fund prices don't always move in the same direction, so if you own a bond fund, it could cushion the blow of losses in your stock funds or other investments.

> ➤ **Money funds.** Money funds generally are a stabilizer. When interest rates rise, you earn higher yields from a money fund.

> ➤ **International stock or bond funds.** Foreign stock markets don't always perform like ours. Often, but not always, international bond or stock funds gain in value while U.S. funds perform poorly.

Some funds do the diversification for you. They are known as *asset allocation funds* (see Chapter 14, "Building Your Wealth with Stock Funds").

Hot Tip!
Mutual fund families have excellent booklets or computer software to help you find the right funds based on your comfort level. Call

T. Rowe Price, 800-638-5660

Vanguard, 800-662-7447

Scudder, 800-225-2470

Fidelity Investments, 800-544-8888

Dreyfus, 800-645-6561

Neuberger & Berman, 800-877-9700

Simple Mixes

The following suggested mixes of different kinds of mutual funds, based on your age and risk tolerance, should give you solid returns while helping to protect you if the market nose-dives:

➤ **Aggressive investors.** When you are young and just starting out in the work world, or you have built up a nest egg and you still have a long time before you retire, you can afford to invest aggressively. You have plenty of time for losses to be offset by gains in the share value of your mutual fund. That's why aggressive investors between the ages of 20 and 49 can invest 80 percent in stock funds and 20 percent in bond funds.

➤ **Moderate investors.** Investors between the ages of 50 and 59, who want to see the share value of their mutual funds grow but want to protect their principal, should invest 60 percent in stocks and 40 percent in bonds. Ages 50 through 59 are key savings and investing years. Because retirement is more than 10 years away, growth in the value of the investments is important to building a retirement nest egg. This group invests in stock funds for growth in the share value of their investments, but they also need to temper the risk of losing a lot of money.

➤ **Conservative investors.** Investors between the ages of 60 and 74 still need some growth so that the share value of their investments keeps pace with inflation. Then, they can protect the purchasing power of their money. Consider a mix of 40 percent stocks, 40 percent bonds, and 20 percent money funds.

➤ **Senior citizens.** Investors age 75 and older, who need income but also need to preserve their principal, should keep 20 percent in stocks to help maintain the purchasing power of the money, 60 percent in bond funds, and 20 percent in money funds. The biggest fear senior citizens face is the fear of outliving their money. That's why it's still important to keep a small percentage of investments in a well-managed stock fund.

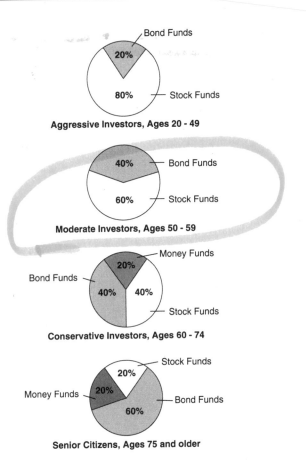

Suggested ways to slice the investment pie.

Aggressive Investors, Ages 20 - 49

Moderate Investors, Ages 50 - 59

Conservative Investors, Ages 60 - 74

Senior Citizens, Ages 75 and older

Spicing It Up

Want even more diversification? Invest in different kinds of stock and bond funds. A really aggressive investor can divide stock funds among aggressive growth funds, small company stock funds, or similar funds that invest overseas.

More moderate investors can split stock fund investments between growth and income funds and international funds or keep a teeny-weeny bit in a well-diversified growth stock fund.

Conservative investors can invest in U.S. and overseas growth and income funds, equity income funds, and short- or intermediate-term bond funds. (A wide variety of bond funds is discussed in Chapter 4 and Part 2, "Getting Started.")

It's always a good idea to mix and match your bond funds. If you need easy access to cash, you might want a money fund. Long-term bond funds typically pay higher yields than short- or intermediate-term bond funds, but the short/intermediate funds are less

71

risky because their share value fluctuates less when interest rates change. For high yields, look at government mortgage bond funds, as well as corporate and international bond funds.

If you're thoroughly diversified, you might have several kinds of funds. How much you invest in each type depends on your goals, how long you have to invest, and your risk tolerance.

Here are several types of funds you should consider when you want to diversify:

➤ A small company stock fund or aggressive stock fund

➤ A growth or a growth and income fund

➤ An international stock fund

➤ A corporate bond fund

➤ An international bond fund

➤ A money fund

Don't put all you eggs in one basket, please. If you rely on one mutual fund to make your fortune, you also could wind up in the poor house. Best to own stock funds, bond funds, and money funds to spread out your risk.

The Least You Need to Know

➤ Learn how much risk you can tolerate.

➤ Match the investment objectives of the funds with your tolerance for risk.

➤ Diversify your investments. By splitting up your investments among different types of mutual funds you are comfortable with, you can lower your overall risk, even though you may be investing in some riskier funds.

➤ Almost everybody should have some money invested in stock funds. Why? Stock fund share values grow more than the rate of inflation over the longer term.

Chapter 7

The Cost of Investing

In This Chapter

➤ Who sells mutual funds?

➤ How can you choose a qualified financial advisor?

➤ What do mutual funds cost?

➤ Should you invest with a discount broker?

➤ How do you invest on the Internet?

How much do you pay for mutual funds? That's a good question. Many mutual funds charge commissions and fees that can significantly reduce the amount of money you actually have to invest. Unlike with your bank checking account, your sales representative may not necessarily spout off all the fees charged by your mutual fund up front. Just because there are no fees or commissions to open a mutual fund, it doesn't mean that they don't exist.

What you pay for a mutual fund largely depends on who you buy it from and what types of securities you buy. You need to balance the level of professional service you require with how much you're willing to spend.

Keeping your fees under control is a key ingredient to investing profitably. To do this, you need to decipher a mutual fund's charges and know when you're paying too much. In this chapter, you will learn what mutual funds cost, how you can save a bundle, and how to get your money's worth when you must pick a financial advisor.

Who Peddles Mutual Funds?

Too many people have the mistaken idea that the only place to buy mutual funds is through a stockbroker. Wrong! Today, you can get mutual funds from a fistful of sources. You can open a mutual fund account at your local bank or through an insurance agent or financial planner or deal directly with a mutual fund company. Stockbrokers, financial planners, insurance agents, and registered investment advisors all sell mutual funds.

It's also possible to buy mutual funds directly from the mutual fund company and save the commission charged by a broker or other licensed pro. By telephoning the mutual fund company directly, you skip the middleman. Mutual fund investment companies already have a trained staff on hand to help.

On the other hand, investing directly through a mutual fund company can be pretty complicated. Perhaps you want a little more hand-holding, which a financial professional can provide. In that case, it's important to get your money's worth. You want to hire someone who has a lot of experience and knows his or her stuff!

Hiring a Professional

There are more than 50,000 financial planners in the U.S. Many are also stockbrokers, insurance agents, or registered investment advisors. When you do business with these people, you're supposed to get an extra level of service for which you'll pay. A financial planner will look at your whole financial picture and help you set up investment goals and a game plan. A financial planner also can help with insurance coverage and handle tax and estate planning.

News You Can Use

The majority of mutual fund investors actually prefer to pay for the services of a financial advisor. A 1996 study commissioned by the Mutual Fund Forum found that nearly twice as many investors opted to pay for financial help rather than buy mutual funds directly. Three of every five investors use financial advisors.

A recent survey of 4,000 people by Dalbar Inc., Boston, backs up this claim. The survey indicated that the vast majority of those who want help are willing to pay a pro an annual fee to manage their mutual funds. Ninety percent of those with $100,000 to invest said they needed help from an investment professional.

If you choose to use financial planners or other investment professionals, it's important to see whether they have certain qualifications. If they do, they'll proudly display the certificates on their office walls and the acronyms on their business cards. Here are some of the credentials to look for:

➤ **Certified Financial Planner (CFP).** The CFP's course work includes training in employee benefits, insurance investments, and tax and estate planning. To keep the CFP license—which is awarded by the CFP Board of Standards (CFP Board), Denver—the financial planner must have completed intensive financial planning course work, passed a national examination, have a minimum of three years of experience, and agree to a code of ethics. A CFP also must agree to regulation by the CFP Board.

➤ **Chartered Life Underwriter (CLU)** and **Chartered Financial Consultant (ChFC).** These designations, issued by the American College, Bryn Mawr, PA, generally go hand-in-hand. The CLU program requires a candidate to take courses with a specialty in life insurance and personal, estate, and business insurance planning. Candidates must have three years of business experience and agree to a code of ethics. The ChFC adds a 10-course program in financial, estate, and tax planning, in addition to investment management. Both designations require candidates to pass national examinations.

➤ **CPA, Personal Financial Specialist (CPA, PFS).** This designation is awarded to Certified Public Accountants (CPAs) who pass a stringent financial planning examination administered by the American Institute of Certified Public Accountants and have a minimum three years of personal financial planning experience. A CPA must pass a national examination but is licensed by the state where he or she sets up practice. A CPA candidate must have a bachelor's degree and generally must have worked in an accounting firm for at least two years.

➤ **Registered Investment Advisors (RIA).** RIAs must register with the Securities and Exchange Commission or, if they manage less than $25 million, abide by state laws. Although state laws vary, RIAs typically are required to disclose their educational backgrounds and the type of investments they manage and generally must file a financial statement revealing how their business is doing.

➤ **Brokers.** Stockbrokers take a training program, often through their brokerage firms. They also must pass a test called an NASD (National Association of Securities Dealers) Series 6 examination. This exam tests a person's knowledge of mutual funds, as well as the rules for buying and selling investments. An individual who also sells individual securities must pass the even-tougher NASD Series 7 exam. (Regardless of which type of salesperson you choose, anyone selling mutual funds must pass the Series 6.)

Checking 'Em Out

Before you hire anyone to give you financial advice, check his or her educational background and number of years in the business. You want someone with at least three years of experience, but the more years, the better.

Technobabble
An **ADV form**, which is on file with the Securities and Exchange Commission, contains important financial information about a registered investment advisor's (RIA's) money management company.

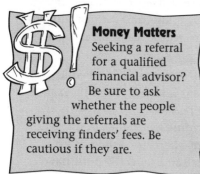

Money Matters
Seeking a referral for a qualified financial advisor? Be sure to ask whether the people giving the referrals are receiving finders' fees. Be cautious if they are.

If you're hiring someone who manages money in addition to peddling insurance, here are some additional steps to take to make sure he or she is qualified:

➤ Check with your state's division of securities, the National Association of Security Dealers, the Securities and Exchange Commission, and state regulators to see if there are any complaints against him or her. (See Appendix B, "Resources," for contact information for these agencies.)

➤ If the person is a registered investment advisor who manages at least $25 million in assets, ask to see the *ADV form*, which is on file with the Securities and Exchange Commission. This form contains important information about the advisor's money management company. You can check out smaller advisors with your state securities department.

➤ Ask to speak to some of the advisor's clients. Make certain they are satisfied.

➤ Examine the advisor's performance in both up and down markets. Pay particular attention to how he or she did in bad markets (such as those of 1987, 1990, and 1994).

Finding a Pro

You can obtain a list of CFPs in your area, along with the booklet "Selecting a Qualified Financial Planning Professional: Twelve Questions to Consider," by contacting the Institute of Certified Financial Planners (ICFP). Write to the ICFP at 3801 East Florida Ave., Suite 708, Denver, CO 80210, call 800-282-7526, or click onto its Web site at www.icfp.org.com.

Another source of free information on how to pick a financial planner is the American Association of Retired Persons, 601 E St. NW, Washington, DC 20049. Finally, the International Association for Financial Planning (IAFP), 5775 Glenridge Dr. NE, Suite B-300, Atlanta, GA 30328, 800-945-4237 (www.iafp.org), also has a consumer referral program.

You can also use referral services to help you locate qualified professionals in your area. Here are some services to try:

➤ **AdvisorLink.** This national money manager evaluation and monitoring service evaluates the performance, risk management, and administrative qualifications of a large number of financial advisors. It then matches investors with one or more of its top-rated advisors. The advisor pays the company a referral fee. Call 800-348-3601.

➤ **National Association of Personal Financial Advisors (NAPFA).** NAPFA members are fee-only financial advisors. Typically, they charge a fee of 1 percent of the assets they manage. They do not charge commissions. NAPFA will send you a list of financial advisors in your area. Call 888-333-6659.

➤ **LINC Society for CPA Financial Advisors.** This is a professional organization of Certified Public Accountants who also manage money for fees or commissions. Call 800-737-2727.

➤ **Charles Schwab.** This discount brokerage firm offers a referral service called AdvisorSource. Schwab has a network of more than 5,000 financial advisors and will help connect investors with one or more professionals. All the advisors in the AdvisorSource system must have been in business for at least three years and must manage a minimum of $25 million. For more information, call your local Charles Schwab office.

Remember, in addition to choosing an advisor who is qualified, you also want an advisor whose investment philosophy matches your own. In other words, if you're conservative and you want to preserve what you have saved over the years, you certainly don't want to invest with a hot-shot advisor who takes a lot of risk.

What's the Price Tag?

There's no free lunch when you invest in mutual funds. You pay several kinds of fees when you invest. How much you pay depends on how the fund is sold.

Load Funds

When you buy a mutual fund from a stockbroker, financial planner, or insurance agent who is registered to sell mutual funds, you'll typically pay more. Often, these professionals will charge a commission, which also is known as a *load*. Loads generally range from as little as 3 percent to as much as 8.5 percent of the amount you invest. The average load on a fund sold by a broker is about 4.5 percent.

You might not realize you're paying this commission because of all the different ways you can be zapped. Get out your Sherlock Holmes hat and investigate. Here's the lowdown on loads:

➤ Some funds charge *front-end loads*, in which the commission is taken out before the money is invested. Front-end loads range from 3 percent to 8.5 percent.

Technobabble
When you purchase a mutual fund from a financial professional, you may have to pay a commission, also known as a **load**. A **front-end load** is an up-front fee. A **back-end load**, or **contingent-deferred sales charge**, is charged only if you leave the fund within a specified time period. A **level load** charges you an annual percentage.

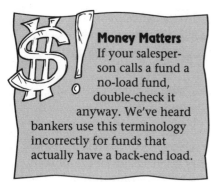

Money Matters
If your salesperson calls a fund a no-load fund, double-check it anyway. We've heard bankers use this terminology incorrectly for funds that actually have a back-end load.

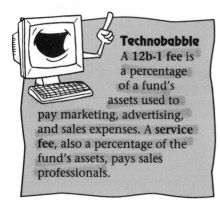

Technobabble
A **12b-1 fee** is a percentage of a fund's assets used to pay marketing, advertising, and sales expenses. A **service fee**, also a percentage of the fund's assets, pays sales professionals.

➤ Some funds have *back-end loads*. These loads kick you in the rear. You pay this commission only if you take out money within the first four to six years you invest in the fund. If you keep your money invested longer, you're not charged. Back-end loads usually start at 4 to 6 percent.

➤ Funds also may charge a *level load*. You pay a flat ongoing annual fee, typically 1 percent, deducted from your fund's earnings.

➤ Some mutual funds may also charge a 12b-1 fee to pay for the fund's advertising and marketing expenses and a service fee to pay sales professionals. The 12b-1 fee, though, cannot exceed .75 percent and the service fee is limited to .25 percent. If a mutual fund calls itself a "no-load fund," it is prohibited from charging 12b-1 fee and/or service fee that total more than .25 percent of the fund's assets.

What's the Best Way to Get Stiffed on Your Load?

What's the best way to pay? If you think you're going to hold on to the fund for longer than six years, pay the back-end load. Why? After the six years have expired, you can take money out of your fund free of charge and you avoid paying that front-end load.

If you don't know how long you're going to hold the fund and you must pay a load, it's better to pay the commission up front and be done with it. That way, if you have to cash out, you won't have to pay an exit fee. Why don't we like back-end loads? Most people panic when the fund declines in value, and they sell. Then, they get double-whammied because they not only lose money, but they also must pay the back-end load.

News You Can Use

As more banks get into the brokerage and mutual fund business, it is becoming increasingly common to find salespeople on salary rather than commission. Also, more brokers and financial planners are charging fees as a percentage of assets under their management rather than as loads. In the future, investors will pay less loads. They will pay fees for the amount of money that is managed.

The worst choice is the level load fund. Pay 1 percent a year over 20 years and you're paying the equivalent of a 20 percent front-end load. Why pay this annual charge when you can buy a fund for a maximum 8.5 percent front-end load or 6 percent back-end load?

Paying the Fees

Although you have control over whether you pay commissions, you're not likely to escape the other charges for owning mutual funds. All fund companies deduct these expenses from the assets of the fund before it distributes dividends and interest income to shareholders. Everyone who has a mutual fund pays the following:

➤ **Fund management fees.** On average, you pay an annual charge of .5 percent in management fees, although this charge may vary. This covers the cost of hiring people, researching, and investing your cash.

➤ **Administrative operational expenses.** This is a small charge for maintaining your account. It's important to look at the fund's *expense ratio*, which indicates how much the fund deducts annually as a percentage of the fund's average net assets. These annual expenses represent the fund management fee and administrative operational expenses, including legal, accounting, and 12b-1 fees (usually stated separately from other operating fees). Excluded from the expense ratio are fund loads or redemption charges and brokerage costs. Stock funds typically have higher expense ratios than bond funds; international funds have higher expense ratios than U.S. funds because of the added cost of doing business overseas.

Technobabble
A **management fee** is the charge for running the fund. The **expense ratio** tells you the total charges on the fund, excluding commissions.

The average stock fund sports an expense ratio of 1.2 percent, and the average bond fund's expense ratio is .75 percent. By contrast, the average international stock and bond funds have expense ratios of 1.5 percent and 1.13 percent, respectively. Chapter 9, "Seeking a Second Opinion," and the chapters in Part 3, "Zoning In on the Picks," present more on expense ratios and how to use them to help pick the right funds.

Hot Tip!
To make sure you're not missing any fees, ask your broker or fund representative to give you the fund's expense ratio. Except for loads or commissions, this figure tells you the total percentage of your fund's average assets on an annual basis that is deducted to cover expenses.

Bargain-Basement Funds

Do it yourself, and you can save a bundle. More than 2,000 no-load funds charge no commissions. You simply buy them directly from the mutual fund company rather than a broker. This way, you have 100 percent of your money invested from day one! Be advised, however, that even no-load funds charge fees.

Remember, investing in no-load funds doesn't mean you won't get any financial information. Fund groups have service representatives that explain how the funds work, what they invest in, and whether they are the right type of investment for you.

Money Matters

Watch for hidden charges in mutual funds. Regardless of whether you pay a commission or load, your fund may still charge 12b-1 fees and service fees.

In addition, look out for redemption fees, which zap you for cashing out when you leave the fund, and exchange fees, which charge you for switching from one fund to another within the same fund family. Plus, there may be fees if you fall below a minimum balance threshold or if you write a check for less than a specified amount on your fund.

Some fund groups, such as Neuberger & Berman (800-877-9700), have in-house financial planners who provide help free of charge. Others, such as the Stein Roe Group of Funds (800-338-2550) and Fidelity Investments (800-544-8888), give you free ongoing professional advice if you have $50,000 to $100,000 to invest. In addition, all fund groups have easy-to-understand self-help booklets to help you get started.

No-load funds can save you money. If you invest $1,000 and pay a 5 percent commission, you've actually slashed your investment to $950. Suppose your mutual fund grows at a 10 percent annual return for 15 years. Your $1,000 investment will grow to $3,968. Invest in a no-load fund at the same 10 percent annual return, on the other hand, and your $1,000 grows to $4,177. You make an extra $209 for every grand you invest.

Not all no-load funds are alike. The 100 percent pure no-loads do not charge commissions or 12b-1 fees. By contrast, some so-called no-load funds still sock it to you with a 12b-1 fee. Low-load funds charge 3 percent commissions and 12b-1 fees. The 12b-1 fee doesn't sound like much, but paying a .5 percent 12 b-1 fee every year for 10 years is the same as paying a 5 percent front-end load.

The following chart shows the difference a 5 percent load can make on a $1,000 investment over 15 years.

Earn more with no-load mutual funds

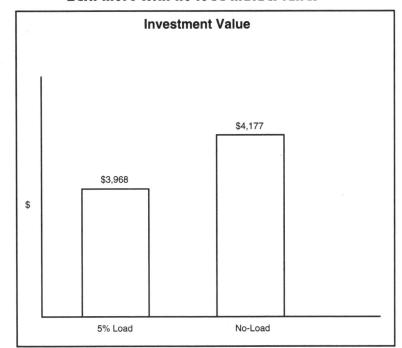

Investment Value

$4,177

$3,968

$

5% Load   No-Load

This chart compares the growth of $1,000 invested in two funds, one with a 5 percent load and one with no load. The bars represent the value of each investment after 15 years if each returned 10 percent annually.

News You Can Use

The 100 percent No-Load Mutual Fund Council publishes a directory of pure no-load mutual funds for $5, which is available by writing to the council at 1501 Broadway, Suite 1809, New York, NY 10036. You can also order the directory through its Web site at www.100noloadfunds.com. Call 212-768-2477 for more information.

The Mutual Fund Education Alliance also publishes a directory on no-load and low-load mutual funds. For more information, call 816-454-9422 or visit its Web site at www.mfea.com. The Handbook for No-Load Investors, by Sheldon Jacobs, is another handy guide. Call 914-693-7420 for more information.

Save Through a Discount Broker

Another way you can buy no-load mutual funds is through a discount brokerage firm's *No-transaction fee (NTF) account.*

Technobabble
A No-transaction fee account (NTF) is an account you set up with a brokerage firm that lets you buy no-load mutual funds without paying a fee for executing the transaction.

You even can invest in no-load mutual funds by opening a brokerage account with companies such as Charles Schwab, Fidelity Brokerage, and Jack White & Company. Ten additional discount brokers offer similar programs with a limited number of funds. Some banks also offer similar services.

Check out the following advantages to one-stop mutual fund shopping:

> ➤ It offers centralized buying and selling. This makes it easy to invest because you buy all your funds at one place. You don't have to call several fund groups to conduct business.

➤ You'll get consolidated statements reflecting all your transactions and account balances. You don't have to sort through several different statements each month. Receiving one statement makes it easy to keep records.

➤ A consolidated 1099 form at the end of the year summarizes all capital gains and dividend income from all the mutual fund investments in your account. (You also get separate statements for your retirement savings accounts and specialized accounts.) One set of forms covers the taxes due on all your investments.

On the downside, one-stop mutual fund shopping also has some disadvantages:

➤ Some of the lowest-cost fund families, such as the Vanguard Group, don't participate in brokerage's no-transaction fee programs.

➤ You might wind up paying higher expenses if you buy a fund through a broker rather than directly from the company.

➤ You have to call your mutual fund group directly to get specific information about the fund holdings and portfolio positions.

➤ You get financial reports more quickly when you deal directly with the mutual fund group.

➤ You do not receive free educational material from the fund family if you do business through a discount broker.

➤ There may be limits on trading funds. If you go over the limit, you can end up paying a transaction fee.

Here are some specific choices for one-stop mutual fund shopping:

➤ **Charles Schwab OneSource (800-435-4000).** Schwab currently offers more than 1,500 funds in its mutual fund marketplace. Eight-hundred-and-seventy of the funds are NTF.

➤ **Fidelity FundsNetwork (800-544-9697).** Fidelity currently offers more than 820 funds from more than 110 fund families on a no-transaction-fee basis. Overall, you can pick from more than 3,300 funds. There's a big advantage to this program: You can invest in most Fidelity funds at no load in tax-qualified accounts such as IRAs, 401(k)s, and profit-sharing plans.

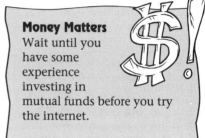

Money Matters
Wait until you have some experience investing in mutual funds before you try the internet.

➤ **Jack White & Company (800-233-3411).** Jack White offers 1,275 funds from 210 fund families on an NTF basis. Overall, there are 6,600 funds to pick from.

Internet Investing

Nowadays, you even can invest in mutual funds with your computer. Many brokerages let you invest online, and other investment companies are expected to follow suit with this service. Because it's cheaper for them to let you trade online than it is for them to set up an office in your neighborhood, it ultimately may cost you less to buy and sell your mutual funds online.

Brokers that currently let investors buy and sell funds online include:

➤ Charles Schwab at www.schwab.com

➤ Jack White at www.jackwhiteco.com

➤ Fidelity Investments at www.fidelity.com

You can also pull up a lot of information about your mutual funds online. To conduct a general search of mutual-fund–related sites, use these Internet search engines:

Yahoo at www.yahoo.com	Excite at www.excite.com
Altavista at www.altavista.com	InfoSeek at www.infoseek.com
Lycos at www.lycos.com	Magellan at www.mckinley.com
Metacrawler at www.Metacrawler.com	Netscape at www.netscape.com
Web Crawler at www.webcrawler.com	

Just enter "mutual funds." You'll get a list of tons of Web sites. Click on.

Many popular Internet sites are devoted to general information on mutual funds; you can find helpful educational and news items on these sites. Most have calculators that let you figure your total return, dividend yields, and how much you should invest for the return you want. They also allow you to set up a file that keeps tabs on your investments. Some of the most popular sites include:

➤ The Mutual Fund Home Page at www.brill.com

➤ Investors Square at www.investorsquare.com

➤ Lipper Analytical Services at www.lipperweb.com

➤ Morningstar Research at www.morningstar.net

➤ Value Line Mutual Fund Survey at www.valueline.com

➤ Mutual Funds Magazine online at www.mfmag.com

You also can get mutual fund information on America Online at www.aol.com.

If you've got in mind a specific mutual fund company, you can call the fund group and ask for the Web address. Some of our favorite no-load mutual fund Web sites include:

➤ T. Rowe Price at www.troweprice.com

➤ The Vanguard Group at www.vanguard.com

➤ American Century at www.americancentury.com

➤ Janus Funds at www.janus.com

➤ Strong Funds at www.strongfunds.com

➤ Stein Roe Mutual Funds at www.steinroe.com

➤ Founders Funds at www.founders.com

➤ Jones & Babson at www.jbfunds.com

Hot Tip!
Looking online for the latest information on money market mutual funds? Check out IBC Financial Data's Money Fund Selector site at www.ibcdata.com. You get educational information, news, and a list of the best-performing money funds for the week. It also features an interactive questionnaire, "How to Select a Money Fund." Plus, it provides yield, asset, and average maturity data on 1,300 money market mutual funds, as well as fund profiles and links to mutual fund sites.

Compare Costs Before You Invest

Now that you know all the costs associated with mutual fund investing, use this handy checklist to zero in on the cost of potential funds.

Compare Fund Fees

Fund Name	Load Percentage (if any)	Management Fee Percentage	Expense Ratio

Compare the fees for different funds before you choose which one to buy.

Load or No Load? That Is the Question

Ask yourself how much professional help is worth. If you invest $5,000, is it worth paying a broker or financial planner $250? What will that person do for you?

➤ Will your pro help you evaluate your goals and risk tolerance and find the best fund?

➤ Will he or she look at a number of different funds before recommending one?

➤ Will you get an explanation of the fund's investment objectives?

➤ Will he or she look at your tax situation if you are in a high tax bracket?

If you answer positively on all these questions, the professional advice may be worth it, but if a broker or planner tries to talk you into a hot-performing fund that charges fat commissions, don't do it.

If you feel comfortable going it alone, the no-load funds are right for you. You make all your money work for you, not your stockbroker. Studies by Morningstar, Inc., a Chicago-based mutual fund service, show that you're not necessarily getting better performance from mutual funds that charge loads. For every well-performing load fund, there is a comparable no-load fund. Why not save and forgo paying someone?

Of course, you'll have to do some careful homework and read up on the funds if you shun the pros. Chapter 9 discusses some valuable resources you can tap.

The Least You Need to Know

➤ Load funds charge an average commission of 4.5 percent.

➤ All your money goes to work for you when you invest in no-load mutual funds.

➤ You should compare fund price tags before you invest. Check the load and expense ratio.

➤ Everyone pays a fund management fee of about one-half of one percent. It can be more or less depending on the size of the fund and the type of investments it owns.

➤ If you choose to use a financial professional, make sure he or she has the right education and credentials, enough years of experience on the job, and an investment philosophy that you feel comfortable with.

Chapter 8

Secrets of Mutual Fund Shopping

> **In This Chapter**
>
> ➤ How many mutual funds should you own?
>
> ➤ Understanding how a fund invests
>
> ➤ Interpreting quarterly and annual fund reports
>
> ➤ Reading mutual fund tables in the newspapers

Do you routinely check the Sunday newspaper for sales on clothes and electronic gizmos? Smart shoppers do the same with mutual funds. Before you go to the shoe store for that year-end clearance sale, you first figure out how many pairs of shoes you need. Then you compare prices. Picking a mutual fund works almost the same way. Before you shop, you figure out how many mutual funds you want to own. You also compare sales charges. Just as you don't want to overpay for that CD player, you don't want to overpay for a mutual fund either.

This chapter is a shopper's guide for mutual funds. You'll learn about the important documents you need to review before you invest in mutual funds. Then, you'll discover a few quick ways to decide whether a fund meets your own personal needs.

How Many Funds Should You Own?

How many mutual funds should you own altogether? Just one? Or five or six? One fund may not be enough. If you put all your money in one stock fund and the market tumbles, you could take a licking. That's why it's best to split your investment among at least two or three different kinds of funds.

If you buy a baker's dozen, on the other hand, you have probably bought too many. Then, you run the risk that all your mutual funds own some of the same stocks. Not only that, but some of your mutual fund managers could be buying the same stocks that your other mutual fund managers are selling. In fact, you actually could end up with the same investments that you started with. Plus, you'll be overwhelmed with paperwork.

If you never have put your money in anything other than bank accounts, it might be best to get your feet wet by first investing in a money fund. After you've accumulated a few thousand dollars, you can take a big step toward building your wealth by investing in a growth and income fund. Once you've gotten comfortable with your growth and income fund, you can begin investing among a few types of funds.

The Magic Number

Five or six funds is a good number to have, but as you learned in Chapter 6, "Which Funds Are Right for You?," it's critical that you spread the investments among different types of funds. Your choices, depending on your investment comfort level and how long you intend to invest, probably should include the following:

➤ Aggressive growth or small company stock fund

➤ Growth fund

➤ Growth and income or balanced fund

➤ International stock fund

➤ Bond fund or income fund

➤ Short-term bond or money fund

When you own a wide variety of funds, it's easy to change your investment mix as financial conditions shift. Recall that younger investors can start building their nest eggs with stock funds. As they get older and build up a hefty stash, they may want to preserve what they have by reducing their risk. Then, they can put more into bond and money funds, and when they retire, they'll start looking for funds to give them income and low risk.

You also can split up your stock fund investments according to your investment style. Chapter 4, "Mutual Funds for Everyone," discussed the difference between stock funds that invest for growth and funds that invest for value. It isn't a bad idea to own at least one fund that buys growth stocks and one fund that invests in undervalued stocks. These types of funds take turns outperforming each other, so if you own both of them, you have a better chance of having a winner.

News You Can Use

Don't want to go through the hassle of owning several funds? Yes, Virginia, it is possible to own just one fund that does all the work for you. With *asset-allocation funds*, you invest in a wide variety of securities under one roof.

Asset-allocation funds are a hybrid type of balanced fund. Some invest both in U.S. and overseas stocks and bonds. Some also invest in large or small company stocks. Asset-allocation fund managers usually make adjustments in their funds' mix of investments, based on their professional evaluation of how the stock and bond markets will perform.

Yuck! Read the Prospectus Before You Invest

Before you take one cent of your money and put it in a mutual fund, we sentence you to one of life's unpleasant little tasks: reading the fund's prospectus. As you know, the prospectus is the legal document that explains what you need to know about the fund before you fork over your money.

Fortunately, by the time you read this, many investment companies will have revamped their prospectuses to make them easier to figure out. In fact, investment companies are currently developing shorter *fund profiles*, which, in three to six pages, summarize a lot of the important information about the fund.

Keep in mind that fund profiles may be written, in part, by the marketing departments of the mutual fund companies. Their job is to get your business, so they will try to portray their fund in the most flattering light. Nevertheless, the same regulations against fraud and manipulation that pertain to full-blown prospectuses apply to fund profiles, so you have some protection.

As of this writing, the new fund profile format has not been fully developed. But for now, here are some of the important pieces of information you should examine in the new fund profile:

➤ A standardized summary containing information about a fund's investment objectives, principal strategies, risks, performance, and fees.

➤ A bar chart to graphically illustrate the volatility of the fund's total return over the past 10 years.

Hot Tip!
Good news: Soon, you'll no longer have to wait for snail mail to get information about a mutual fund. Under regulations adopted in 1998, investment companies will be able to distribute their fund profiles through any media—including the Internet and newspapers.

Technobabble
The **prospectus** is a legal document that provides important information about the fund, such as investment objectives, risks, fees, and who runs the fund. The **annual** and **quarterly reports** are fund updates that tell you what the fund did and how it performed for the period.

Money Matters
Specific fund investments are not included in the prospectus. Make certain you obtain quarterly and annual reports to see exactly what your fund is investing in.

➤ A table comparing the fund's total return to those of appropriate broad-based securities market indexes. (For example, if you are looking at a growth and income fund, you will compare the fund to the performance of the S&P 500 market index.)

➤ A discussion of the risks that could adversely affect the fund.

By the end of 1998, the fund will be required to send you the full-blown prospectus only upon confirmation of your mutual fund sale. But we suspect that some investment companies will continue to send you the whole care package—a simple prospectus, a fund profile, and the full prospectus—when you're inquiring about a fund.

Read All About It: the Prospectus

Always ask for the full prospectus and read it carefully—even if you don't get it automatically. It could spare you from a bad investment and some sleepless nights. The full prospectus contains more detailed information than the fund profile.

Here's what you might learn in the full prospectus, for example, that may or may not be in the fund profile:

➤ You'll learn about the tactics a fund manager uses to find attractive stocks. "Who cares about this?" you ask, figuring you're already handing over your trust to a seasoned professional. You do.

Say you desperately need income from a fund to pay monthly bills. A couple of years ago, the Fidelity Dividend Growth Fund might have seemed like the ideal selection. By looking at its name, you'd think it pays bigger and bigger dividends each month. Sounds great for your ever-mounting bills, right? If you look closely at the fund's prospectus, however, you'll uncover a whole different story.

The Fidelity Dividend Growth Fund invests in small companies that may pay little or no dividends now but are expected to one day become big profitable companies that do pay shareholders dividends. Oops!

FUND PROFILE

T. Rowe Price
Equity Income Fund

Important
Information
About This Fund

As of 12/31/97

*This profile contains key
information about the fund.
If you would like more information before you invest,
please consult the fund's
prospectus. For details about
the fund's holdings or recent
investment strategies, please
review the fund's most recent
annual or semiannual report.
The prospectus and reports
may be obtained at no cost
by calling 1-800-638-5660.*

Invest With Confidence
T.RowePrice

The cover of a
sample fund
profile. (Source: T.
Rowe Price Associ-
ates, Inc.)

The fund profile describes the fund's investment strategy and potential risks and rewards. (Source: T. Rowe Price Associates, Inc.)

FUND PROFILE

1. What is the fund's goal?

The fund seeks to provide substantial dividend income and also long-term capital appreciation.

2. What is the fund's investment strategy?

This conservative stock fund uses a "value" strategy in selecting investments. It seeks out stocks whose prices appear low relative to their potential. Value investors hope to realize capital appreciation as other investors recognize a stock's intrinsic value and drive its price higher.

The fund invests primarily in the common stocks of established U.S. companies that pay above-average dividends. However, it may also invest in bonds, preferred stocks, and convertible securities, as well as foreign and other securities, in keeping with its investment goal. Most holdings will provide income.

The fund expects to generate a yield higher than that of the S&P 500 Stock Index.

3. What is the fund's risk/reward potential?

Risk:

- The Equity Income Fund is primarily a stock fund; like all stock investments, it exposes the investor to potential drops in stock prices.
- In bull markets, this fund's focus on income-producing securities could dampen its performance.
- The market's long rise over time has been punctuated by declines; even in rising markets, the share prices of the most profitable companies can fall.
- The fund's price will fluctuate; there is no assurance you will be able to sell your shares at a profit.

Reward:

- Shareholders will participate in the long-term growth potential of investing in common stocks.
- Advantages of the fund's focus on income:
  - for stocks, dividends are normally a more stable component of total return than capital appreciation;
  - securities that pay higher levels of income tend to fluctuate less in price than those paying little or no income;
  - the compounding effect of reinvested dividends can substantially increase investment returns over time.

4. How can I tell if the fund is appropriate for me?

The fund is designed for individuals seeking a conservative approach to investing in stocks – one that provides income in addition to the prospects of capital appreciation over time.

Because of its long-term orientation, the fund is appropriate for both regular and tax-deferred accounts (IRAs and Keoghs).

All investors in the fund should be willing to ride out inevitable market downturns, which may last for extended periods.

The fund profile explains the fees and past performance of the fund. (Source: T. Rowe Price Associates, Inc.)

5. What fees or expenses will I pay?

This fund is 100% no load. There are no fees or charges to buy or sell fund shares, reinvest dividends, or exchange into other T. Rowe Price funds. There are no 12b-1 marketing fees.

Annual fund expenses as a percentage of average net assets	
Management fee	0.59%
Other expenses	0.26%
Total fund expenses	0.85%

These costs are deducted from the fund's total assets before the daily share price is calculated and before distributions are made. You do not pay them directly.

Sample expenses over time			
(assuming $1,000 investment earning 5% annual return):			
1 year	3 years	5 years	10 years
$9	$27	$47	$105

This is an illustration only; actual expenses and returns will vary.

6. How has the fund performed in the past?

The bar chart shows the fund's actual performance for each of the last 10 calendar years through December 31, 1997. It indicates the relative volatility of returns from one year to the next.

The fund's average annual compound total returns for various holding periods through 12/31/97 are compared with its Lipper peer group average in the other chart. These average returns smooth out the year-to-year variations in actual returns. Of course, the fund's past performance is no guarantee of its future returns

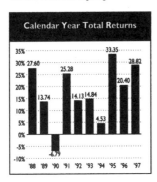

Calendar Year Total Returns

Average Annual Compound Total Returns as of 12/31/97		
	Fund	Lipper Average*
1 year	28.82%	27.51%
5 years	19.95%	17.01%
10 years	16.99%	14.66%
*Lipper Equity Income Funds Average		

These figures include changes in principal value, reinvested dividends, and capital gain distributions. Investment return and principal value will vary, and shares may be worth more or less at redemption than at original purchase.

7. Who manages the fund?

The fund is managed by T. Rowe Price Associates. Founded in 1937, T. Rowe Price and its affiliates manage over $120 billion for approximately six million individual and institutional investor accounts. The company offers a comprehensive range of stock, bond, and money market funds directly to the investing public. Brian Rogers has day-to-day responsibility for the fund and has managed investments for T. Rowe Price since 1983.

The fund profile shows you how to open an account and buy and sell shares. (Source: T. Rowe Price Associates, Inc.)

8. How can I purchase shares?

Fill out and return the New Account Form in the postpaid envelope, along with your check for a minimum of $2,500 or more ($1,000 or more for retirement plans and gifts or transfers to minors) or $50 if investing through Automatic Asset Builder. You can also open an account by bank wire or by exchanging from another T. Rowe Price fund.

9. How can I sell shares or close my account?

You may redeem or sell any portion of your account on any business day. Simply write to us or call.

We also offer easy exchange among our entire family of domestic and international funds. Restrictions may apply in special circumstances, and some redemption requests need a signature guarantee.

10. When will I receive distributions?

The fund distributes income quarterly and net capital gains, if any, at year-end. Income and short-term gains are taxable at ordinary income rates, and long-term gains are taxable at the current capital gains rate. Distributions are reinvested automatically in additional shares unless you choose another option, such as receiving a check.

11. What services are available?

A wide range, including but not limited to:
- easy exchanges;
- retirement plans for individuals and large and small businesses (e.g., IRA, SEP, Keogh, 401(k), 403(b), etc.);
- automated information and transaction services by telephone or personal computer;
- electronic transfers between your fund and bank accounts;
- automatic investing and automatic exchange;
- discount brokerage.

To Open an Account
Investor Services
1-800-638-5660

For Existing Accounts
Shareholder Services
1-800-225-5132

For Yields and Prices
Tele*Access®
1-800-638-2587
24 hours, 7 days

For Information via the Internet
www.troweprice.com

T. Rowe Price OnLine
Call us at 1-800-541-3036 for more information on this complete financial management service.

T. Rowe Price
100 East Pratt Street
Baltimore, MD 21202

Invest With Confidence
T.RowePrice

T. Rowe Price Investment Services, Inc., Distributor

F71-042 12/31/97

➤ You'll learn more about all the risks of investing overseas—lessons that might have prevented a lot of mutual fund investors from crying in their beer over the years. By simply turning a few extra pages in a full-blown prospectus, they might have learned in advance about brewing foreign currency risks, political risks, or economic risks that might trigger an investment disaster.

News You Can Use

Here are some real-life risks faced by investors who plunked their money into international investments:

Over a decade ago, the Philippine government under Ferdinand Marcos declared an asset freeze on all foreign investments. That meant investors couldn't sell their holdings held in custody in Philippine banks.

In Latin America in 1994 and 1995, the Mexican economy collapsed, interest rates rose to more than 22 percent, and the Mexican market took a nose-dive. Other Latin markets followed suit. Investors in Latin American stock funds lost more than 50 percent in those two years. It took more than two years for them to break even—assuming that they stayed fully invested in their funds.

➤ You can learn whether a fund manager invests in *derivatives*—another type of risky investment. Derivatives are highly specialized securities that brokers manufacture from known securities. We'll discuss these a little more in Chapter 11, "Money Funds: Better Than a Bank Account?", but derivatives, which may include futures and options, generally are riskier than owning a stock or bond because their prices can swing as quickly as Tarzan jumps from vine to vine throughout the jungle.

You'll also learn whether the fund can use borrowed money to invest in hot stocks—another risky practice that many investors in past years wished they had stayed away from.

➤ By reading the full-blown prospectus, you'll be able to put some of the advertising hype you're apt to get in the fund profile in its proper perspective.

John C. Bogle, founder and senior chairman of the Vanguard Group, complains that outside the

Money Matters
At least 99 percent of investment companies never discuss the role of costs in the detail they should, warns John C. Bogle, founder and chairman of the Vanguard Group. They present only figures that are legally required and even those only where they are required. "They offer numbers of the actual and expected cost of portfolio turnover and taxes and provide expense ratios only in prospectuses and annual reports," he says.

prospectuses, too many investment companies promote recent performance but fail to adequately disclose the accompanying risks. "We have leaned on massive advertising to promote sales of our relative handful of funds that have had outstanding records of past performance, even though we know that few if any of those records will be repeated," Bogle complains.

A Brief Tour of a Prospectus

All prospectuses are required to present the same information to investors. Each prospectus has a table of contents to make your life a little easier. (An example appears as an illustration.)

A sample table of contents from a prospectus. (Source: Markman Capital Management.)

It's a good idea to get a yellow marker or highlighter to underline the most important information. Read the entire prospectus and pay close attention to the following sections. (Keep in mind that they may be called different things in different prospectuses.)

Investment Objectives

The investment objectives section tells you how the fund intends to make money. It contains a statement about the investment objectives and investment policy of the fund that you can compare against your own investment objectives (see Chapter 6).

Right off the bat, you can tell the type of fund you are looking at. When you see words such as *maximum capital appreciation* or *capital growth*, for example, you know you are dealing with an aggressive growth fund. When you see *long-term growth*, that's a sign it's a growth fund. *Growth with income* as a secondary consideration tells you it's a growth and income fund.

General Description

Exactly how the fund invests is discussed in the general discussion section. Here, you will learn about how the fund invests in stocks or bonds. For stock funds, you may read that the fund invests in large company stocks that should raise their dividends. You might see something like, The fund invests in companies that show a catalyst for change and should dominate their competitors.

With bond funds, you may read something like, "The fund will invest 65 percent of its assets in U.S. Government securities, but the fund may also invest in high-quality corporate bonds."

Fund Expenses

The fund expenses section explains the fees charged by the fund. You'll learn whether the fund has a load or whether it's no-load with no commission. If the fund has a front-end load, you'll probably find a table showing the load based on the amount invested. (See Table 8.1 for an example.)

You'll also discover the fund's management fee, 12b-1 fee, and other fees. (See Chapter 7, "The Cost of Investing," for an explanation of these fees.) Another table shows the fees you pay, excluding any load, on a $1,000 investment, assuming that the fund earns 5 percent and you cash in the fund after 1 to 10 years. (Beginning in late 1998, the prospectus will provide a table based on a $10,000 investment.)

With this information, you can compare the cost of different funds. For example, one stock fund may sock it to you with a total of $50 in fees after 10 years for every $1,000 you invest. Another may hit you up for $65. All other things being equal, cheaper is better.

Example of a Fund Expense Information Table

er Transaction Expenses

~a.es load imposed on purchases	None
Sales load imposed on reinvested dividends	None
Deferred (back-end load)	None
Exchange fee	None
Wire redemption processing fee	$15
Other redemption fees	None

Annual Fund Operation Expenses (as a Percentage of Average Net Assets)

Management fee*	0.95%
12b-1 fees	None
Other expenses	0.00%
Total fund operating expenses	**0.95%**

*The fund will voluntarily waive each of the fund's fees and expenses to the extent necessary to keep the total fund operating expenses no greater than 0.95 percent. Management fees paid by the fund do not include brokerage commissions, taxes, interest, or extraordinary expenses.

For example, you would pay the following expenses on a $1,000 investment, assuming a 5 percent annual return and redemption at the end of each time period: $10 at the end of one year and $30 at the end of three years.

The Funds

The funds section helps you determine how much income you may receive from the fund, what expenses are taken out, and how the fund performed annually. You'll see a table that lists up to 10 years of very important year-by-year information, including the following:

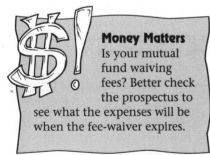

Money Matters
Is your mutual fund waiving fees? Better check the prospectus to see what the expenses will be when the fee-waiver expires.

➤ How much was paid per share in distributions from dividends, interest, and capital gains

➤ The fund's total return, year-by-year

➤ The fund's yield, year-by-year

➤ The fund's year-by-year expense ratio, the total percent of charges taken out of the fund, excluding the load

Risks and Other Considerations

The risks and other considerations section tells you how the fund could lose money and what investments the fund cannot make. This section should explain whether the fund uses risky investment tactics or borrows to invest in speculative stocks. You'll learn whether the fund is exposed to foreign currency risk or whether it invests in bonds issued by companies with poor credit ratings. You'll also find federally imposed restrictions, some of which we discussed earlier.

Fund Management

In the fund management section, you'll find information about the fund manager, the board of directors, and officers of the fund. It's important to know how long the fund manager has been at the helm. This part of the prospectus should describe the portfolio manager's experience and how he or she gets paid.

Share Purchase and Redemption

The prospectus should offer information about how to buy and sell shares. The share purchase and redemption sections tell you how to set up an account with the fund and explain whether the fund allows you to buy and sell shares by telephone or whether you must send notarized instructions, guaranteeing your signature. This section also contains information on automatic investment programs and wire transfers.

Shareholder Services

The shareholder services section explains how to reinvest a fund's income, as well as provides information on automatic investment and withdrawal programs. Also covered is information on retirement savings plans such as IRAs, Keoghs, SEPs, and pension plans (which you'll learn about in Part 5, "Mutual Fund Investing for Special Situations").

Hot Tip!
Examine the prospectus to determine whether the fund manager receives a bonus for doing a good job. Many investment companies reward a fund's portfolio manager for outperforming the market averages on similar funds. On the other hand, such a bonus could prompt the manager to take greater risks to show a more impressive return. Also see if the manager has his own money invested in the fund.

Money Matters
Do not invest in a mutual fund until you have a thorough understanding of how the fund will affect your tax situation. You could be socked with a stiff tax bill, for example, if a fund manager does a lot of profitable stock trades—even though you're a buy-and-hold investor.

Tax Information and Distributions

The tax information and distributions section tells you that the fund is required to distribute 98 percent of the income earned by the fund to its shareholders. This section contains other information about taxes, as well as important information stating the dates and frequency that distributions are paid to shareholders.

Several other sections of the prospectus present an auditor's report on the fund's financial condition and legal information regarding any lawsuits.

Read the Updates

Periodically, you get progress reports on your fund, known as *quarterly* and *annual reports*. You'll find out how the fund is doing and what stocks or bonds it owns.

Technobabble
The annual and quarterly reports are fund updates that tell you what the fund did and how it performed for the period.

Money Matters
Make certain the fund sends the "Statement of Additional Information" along with the prospectus. This document might have some important details about risk and investment strategies that aren't in the prospectus. Check the litigation section of the prospectus to determine whether there are any current or pending legal actions against the fund.

There are several important sections to the reports:

➤ First, you get a message from the president of the fund recapping how the fund did in the past, including why the fund did or did not perform well. For example, a stock fund's share value might have increased because interest rates are low and corporate profits are high. A bond fund's share value might have declined because interest rates rose and the value of the fund's long-term bonds dropped.

The last part of the section tells shareholders what the fund expects in the future. Sometimes the news is good, and sometimes it's bad. A fund's president may say that the near-term prospect for stocks isn't rosy due to the prolonged recession. Over the longer term, however, as business conditions improve, the outlook for the fund's investments might improve.

➤ You'll also get a comparison of how the fund performed versus its peer group's average and the market averages is also provided. Aha! There is usually a bar chart that shows you how the fund did versus the stock or bond market average over several time periods. You may also learn how the fund performed against an average of similar types of funds.

➤ A stock fund's financial report will list the percentage of the fund's assets invested in different industries, such as financial services, natural resources, leisure, and technology. That way, you can see in which type of business your hard-earned money is invested.

➤ You also get a list of all the fund's investments and how much money is invested in each security. Usually, there is a list of the top 10 holdings. You might write down the names of the stocks or bonds and look them up in other reports. That way, you can get a feel for the types of investments a fund makes.

If you see a fund that invests in AT&T, Coke, Walt Disney, Pepsi, IBM, Merck, and Exxon, for example, you know you are investing in blue-chip stocks. By contrast, if you see a list of names such as Broderbund Software, LSI Logic, and Orbital Sciences, you are investing in small company stocks.

➤ If you invest in a growth and income fund, income fund, or bond fund, you'll find information on how much dividend or interest income you received. If you invest in a small company stock fund or aggressive growth and growth funds, however, you may not see this information.

Check a Fund Every Day

You can check on your mutual funds even more frequently by reading the mutual fund prices in your local newspaper's business section.

Every newspaper presents this information a little differently, but here's the way most work:

➤ To the far left, you'll see the name of the fund group or family. Underneath is the name of the fund (Pal Fund, in our example).

➤ Some tables do not list the investment objective of the fund; others do.

➤ Next is the Buy price of the fund, the sales price. If you are buying a no-load fund, the buy price equals the net asset value (NAV), which is the share price of the fund less fund expenses. If you are buying a load fund, this is also known as the *offering price* you have to pay for the fund, including the load.

➤ Next is the Sell price, or the price of the fund minus the commission. Some tables list this as the fund's NAV.

➤ To find out whether an investor pays a load, subtract the sell price from the buy price and divide by the buy price. For example, suppose the fund has a buy price of $21 and a sell price of $20. That means you pay a 1-buck commission on each share of the fund. One dollar divided by $20 means that you are paying a 5 percent front-end commission. If you invest $1,000 in this fund, the broker takes $50. You actually have $950 invested.

➤ How can you tell whether the fund charges a 12b-1 fee? You will see footnotes after the fund's name, which refer to information that tells you about the fees and charges.

➤ Change means the number of cents the price of the fund went up or down, based on its buy price (the NAV) the previous day.

➤ Return is the total return of the fund. Some tables list the total return year-to-date, for one year, or as an annual average total return for three to five years.

Table 8.2 offers an example of a typical newspaper listing. According to the table, you can buy Investors Friends' Pal Fund for $10 a share and there is no load. The fund went up 25 cents in value yesterday, and this year-to-date, the total return is 8 percent.

Table 8.2   Mutual Fund Newspaper Quotations

Fund	Buy	Sell	Change	Year-to-Date % Return
Happy Growth Group's Giggle Fund	$21	20	–.05	5.5
Investors Friends' Pal Fund	$10	10	.25	8

Five Important Questions You Need to Answer

Now that you know what to look for in the prospectus and the mutual fund tables in your newspaper, make certain you've nailed down the answers to the following questions about a particular fund and that you are satisfied with those answers before you buy shares:

1. Is this a fund that invests only in stocks? Or is it a lower-risk fund that invests in both stocks and bonds? Does it invest both in this country and abroad?

2. What's this going to cost me? Is there a load? If so, how much?

3. Do I want income from this fund? If so, what's the yield over the past several years?

4. Do I want to see my money grow over the years? If so, what's the fund's total return over at least the last 5 or 10 years?

5. How many years has the portfolio manager been at the helm of the funds? What's his or her background?

The Least You Need to Know

➤ It's generally best to own at least five or six funds, but no more than a dozen.

➤ Read the fund's prospectus to learn the objective and risks of the fund before you invest.

➤ The prospectus fee table shows how much the fund costs.

➤ Many investment companies are developing a new fund profile that makes it easier to invest.

Chapter 9

Seeking a Second Opinion

In This Chapter

➤ Where to get a second opinion on a mutual fund

➤ The best sources of information on funds

➤ What to look for in the reports

➤ The best newsletters for ongoing advice

You have already learned about many of the tools you need to select a mutual fund on your own, but let's face it, you're no idiot. Why venture into totally unknown territory when the experts have already been there? It pays to see what the pros have to say about the mutual fund strategy you're considering.

This chapter takes a look at some important sources of mutual fund information. You'll learn what reports can help you pick funds and keep you up to date.

Mutual Fund Reporting Services

At the library, you can find several excellent sources of information on mutual funds. In the mutual fund section, you'll see a long table with a group of binders filed neatly in rows. Here you can often find mutual fund reports, which will provide you with sufficient information to make a knowledgeable investment decision.

No matter what report you look at, you'll get the following information about a fund:

Money Matters
Not all mutual fund reporting services say the same things about the same funds. They all measure things a little differently. Look for a consensus of opinion from the reports or just stick with one report over the long haul.

➤ Past performance. This covers both total return and yield.

➤ Investment objectives.

➤ How funds rank in rate of return over fixed periods of time relative to other funds. (Funds are ranked against all funds, as well as against funds with the same investment objective.)

➤ Risk ratings.

➤ How much funds have made in total return when the market has gone up and how much they have lost when the market has gone down.

➤ Funds' fees, expenses, amounts needed to invest, addresses, and toll-free phone numbers.

SShhh...Go to the Library

Take a friend to the library. It's always good to have some help until you get the hang of looking up things. You'll know when you're near the mutual fund section. You'll see a long table with a group of binders filed neatly in rows. The following reports, which can help with your investment decisions, also provide the funds, toll-free numbers, addresses, and investment minimums.

➤ **Morningstar Mutual Funds.** These reports are published every other week and cover more than 1,800 stock and bond funds. You get a comprehensive one-page report on each fund, including ratings of each. Funds rated with four or five stars offer the best returns with the least amount of risk for funds in their category. In addition, there's a list of each fund's 25 largest stock or bond holdings. You get a written evaluation of each fund plus information on how the fund does in down markets in relation to similar funds.

➤ **The Value Line Mutual Fund Survey.** This report provides information on more than 2,000 funds by investment objective. Funds are rated by number: One is best and five is worst. In addition, Value Line shows how each fund did in both up and down markets and lists each fund's holdings. A written evaluation included for each fund might help you choose whether to invest.

Don't forget: Although all these services are helpful for second opinions, you need to first do some homework to determine whether the fund fits in your own game plan and tolerance for risk. Omit this exercise, which we discussed in Chapter 6, "Which Funds Are Right for You?," and all the second opinions in the world won't necessarily help you make money on your investment.

Tips on Using Mutual Fund Reports

You should pay particular attention to the following key items when examining either the Morningstar or Value Line mutual fund services:

➤ The written commentary on the funds, which tells how the fund has been managed. You will learn how the fund manager is investing the shareholders' cash.

➤ Annual rates of return over 1, 3, 5, and 10 years. This makes it easy to compare funds.

➤ How the fund performed in good and bad markets.

➤ The beta value of a stock fund, which, as you learned in Chapter 5, "Is a Fund a Winner or Loser?," tells how volatile the fund is compared with the overall stock market.

➤ An overall risk rating of the fund.

➤ The duration of the bond fund. This, as you'll recall from Chapter 5, tells how much the fund will change in value if interest rates rise or fall.

Ratings Aren't Everything

Although the Morningstar and Value Line mutual fund services are extremely helpful, please—we repeat, please—don't invest in a fund just because a report gives a fund a high ranking or rating. Often, the ratings don't last.

A study by Putnam, Lovell, and Thorton, a New York-based investment company, showed that of the 207 funds rated five stars in the fourth quarter of 1994, only 87 were still rated five stars in the fourth quarter of 1996, whereas 92 dropped to four stars and 21 dropped to 3 stars. Just 42 percent and 45 percent of the five-star and four-star rated funds kept their ratings.

A little fact-checking by Jerry Tweddell, a Sonora, California, money manager, found that once a mutual fund makes the Forbes Honor Roll list or gets a five-star Morningstar rating, the fund tends to underperform.

In his book, *Winning with Index Mutual Funds*, Tweddell notes that over five-year periods from 1980–1984 and 1986–1990, the Honor Roll Funds outperformed the S&P 500 only once in seven years. From 1974 to 1992, the Forbes Honor Roll funds grew at an 11.2 percent annual rate. By contrast, the average stock fund gained 12.5 percent, whereas the Wilshire 5000, an index of all stocks, grew 13.1 percent annually.

Meanwhile, data supplied by Lipper Analytical Services, New York, shows that in each of the prior four years, stock funds that had been awarded Morningstar's five-star rating underperformed their peers over the next year.

The lesson, Tweddell says: Chasing after hot returns is flawed thinking. It is not unusual for a large fund family to funnel "hot deals" into one or two smaller funds to boost returns. The funds buy up the stock before the retail stockbrokers get their hands on it. But if the initial public offering market cools off, the fund family's management tends to divert the hot deals to its other funds.

Performance also can suffer when tons of money flow into a hot-performing fund. The fund's assets increase so much that hot-performing stocks have little impact on a fund's total return.

The more money that comes into a fund, the less the fund manager swiftly can profit from small, but nimble trades. Often, managers must skip buying attractive stocks because they have to buy too much of it. Buying large blocks of stocks will in itself drive the price up. Selling drives the price down too much.

Although it may help to refer to a rating service before you invest, it pays to stay well-diversified. As we've stressed throughout this book, the best idea typically is to divide your money up into stocks, bonds, and money funds. Chapters 18 through 21 in this book will show you how to manage your money to get the best return with the least amount of losses—without necessarily betting on the single best-rated fund.

Read All About It: Newsletters

Several top-notch mutual fund newsletters can show you what professional money managers say about your mutual funds. Mutual fund newsletters make recommendations and track how their picks do over the years. The newsletters cost from $50 to $125 annually. That's not exactly small potatoes (but your subscriptions can be tax-deductible). If you need to split the cost, get a couple of investment-minded friends to chip in for a subscription. You can also find many newsletters in the library.

Find the Right Newsletter

You might have a rough time picking from the dozens of mutual fund newsletters on the market. Some suggest making several trades a year; others take a longer-term perspective and recommend funds with long-term track records. These reports also give asset allocation advice on how to slice the investment pie. Some newsletters specialize in sector funds or funds that invest in specific industries; others track fund groups.

Before you subscribe to a particular newsletter, it's important to find out what it is all about. Many libraries carry the Hulbert Financial Digest. This monthly report and directory tracks the performance of several hundred newsletters so you can see how well the advisors' fund picks have panned out. If the library doesn't carry this important report, you can purchase a trial subscription to the Hulbert Financial Digest for $35 (703-683-5905).

The Hulbert Financial Digest also offers profiles on newsletters of interest. It will prepare customized reports for investors. Although it could cost you a few bucks for the information, it is well worth it.

The Hulbert profiles include the following helpful information:

➤ Complete performance ratings telling how a fund has done based on its level of risk as far back as 15 years.

➤ Information about what specific funds the newsletter recommends.

➤ A graph that shows how the newsletter picks have performed over time.

➤ Commentary about the newsletter, its good and bad points, as well as information about the people behind the newsletter.

For more information on the Hulbert Financial Digest service, call 888-485-2378. Here are some more tips on choosing a newsletter that's right for you:

➤ Request a free sample copy of the report before you subscribe.

➤ See whether the newsletter's investment philosophy is the same as yours. If you're a conservative investor, for example, you don't want to use a newsletter recommending a high-risk market-timing strategy.

➤ Determine whether the report includes news and information about the financial markets and the mutual fund industry.

➤ Make sure the newsletter gives advice on how to diversify based on your tolerance for risk, age, and investment goals.

➤ Compare the newsletter's returns versus the stock and bond market averages rather than rely on the newsletter's hype about its record.

➤ Consider a newsletter that has tracked mutual funds through at least one bull market and one bear market over the past three to five years.

➤ Subscribe only to a newsletter you can understand. Some are very technical and written for sophisticated traders. Others are written for the average investor.

Hot Tip!
You can call the publishers of most mutual fund newsletters and get a free copy of their publications. That way, you can tell whether a newsletter is right for you.

Money Matters
Don't expect to hit a home run when you follow mutual fund newsletter advice. The good ones help you set up a solid long-term investment program. They're not interested in picking hot funds for those who want to get rich quick. At best, a good newsletter recommends well-managed stock and bond funds. It fills you in on the latest news and suggests ways to diversify your investments.

➤ Call the newsletter before you subscribe. Find out whether the editor or investment advisor will answer any question you may have during the year.

Before you subscribe to a newsletter, we suggest you ask whether it has a 24-hour toll-free telephone hot-line service you can call to get the most up-to-date financial and investment information. We don't know about you, but based on the speed at which we get our mail from the U.S. Post Office—that is, *if* we get our mail—we'd certainly prefer another communication option. You might also inquire about having the newsletter faxed to you. Many newsletters now have Web pages, too, so you also can check out the information online. Most newsletters offer an inexpensive trial subscription.

Our Favorite Newsletters

Several newsletters are published by some of the most highly respected mutual fund financial advisors in the country. Our favorites include the following:

➤ *No-Load Fund Investor* (510-254-9017). Sheldon Jacobs puts together a great monthly report. He evaluates no-load funds and tells which funds are best for the short or long term. Jacobs also discusses any important changes in mutual funds. The newsletter has a section on useful news. One section tracks the performance of no-load funds and adds recommended investment mixes or portfolios. Jacobs also publishes *The Handbook for No-Load Investors*, a directory of no-load fund track records.

➤ *The Mutual Fund Letter* (800-326-6941). This newsletter by Gerald Perritt, Ph.D., is good for those who want to learn more about the ins and outs of investing and how the financial markets work. The newsletter focuses on no-load mutual funds that you can buy and hold for your lifetime. Perritt also publishes *The Mutual Fund Encyclopedia*, a directory of no-load mutual funds.

➤ *Mutual Fund Forecaster* (800-327-6720). We can't help taking a peek at Norm Fosback's newsletter every month. This report publishes estimates of how more than 1,000 mutual funds will perform over the next year and next five years. Fosback has an excellent track record in predicting the future performance of the stock markets, so his mutual fund recommendations will give you an idea of where a fund stands.

➤ *No-Load Fund Analyst* (415-989-8513). If you're looking for low-risk funds to invest in for the long haul, consider this report. Publisher Ken Gregory shows how to split up your investments and invest for the long term. The report tracks funds that buy undervalued stocks. Gregory interviews fund managers monthly. He also keeps close tabs on international funds.

➤ *Fund Exchange* (800-423-4893). Every month, this newsletter gives you buy, sell, and hold advice on your mutual funds. Paul Merriman, publisher, has developed a market-timing method for aggressive as well as conservative investors. He also manages a series of no-load mutual funds that use the same system. His funds are noted for being low risk. You get information each month about how much to put in stocks, bonds, and money-market mutual funds. Merriman focuses on getting his subscribers out of down markets to protect them against large losses. You can also access his Web site at www.paulmerriman.com.

Some other well-read mutual fund newsletters recommend specific funds and model portfolios. They include IBC *Moneyletter* (508-881-2800), *Funds Net Insight* (617-369-2000), *The Independent Advisor for Vanguard Investors* (800-435-3372), and *The Sagami Report* (800-289-9222).

Newsletters for the Brave Investor

Aggressive mutual fund investors check out several newsletters for advice about when to buy and sell funds to profit from changing share prices. Most of these newsletters have investor hot-line phone numbers. You can call and get the latest recommendations toll-free. Some of the best include the following:

➤ *Stockmarket Cycles* (707-579-8444). This newsletter looks at market trends and cycles and tells you when to switch between stock funds and money funds.

➤ *InvesTech Mutual Fund Advisor* (406-862-7777). This report looks at a number of economic and fund performance trends and recommends how much you should invest in stock funds, bond funds, and other types of mutual funds.

➤ *Growth Fund Guide* (605-341-1971) tells when to move into money funds, conservative stock funds, or aggressive stock funds depending on the newsletter's forecast of the stock market.

➤ *NoLoad Fund X* (415-986-7979). This newsletter recommends that you always invest in the funds with the best current performance. The idea is that if a fund is doing well today, it will do well tomorrow.

➤ *Fabian's Investment Resources* (800-950-8765). This newsletter uses market indicators so that you can switch between money funds and stock funds.

➤ *Jay Schabacker's Mutual Fund Investing* (800-777-5005). This newsletter recommends when to change the mix of funds based on the newsletter's forecast of the stock and bond markets.

When you invest with these newsletters, be prepared to stay on top of your investments and do some fund switching. Each month, the reports will tell you what to do. You also have to keep good records of your transactions because trading funds can have tax implications.

Make the Best Use of a Newsletter

There are two ways to use an investment newsletter. You can see what the newsletter recommends and then do your own homework. Not all funds are for all investors, so a blanket newsletter recommendation isn't always the best advice. Look at how the funds invest, what they hold in their portfolios, and their performance. Other funds might best fit your needs.

The other way is to pick funds and look to the newsletters to validate your selections. If a newsletter doesn't report on a fund you like, you shouldn't necessarily avoid that fund. The newsletters often cover just a small group of funds. Meanwhile, if a fund also is picked by the newsletter, there's a good chance you're on the right track.

The Least You Need to Know

➤ It never hurts to see what the experts say about the mutual funds you're interested in.

➤ Morningstar Mutual Funds and The Value Line Mutual Fund Survey are two of the best mutual fund reports. They're available at most public libraries.

➤ Get a newsletter with a toll-free phone number so you can get updated information any time you want.

➤ Get your friends to chip in for a subscription to a mutual fund newsletter. You can use a newsletter as a source of information on the best funds to invest in, or you can use the newsletter to confirm your opinion of a fund you've already checked out.

Chapter 10

Opening Your Mutual Fund Account

In This Chapter

➤ Filling out application forms

➤ How to send money to the fund

➤ Avoiding the most common application errors

➤ Adding new services

It may *seem* like a simple case of fill-in-the-blanks, but fill out incorrect information on a mutual fund application, and you could find yourself in a mess. The way you fill out the application form also can make a difference in the taxes you or your loved ones pay, as well as who inherits this impressive mix of investments you're so diligently working to develop.

It's easy to tell that lawyers had a major hand in developing mutual fund application forms. They don't always ask the easiest-to-understand questions.

That's why this chapter is here. It will help put those questions on your mutual fund forms into simple language.

You'll learn about the types of forms you need to transfer an account or move an IRA to a new mutual fund family. You'll also find out where people get into the most trouble on their mutual fund forms—and what steps you can take to avoid it. If you get the basic forms filled out right, you're on your way!

Sharpen Your Pencil: Filling Out Forms

Filling out forms may not be the sexiest part of investing in mutual funds, but it sure is important. You can't get started in a mutual fund until you obtain and fill out all the right forms.

You'll need the following:

➤ The prospectus and application form for the fund or funds you're interested in. You need to read the prospectus before you invest to determine whether the fund is right for you. (See Chapter 8, "Secrets of Mutual Fund Shopping," for more information on what to look for in a prospectus.)

➤ An IRA application form if you're starting an IRA (a retirement savings account).

➤ An IRA transfer form if you're moving your IRA from one fund group or family to another.

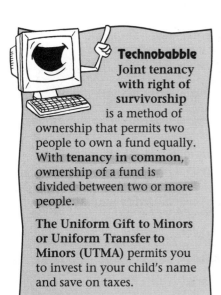

Technobabble
Joint tenancy with right of survivorship is a method of ownership that permits two people to own a fund equally. With **tenancy in common**, ownership of a fund is divided between two or more people.

The Uniform Gift to Minors or Uniform Transfer to Minors (UTMA) permits you to invest in your child's name and save on taxes.

With a broker or discount broker, often you can just walk into the nearest office and get all these forms. If you are buying funds directly from your mutual fund company, call the mutual fund group's toll-free number and ask for what you need.

The Application Form

The following is a list of questions you're likely to encounter on a mutual fund application form and a step-by-step guide on how to respond:

1. The Account Registration, or who owns the account, is no Mickey Mouse subject. The most common way to own a mutual fund is to put it in your name or to own it jointly with another person, such as your spouse. Officially known as *joint tenancy with right of survivorship*, this method of ownership permits you both to own the fund equally. If one person dies, your partner automatically gets your share of the whole investment.

Do not use this Application for IRA or Keogh Plans.
For special forms or if you need assistance completing this
Application, please call us at 1-800-782-6620.

Please print all items except signatures.

Please use blue or black ink only.

1   Account registration   *Please choose one.*

☐ **Individual or Joint* account**

Owner's name (first, middle initial, last)

and

Joint owner's name (first, middle initial, last)

*   *Joint tenancy with right of survivorship presumed, unless otherwise
indicated.*

OR
☐ **Uniform Gifts/Transfers to Minors (UGMA/UTMA)**

as custodian for
Custodian's name (one custodian only)

under the
Minor's name (first, middle initial, last/one minor only)

Uniform Gifts/Transfers to Minors Act
State

OR
☐ **Trust***

as trustee(s) of
Trustee(s) name

for the benefit of
Name of trust agreement

dated
Beneficiary's name (if applicable)   Date of trust agreement

*   *For Trust Accounts, a multipurpose certification form may be
required to authorize redemptions and add privileges. Please call
1-800-782-6620 to determine if a multipurpose certification form is
required.*

OR
☐ **Corporation, Partnership, Estate or Other Entity***

Name of Corporation, Partnership, Estate or Other Entity

Type of Entity

*   *For Corporations, Partnerships, Estates or Other Entities, a
multipurpose certification form is required to authorize redemptions and
add privileges. If you have any questions please call Business
Advisors at 1-800-842-3629.*

**2   Social Security number or Taxpayer
Identification number**

This section must be completed to open your account.

* **Individual accounts** specify the Social Security number of the owner.
* **Joint accounts** specify the Social Security number of the first named
owner.
* **Uniform Gifts/Transfers to Minors accounts** specify minor's Social
Security number.
* **Corporations, Partnerships, Estates, Other Entities or Trust
Accounts** specify the Taxpayer Identification number or Social
Security number of the legal entity or organization that will report
income and/or gains resulting from your investments in the Fund.

3   Address

Street or P.O. Box   Apt. No.

City   State   Zip Code

(   )   (   )
Daytime phone number   Evening phone number

☐ If you are not a U.S. citizen, please check box and specify
country of legal residence.

Country of legal residence

4   Investment method   *Minimum investment: $2,500*

☐ **Check**
Enclosed is a check payable to   **Family of Funds.**
*Neither initial nor subsequent investments should be made by
third party check.*

for $
         Amount

OR
☐ **Wire**
You may request your bank to wire your investment to
The Bank of New York, DDA #8900051906,

* your account is in a commercial bank that is a member of the
Federal Reserve System, or
* your account is in any bank that has a correspondent bank
in New York City.
The wire must include your account registration, address and
Social Security number or Taxpayer Identification number. It
should also indicate that you are opening a new account.

Funds were wired on
                        Date

for $ into account
         Amount   Account number

**5   Dividend and capital gains distribution
options**

*Unless you choose an option below, all dividends and capital gains
will be reinvested.*

☐ Pay all dividends and capital gains by check.

☐ Pay all dividends by check and reinvest all capital gains.

Please turn over to complete this application.

The first page of a sample mutual fund application form.

Hot Tip!

When you invest in a money fund or a bond fund, you may get check-writing privileges. You have to check the right box on the application form and then sign your name, much as you do when you open a bank checking account. Be advised, however, that when you write a check from your bond fund, it is a taxable event. Bond fund shares are sold in your account to cover the dollar amount of the check. You also have to keep good records.

Hot Tip!

Rather than send a check, you can also have your bank send the money to the fund electronically by what is called a wire transfer by checking the Wire box or a similarly named box. You'll probably pay a fee for this, but because fund prices change daily, it could make a difference. Why? When you pay electronically, you can invest the same day. Pay by check, and it might be three to five business days before the money is invested. but it will cost you about $15 for a wire transfer.

Don't get joint tenancy with right of survivorship confused with *tenancy in common*. With tenancy in common, ownership is divided between two or more people. If one person dies, that person's portion of the investment goes to his or her heirs based on the deceased's will. By contrast, with joint tenancy with right of survivorship, the property automatically goes to the joint owner.

If you're taking the wise step of investing in a mutual fund for a minor child, pay particular attention to the *Uniform Gift to Minors* or *Uniform Transfer to Minors* section of the application.

This portion of the application allows you to pay taxes based on your child's tax bracket once the child is over 14. If your child is under age 14, the first $650 of income is not taxed. The next $650 is taxed at the child's tax rate of 15 percent. Investment income over $1,300 is taxed at your rate. However, if your child is 14 years or older, all the investment income is taxed at his or her rate, which usually is 15 percent.

Assuming your child is in a lower tax bracket than you are, this arrangement could be to your advantage tax-wise. However, you might want to consult with your tax advisor to be certain.

These accounts are always established under the child's name and under the child's Social Security number. If you decide to complete this portion of the application, list yourself as the custodian. This means you're in charge of the account until your child becomes an adult, generally age 21. Then, it's transferred automatically.

You also can register the account so that a trust or a business owns the mutual fund. If you choose a business, you have to fill out the business name and explain the type of work the business performs.

2. You have to write down your Social Security number or taxpayer identification number. Unfortunately, that's so the IRS can keep track of the income you earn from the fund.

3. Next, fill in your name and address. If you're not a U.S. citizen, you have to check the box and list the country in which you are a legal citizen.

4. Send the fund a check for the amount of your investment along with your application.

5. Next, check the box indicating whether you'd rather have any income reinvested in new shares of the fund or sent to you by check.

6. In the Automatic Asset section, you can set up an automatic investment plan by checking the Yes box. Check this if you want to invest a regular amount each month to be deducted from a designated bank account.

   If you select this option, attach a canceled or voided check to your application so the fund can instruct the bank to send money automatically to your mutual fund. Be sure to note the time of the month you want the money automatically invested.

7. There are two parts to the Teleservice Privileges section, requiring you to indicate whether you want the convenience of phoning a fund group and telling it to move, buy, or sell shares of your fund. You must check Yes or No to two separate questions.

   The first part queries whether you'd like your fund group to transfer or wire money between the fund and your bank account. If you check yes, you must attach a voided or canceled check. Funds will be automatically directed to the bank account number on your check. The second part, which refers to fund exchanges, asks whether you'd like the capability of phoning in orders to transfer money between funds in the family.

8. It's not necessary to fill in the Optimal Information section. This part just seeks voluntary information that fund groups use to get an idea of what kind of people invest in their funds.

9. Finally, put your John Hancock on the bottom line—the Signature and Taxpayer Identification Certification section. Your signature verifies that you're legally able to invest in the fund and you're the lucky person who gets to pay taxes on the fund's earnings.

> **Hot Tip!**
> Application forms can be for one specific fund or for a number of funds. That's why some application forms have a section for you to check off the specific funds you want and the amount you want to invest in each.

6 Automatic Asset

Permits you to purchase shares automatically, on a regular basis by electronically transferring a specified dollar amount from your bank account to your mutual fund account. Your bank must be a member of the Automated Clearing House (ACH).

☐ Yes, you want Automatic Asset

You must attach a voided check to this Application in the area designated next to section 7. Money will be transferred only from the bank account indicated on the voided check.

Check the day of the month most convenient for you to have your bank account debited. You can invest once or twice a month.

☐ 1st ☐ 15th ☐ Both Dates

Amount you would like to invest each time: $ ______________
Minimum $100

This service is governed by Prospectus provisions as well as by Automated Clearing House rules and is established solely for your convenience. This service may be terminated or modified at any time without notice by Dreyfus or the Transfer Agent.

7 Teleservice privileges

TeleTransfer
Permits electronic transfer of money between your designated bank account and your mutual fund account by telephone.

Wire redemption
Permits proceeds of redemption requests initiated by wire, telephone or letter to be transmitted by Fed wire to your designated Federal Reserve Member Bank.

☐ Yes, you want *TeleTransfer* and wire redemption privileges.

You must attach a voided check to this application. Money will be wired or transferred only to the bank account indicated on the voided check.

☐ No, you do not want *TeleTransfer* and wire redemption privileges.

Fund exchanges
Permits exchanges by telephone among certain fund accounts with the same registration.

☐ Yes, you want fund exchanges by telephone.

☐ No, you do not want fund exchanges by telephone.

The Fund will require its Transfer Agent to employ reasonable procedures, such as requiring a form of personal identification, to confirm that instructions relayed by telephone are genuine and, if it does not follow procedures, it may be liable for any losses due to unauthorized or fraudulent instructions.

PLEASE ATTACH VOIDED CHECK HERE.

8 Optional information *We are required by the National Association of Securities Dealers, Inc. to request this information.*

Owner's occupation ______ Owner's date of birth ______

Employer's name ______

Employer's address ______

Joint owner's occupation ______ Joint owner's date of birth ______

Joint owner's employer's name ______

Joint owner's employer's address ______

9 Signature and Taxpayer Identification number certification

By signing below, you certify and agree that:

- You have full authority and are of legal age to buy and redeem shares (custodians certify they are duly authorized to act on behalf of the investors).
- You have received a current Fund Prospectus and agree to its terms.
- Any representations accompanying this application are in conformity with state regulatory requirements.
- TSSG (the "Transfer Agent"), any subsidiary and/or any of their directors, trustees, employees and agents will not be liable for any claims, losses or expenses (including legal fees) for acting on any instructions or inquiries believed genuine.
- You appoint the Transfer Agent, and any successor named at a later time in the Prospectus of the Fund(s) in which you have invested, as the Transfer Agent for receipt of all dividends and distributions.
- **You understand that mutual fund shares are not deposits or obligations of, or guaranteed or endorsed by, any bank or the U.S. Government, and are not federally insured by the Federal Deposit Insurance Corporation, the Federal Reserve Board or any other agency. The net asset value of funds of this type will fluctuate from time to time.**

Taxpayer Identification Number Certification

The IRS requires all taxpayers to write their Social Security number or Taxpayer Identification number in Section 2 of this Application, and sign this Certification. Failure by a non-exempt taxpayer to give us the correct Social Security number or Taxpayer Identification number will result in withholding of 31% of all taxable dividends paid to your account and/or withholding of certain other payments to you (referred to as "backup withholding").

Under penalties of perjury, you certify that:

1. The Social Security or Taxpayer Identification number on this Application is correct; and
2. You are not subject to backup withholding because a) you are exempt from backup withholding; b) you have not been notified by the Internal Revenue Service that you are subject to backup withholding; or c) the IRS has notified you that you are no longer subject to backup withholding.

Cross out item 2 above if you have been notified by the IRS that you are currently subject to backup withholding because of underreporting dividends on your tax return.

PLEASE SIGN HERE:

X ______________
Owner or Custodian

X ______________
Joint owner (if any), Corporate officer, Partner, Trustee, etc.

____
Date Title

Mailing instructions

Please mail the Application to:

You will receive a confirmation showing your Fund account number, dollar amount received, shares purchased and price paid per share.

This Application must be filed with the Transfer Agent before any redemption request can be honored.

The second page of a sample mutual fund application form.

Send the application along with your check. It can take five business days or more before the account is opened.

IRA Applications

When you open an IRA account with a fund, you have to fill out the IRA application, which is similar to the fund application (see Chapter 23, "Saving for Important Life Goals"). Here's how to fill out this form:

1. First, list your name, Social Security number, and birth date in the proper boxes.

2. Next, write your address and check whether you're a U.S. citizen, resident alien (foreigner), or nonresident alien (foreigner). You must include both day and evening telephone numbers where you can be reached.

3. Check whether this is your regular IRA contribution, and for which year, or a rollover IRA. If it's a rollover from an employer-sponsored plan, you also need to indicate whether your check is enclosed or your employer is sending it.

4. If you are transferring funds from another institution, check the box that tells how you're making the IRA transfer.

5. Next, designate how much of your IRA you want in each fund.

6. You also must state who will inherit your IRA as the *main beneficiary*. You can have more than one beneficiary. Just list the names of the person or persons who should receive the money, what proportion you want each to have, and how each person is related to you (son, daughter, friend, relative). These are your *primary beneficiaries*. You also should select someone to receive the IRA if the primary beneficiaries pass away. These are known as *contingent beneficiaries*.

Money Matters
IRS rules for transferring IRAs are technical. Be certain to check with your accountant or a retirement account specialist at the IRS (800-829-1040) before you make a move. Keep good records of whom you spoke with and when.

Technobabble
Your **main beneficiary** is the person (or people) who inherits your IRA. Your **primary beneficiaries** inherit your IRA if you pass away. Your **contingent beneficiaries** receive the IRA if the primary beneficiaries pass away.

IRA Transfers

Suppose you want to move your IRA from your bank (or another kind of account, such as another fund account or a stock investment account) to a mutual fund. You must fill out the IRA transfer form that you get with your new IRA application. This application asks you to identify the name, address, and telephone number of the institution that has your IRA, your old IRA account number, and which investments you want to transfer.

Signing Up for New Services

Each month, a growing number of investors faithfully send a check to their mutual funds. They could save time and a few dollars in postage by signing up for an automatic investment plan. Others who like to squirrel away money in a bank account until they have a large chunk to invest may suddenly decide to have the money wired electronically to their funds. Still others occasionally might want to have money wired out of their mutual funds into their checking accounts to pay large bills.

Oops! All these people already opened their accounts. Is there any way they can sign up for these services now?

With most investment companies, it's never too late to change the details of the account. You just call the fund and ask for a shareholder services form (see the following example). This form covers several services you might not have signed up for when you initially opened your account.

Here's how to fill out a shareholder services form:

1. The first section of this form asks for your Social Security number or employer identification number, name, address, and telephone number. (Be sure to check the box at the end of this section if you are living at a new address. Otherwise, important investment information and records may not get forwarded to your new digs.)

2. The next section asks how you prefer to do business with the fund family. Do you want the fund to accept telephone instructions from you or other registered account owners? Do you want the option of mailing written instructions without having to get your signature guaranteed by a notary public? If not, check the box that says In Writing Only or something similar. This establishes that all written instructions must have a signature guarantee.

3. The third section asks whether you want to add wire and electronic funds transfer of redemption proceeds to your account. Choose this option if you want to sell shares of your fund and have the money wired electronically to your bank account.

1 Shareholder Information.

Taxpayer Identification Number or Employer Identification Number:

or

Social Security Number   ID Number

Name

Address

City   State   Zip Code

Is this a new address?   ☐ yes   ☐ no

2 How do you want to do business? *Please check the service you want.*

☐ **By Telephone and In Writing.**
I want the fund to accept telephone instructions from me or any other registered owner by telephone or in writing without a signature guarantee to redeem or convert shares

OR

☐ **In Writing Only.**
I want the fund to accept only written instructions signed by me and all registered owners to redeem or convert shares and to require that signatures be guaranteed on redemption requests.

If no box is checked, the fund assumes you want to do business with the fund in writing only.

3 Optional Services. *Please check the service you want.*

☐ **Wire and Electronic Funds Transfer of Redemption Proceeds.**
Check this if you want to have redemption proceeds sent to your bank by wire or electronic funds transfer. Be sure to check the section "By Telephone and In Writing" in Section 2 above.

☐ **Telephone Investments.**
If you want to be able to make telephone investments, check this box to authorize us to draw from your bank account. The minimum is $50.
Please attach a preprinted voided check below.

☐ **Automatic Monthly Investments.**
When do you want your automatic monthly investments to begin?

Month   Day   Year

$ _____

Fund name and account number if known   Minimum $50.

$ _____

Fund name and account number if known   Minimum $50.

Please note: If the date selected falls on a weekend or holiday, investments will be made the next business day. Be sure to attach a voided check below.

☐ **Telephone Access Code.**
Please check if you want to apply for your personal and confidential access code.

Attach Voided Check Here.

4 Signatures

* I authorize the fund to act upon my instructions for the services I have checked on this form.

* I certify under penalties of perjury, that the tax identification number shown on this form is correct and that I am not currently under IRS notification that part of my dividend and interest income is to be withheld as a result of my failure to report all dividend and interest income on my tax return.

* If signing for a personal trust, all trustees must sign with the word trustee following each signature. This form must be accompanied by a copy of the portion of the trust document that names the trustees only if you haven't previously provided this document to the investment company.

* If signing on behalf of a bank (or bank acting as a trustee/custodian), please provide the signature of the office at the level of senior vice president or above.

All registered owners of the accounts listed under the taxpayer identification number shown on this form must sign below.

X _____   _____
Signature of owner, custodian, or trustee   Date

X _____   _____

X _____   _____

Note: In electing to do business by telephone or in writing without a signature guarantee, you have indemnified the fund and affiliated companies from liability for any loss you may sustain. The fund will employ reasonable procedures to confirm that instructions communicated by telephone are genuine. These procedures include personal identification, recording of telephone conversations, and providing written confirmation of each transaction. A failure on the fund's part to employ such procedures may subject us to liability for any loss due to unauthorized or fraudulent instructions.

Example of shareholder services form.

Hot Tip!
If you plan to use your mutual fund investments to pay for your child's college education, or to pay off the mortgage one day, sign up for the fund's wire and electronic funds transfer of redemption proceeds. You can have money transferred to your bank account the same day you need the money.

Most funds also enable you to specify whether to authorize the fund to withdraw money automatically from your checking account and invest it based on your telephone instructions. Always attach a voided check when you choose either this box or the Automatic Monthly Investment box, which instructs the fund to withdraw funds electronically from your checking account and invest them in your fund.

4. If you want a telephone access code number to track your account status 24 hours a day, check the box for this option. (You might not see this option on all mutual fund services forms.)

5. The last part of the form asks for your signature, which is necessary to enable the fund to carry out your instructions.

If Things Can Go Wrong, They Will

Before you send in the forms along with your check, double-check your paperwork. It's easy to write down the wrong number, check the wrong box, or overlook certain questions entirely. It's a good idea to fill out the form and let it sit for a day. Then, return to it. Once you're done filling out everything, make photocopies of all the completed forms for your files.

Money Matters
Be sure to notify your fund group if you change your address. Otherwise, your fund updates and checks will be sent to the wrong place, and it could take a few extra days for the post office to forward them.

In addition to writing the wrong numbers, here are other common errors to avoid:

➤ Registering the fund incorrectly. Registration determines who pays taxes on your mutual fund and who eventually inherits your fortune when you go to the above and beyond. For example, if you plan to open a joint account, make certain you remember to include the name of the joint owner!

➤ Forgetting the ZIP code in the section that includes your address. Do this and your mail could wind up back at your fund group.

➤ Forgetting to check the box asking whether you want income to be mailed to you in the form of a check. If you don't check this, your income automatically gets reinvested in your mutual fund.

➤ Checking the wrong funds when the application applies to several different funds. Use a ruler when you go over this section. Sometimes the fund names appear in small type. There are so many funds nowadays that many have similar names.

The Least You Need to Know

➤ Your application is a record of how you want your money invested.

➤ You can register your fund in your name or share ownership in a joint account or an account set up as tenants in common.

➤ You must fill out a special IRA form to open a retirement savings account for your mutual fund investment.

➤ If you want to move your IRA, you must fill out a transfer form.

➤ Double-check your paperwork. It's easy to write a wrong number, check a wrong box, or overlook an important section of your application.

Part 3
Zoning In on the Picks

This section of the book puts the different types of mutual funds under a microscope. You'll see exactly how money market mutual funds, bond mutual funds, and stock mutual funds stack up against each other and against similar investments. You'll learn how risky each type of fund is and get some idea of which funds are among the most well managed. You'll also learn which funds to avoid like the plague.

Earlier chapters introduced you to the basics of mutual fund investing. Now, get ready for the nitty-gritty.

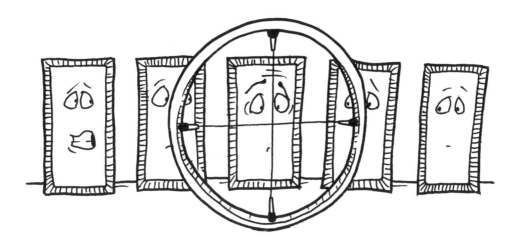

Chapter 11

Money Funds: Better Than a Bank Account?

In This Chapter

➤ How do money funds work?

➤ How you can have a high-yielding checking account

➤ Other advantages of money funds

Money market mutual funds are the closest thing to a bank account that you'll find in the mutual fund world. They are *not* FDIC-insured bank accounts, however. You'll discover the differences in this chapter.

A money market mutual fund, money market fund, or money fund, as this animal frequently is called, generally allows you to write checks against the balance in your account. Money market funds also often pay higher yields than similar bank accounts.

This chapter takes a close look at money market mutual funds. It examines exactly how risky money funds are, whether they are for you, and the best ways to use them in your investment game plan.

Money Funds: Low Risk

Whether you're just starting out in the investment world, looking for a temporary parking place for some cash, or seeking to diversify your investment mix, money funds are a low-risk starting place.

How can money funds be so low-risk if they are not FDIC-insured? As you learned in Chapter 3, "Investing: Your Options, Your Risks, Your Rewards," money funds invest in very short-term debt instruments. These debt obligations include short-term government notes and bills with average maturities of up to 90 days, jumbo certificates of deposit from financially strong banks, and commercial paper issued by corporations. When you loan money for such a short time to financially strong organizations, there's little chance your money fund won't be paid back.

Even more importantly, money market mutual funds have one unique low-risk advantage over all other mutual funds. Whatever money you put into a fund, you should get back. Each share you buy is kept at $1. In effect, this means that exactly what you invest in a money market fund is exactly what you should get back.

(Remember, no mutual funds are risk-free! There have been some 50 instances of a money market fund's share price dropping below $1. However, in most cases, the funds dipped into their own coffers to bring the price back to $1 a share.)

Only one money fund, Community Bankers U.S. Government Money Market Fund, which required a minimum $100,000 investment, failed to meet its obligations entirely and disbanded in 1994. Its investors, mostly community banks, lost six cents on each $1 they invested.

There is no federal law that says money funds must keep their share price at $1, and you must get your principal back. "The culture came about because money market funds were set up to compete with bank accounts," Securities and Exchange Commission spokesman Duncan King told us, "It's self-imposed." On top of that, a money fund pays you interest income. You can take this interest in cash or plow it back into the fund and buy more shares.

News You Can Use

Money funds actually are the babies of the mutual fund industry. They were created in the early 1970s as investors looked for low-risk ways to take advantage of high rates. Bank rates, at the time, were restricted by federal law. By the early 1980s, when short-term interest rates hit double digits, even the most conservative investors began withdrawing money from CDs and putting it into money funds, which dangled check-writing privileges and lower minimum required opening investments than many bank CDs. By year-end 1997, money market funds represented $1 trillion of the more than $4.5 trillion in mutual fund assets, according to the Investment Company Institute.

By investing in a money market fund, you avoid some of the risks associated with stock or bond funds. Here's why:

➤ Recall from our discussion in Chapter 3 that long-term bonds can lose money when interest rates rise. You're unlikely to encounter this problem with money market funds. The average maturity of a money market fund is 90 days.

128

➤ The rules for money fund diversification are even stricter than for other diversified funds. In most cases, no more than 5 percent of a money fund's assets are allowed to be in any one issuer. This way, if one investment does happen to perform poorly, it should not dramatically affect the value of the entire fund.

➤ If a money fund invests in corporate I.O.U.'s, also known as commercial paper, 95 percent has to be rated in the highest-quality instruments. Top-rated commercial paper carries an A1 rating by Standard & Poor's and a P1 rating by Moody's.

➤ The SEC also requires that if a money fund owns an investment that pays a variable rate, the fund's adviser must believe it is stable enough so that your principal won't fluctuate.

Technobabble **Derivatives** are securities manufactured by sophisticated traders whose performance mimics the underlying security. These newfangled investments can be particularly sensitive to interest rate swings. They took a beating in 1994, when interest rates rose and bond prices dropped.

Different Strokes for Different Folks

Assuming you can live without FDIC insurance, you can buy four types of money market mutual funds either from a broker or directly from an investment company. The one you choose depends on your investment comfort level and tax situation.

➤ **U.S. Treasury-only money funds.** These funds invest only in good old Treasury bills, or T-bills, which are short-term IOUs of the U.S. Treasury. The funds typically pay the lowest yields but are considered the least risky investments. Treasury securities are backed against default by the "full faith and credit" of Uncle Sam. U.S. Treasury-only money funds have one added advantage. In most states, their income is exempt from state and local taxes.

➤ **Government-only money funds.** These funds typically limit their investments to T-bills and U.S. government securities, so they are considered among the least risky money funds. They're backed by the U.S. government. The government agency bonds that these funds invest in include those of the Federal Home Loan Mortgage Corporation, the Small Business Administration, the Student Loan Marketing Association, the Farm Credit Program, and the Federal Home Loan Bank. Government-only funds typically pay higher yields than U.S. Treasury-only funds. Funds investing in U.S. Treasury obligations carry the added advantage of paying no state taxes on income earned from these investments.

➤ **General-purpose money funds.** These funds invest in government and corporate loans as well as bank CDs. They generally pay the highest yields. Money market fund yields tend to be highest when investments are concentrated in short-term corporate loans, called commercial paper, and Eurodollar deposits in foreign branches of U.S. banks.

➤ **Tax-free money funds.** Look for the words "tax-free" in the name or investment objective. With these funds, which invest in short-term loans to state governments, cities, and towns, your income is sheltered from federal taxes. Recall that single-state money funds also shelter income from federal and state income taxes.

Watch Those Money Fund Critters

Even though money market mutual funds are considered the least risky mutual fund investments, you must still read the investment objective section of the prospectus, which tells you what kind of money market investments the fund owns. (The investments are also listed in the fund's financial statements.) There are several different kinds of money market investments, and it's important to understand each kind. Here are the types you're likely to see in a general-purpose money fund:

➤ **Certificates of Deposit (CDs).** These are CDs issued by the largest banks in the country. The money fund manager and his or her research staff looks at the credit ratings of the banks to invest in only the financially strongest institutions.

➤ **Yankee Dollar CDs.** These CDs are issued by some of the largest foreign banks in the world that have offices in the United States. They often yield a little more than U.S. bank CDs.

Technobabble
Yankee Dollar CDs are certificates of deposit issued by U.S.-based branches of foreign banks. **Eurodollar CDs** represent deposits in U.S. bank branches overseas. **Bankers Acceptances** are short-term loans used to finance exports. **Repurchase agreements** are collateralized overnight loans to banks.

➤ **Eurodollar CDs.** These are CDs issued by U.S. banks that have branches in other countries. The CDs are in U.S. dollars and tend to have higher yields than domestic CDs.

➤ **Bankers Acceptances (BAs).** These are short-term loans to companies that export worldwide. Bankers Acceptances actually are secured by the goods that are to be sold.

➤ **Commercial Paper (CP).** These are short-term loans to large corporations.

➤ **Repurchase Agreements.** These generally are overnight loans to banks secured by U.S. Treasury securities.

➤ **Treasury bills.** These are short-term debt obligations issued by what most consider the most solid creditor of all: the United States Treasury.

Check Out Your Checking Account

You don't need much cash to invest in a money fund. Generally $500 to $1,000 is enough to start. After that, you can invest as little as $50 at a time.

With a money fund, you receive checks, which frequently must be written in denominations of at least $500. Your money earns interest income until the check clears. For example, if you write a check on a Monday and it doesn't clear your account until Thursday, your money accumulates interest Monday through Wednesday.

If you plan to use your money fund checking account, it's best to limit your purchases to large-ticket items. It can take as long as a week for the money fund check to clear through the banking system. You earn extra interest until that happens.

We Repeat: Money Funds Are Not Bank Accounts!

Yes, money market funds are relatively low risk, but they aren't the same as a bank account. For one thing, they're not FDIC-insured! Nor are they guaranteed by banks. It's easy to get confused about this because you hear the words "money market" refer to so many different things! Take Bertha Biddle's case as an example.

Bertha sure had her mind muddled. She invested in a money fund when she opened an account with a mutual fund family at a branch of Bank Onus. She got a checkbook in the mail along with some investment slips, and she put it next to her bank checkbook on her dresser. When she got statements from both her money fund and the bank, she noticed she earned more interest in her money fund, so she quickly canceled her bank checking account. After all, the money fund sales rep said her money fund was invested in CDs. She needn't worry about the risk.

Bertha, who invested only in banks her whole life, didn't realize that her money market mutual fund was not FDIC-insured until she stopped to chat with her stockbroker neighbor, Jack.

Bertha was a little upset by the fact that the money fund was not insured. But she didn't cash it out. Fortunately, Jack sat down with her, and together, they went over her money fund holdings. Bertha learned that the money fund invested in Treasury bills and CDs from some of the largest and least risky banks in the country. Jack also explained that her money fund was with a company that was so large, it could easily bail out the fund if there were any problems. So, she decided to keep the fund; it was a low-risk investment. However, she also learned that there is always a possibility that the money fund can drop below $1 per share.

Money Matters
Unlike a bank deposit, the federal government does not guarantee money that's invested in a money fund to $100,000!

A Word about Bank Accounts...

In 1982, a federal law was passed that permitted banks to offer a money market deposit account (MMDA) or money market account. This FDIC-insured savings account at a bank actually was designed to compete directly with money market funds.

Bank MMDA yields are lower than those of money market funds because of banks' higher operating costs. Part of that cost is for the FDIC insurance, which bank accounts offer and money market funds do not.

If you opt for FDIC insurance at a bank, remember that you are protected to up to $100,000 per person.

News You Can Use

Although money market mutual funds average higher yields than bank money market accounts, you can get a relatively high rate of return on an FDIC-insured money market account if you shop around. 100 Highest Yields, North Palm Beach, Florida (800-327-7717), tracks the highest yields on money market accounts and CDs nationwide. Some banks may also pay higher yields if you have a large balance or another account at the institution.

Picking a Money Fund

So you've decided to invest in a money fund. How do you pick one that's right for you? Here are a few tips:

➤ **Read the fund's prospectus and annual reports before you invest.** Get the facts!

➤ **Look at the type of investments the fund makes.** The safest funds invest only in U.S. Treasury securities, but these funds may pay lower yields. The highest yielding funds frequently invest in commercial paper, Yankee CDs, and Eurodollar CDs.

➤ **Check the fund's expenses, listed in the prospectus as the expense ratio.** The average money fund has an expense ratio of .5 percent, but there are many funds with lower expenses than that.

➤ **Check the quality of the securities held by the fund.** If you're a conservative investor, stick with funds that hold issues which receive the highest quality ratings by Standard & Poor's or Moody's.

➤ **Check the average maturity of the fund.** The lower the average maturity, the greater chance you have to earn higher yields when interest rates rise. The fund manager will roll over the money into higher-yielding securities.

➤ **Watch out for hidden charges.** There may be charges for check-writing privileges, exchanges, or even withdrawing money.

➤ **Look for the check minimums.** These can range from $100 to $500.

➤ **Seek funds with wire transfer capabilities.** This enables you to move money electronically to and from your bank account and money fund.

TAXABLE RETAIL MONEY FUNDS RANKED BY COMPOUND 7-DAY YIELD as of 5/7/98					

FUND	NOTE	7-DAY	30-DAY	AVG. MAT.	PHONE
Zurich YieldWise Money Fund	k	5.74	5.75	22	(888) 523-4140
OLDE Premium Plus MM Series	k	5.61	5.62	51	(800) 872-6533
Kiewit Mutual Fund/MMP	k	5.56	5.57	29	(800) 254-3948
Aon Funds/Money Market Fund	k	5.55	0	0	(800) 266-3637
Scudder Premium Money Market Shares	k	5.49	5.48	40	(800) 854-8525
Strong Heritage Money Fund	k	5.49	5.51	59	(800) 368-3863
Marshall MMF/Class A	k	5.46	5.47	44	(800) 236-3863
JP Morgan Prime MMF		5.45	5.48	45	(800) 521-5411
Rembrandt MMF/Common Cl	k	5.45	5.46	61	(800) 443-4725
Vanguard MMR/Prime Port/Retail		5.44	5.45	56	(800) 662-7447
Benham Cash Reserve Fund		5.43	5.37	62	(800) 345-2021
Fremont Money Market Fund	k	5.43	5.43	68	(800) 548-4539
Schwab Value Advantage MF	k	5.40	5.40	71	(800) 435-4000
USAA Money Market Fund		5.40	5.40	71	(800) 382-8722
Dreyfus BASIC MMF	k	5.39	5.40	87	(800) 782-6620
T Rowe Price Summit Cash Reserves		5.37	5.37	74	(800) 638-5660
Dreyfus BASIC US Government MMF	k	5.36	5.36	76	(800) 782-6620
Fidelity Spartan MMF		5.36	5.37	72	(800) 544-8888
Vanguard MMR/Federal Port		5.36	5.38	58	(800) 662-7447
Rembrandt Govt MMF/Common Cl	k	5.35	5.36	72	(800) 443-4725
Fidelity Cash Reserves		5.33	5.35	71	(800) 544-8888
Nations Prime Fund/Investor B	k	5.33	5.35	75	(800) 321-7854
OLDE Premium MM Series		5.33	5.35	50	(800) 872-6533
SSgA Money Market Fund/Cl A		5.33	5.36	54	(800) 647-7327
Zurich Money Market Fund		5.33	5.35	28	(888) 523-4140
Putnam Money Market Fund/Cl A		5.32	5.31	58	(800) 225-1581
US Govt Securities Savings Fund	k	5.32	5.33	75	(800) 873-8637
Aetna Money Market Fund/Cl A	k	5.31	5.33	63	(800) 367-7732
Strong Money Market Fund	k	5.31	5.32	57	(800) 368-3863
Dean Witter/Active Assets MT		5.30	5.32	78	(800) 869-3863
Harris Insight Money Fund/Cl A	k	5.30	5.30	72	(800) 982-8782
RBB MMP/Sansom Street Class	k	5.30	5.31	72	(800) 888-9723
Zurich Government Money Fund		5.30	5.30	22	(888) 523-4140
Fidelity US Govt Reserves		5.29	5.30	58	(800) 544-8888
Benham Prime Money Market Fund		5.28	5.29	68	(800) 472-3389
Fidelity Spartan US Govt MMF		5.28	5.29	61	(800) 544-8888
Pacific Hrzn Prime Fund/PacHrzn Shr		5.28	5.29	55	(800) 367-6075
SSgA US Govt MMF/Cl A		5.28	5.32	41	(800) 647-7327
Amer AAdvntge MMF/Plan Ahead Cl		5.27	5.26	50	(800) 388-3344
Prudential/Command Money Fund		5.26	5.27	59	(800) 222-4321

k = waiving some or all expenses.
Source: IBC's *Money Fund Report*, a service of IBC Financial Data, Inc, of Ashland, Mass.
On the Web at http://www.ibcdata.com.

133

100% U.S. TREASURY MONEY FUNDS as of 5/7/98					
FUND	WD	7-DAY	30-DAY	AVG. MAT.	PHONE
Fidelity Spartan US Treas MMF		5.10	5.07	76	(800) 544-8888
Vanguard Treasury Fund/Treas MMP		5.09	5.16	73	(800) 662-7447
Gabelli US Treasury MMF	k	5.03	5.07	75	(800) 422-3554
Benham/Capital Presv Fund I		4.94	4.99	44	(800) 472-3389
T Rowe Price US Treasury MF		4.93	4.97	82	(800) 638-5660
CMA Treasury Fund		4.83	4.86	77	(800) 262-4636
Schwab US Treasury Money Fund	k	4.83	4.88	83	(800) 435-4000
Pacific Hrzn Treas Only/PacHrzn Shr		4.75	4.85	58	(800) 332-3863
Neuberger & Berman Govt MF		4.73	4.78	83	(800) 877-9700
BT Alex Brown Cash Res/Treas		4.71	4.76	59	(800) 553-8080
HighMark 100% US Treas MMF/Retail	k	4.71	4.75	73	(800) 433-6884
Dreyfus 100% US Treas MMF		4.63	4.71	89	(800) 782-6620
CitiFunds US Treasury Reserves	k	4.56	4.59	57	(800) 331-1792
Prudential Govt Sec Tr/US Treas		4.54	4.77	64	(800) 225-1852
Fund for Government Investors		4.50	4.50	47	(800) 343-3355
Reserve Fund/US Treas Fund	k	4.48	4.53	75	(800) 637-1700
US Treasury MF of America		4.46	4.58	56	(800) 421-9900

k = waiving some or all expenses.
Source: IBC's *Money Fund Report*, a service of IBC Financial Data, Inc, of Ashland, Mass.
On the Web at http://www.ibcdata.com.

TAX-FREE GENERAL PURPOSE MONEY FUNDS
as of 5/7/98

FUND	NOTE	7-DAY	30-DAY	AVG. MAT.	PHONE
Benham Tax-Free MMF	k	4.27	4.10	48	(800) 472-3389
Strong Municipal MMF		4.03	3.87	35	(800) 368-3863
Vanguard Muni Bond/MMP		3.89	3.79	36	(800) 662-7447
Calvert T-F Reserves MMP/O Shares		3.86	3.73	21	(800) 368-2748
Fidelity Spartan Municipal MF	k	3.81	3.67	29	(800) 544-8888
USAA Tax Exempt MMF		3.78	3.71	64	(800) 382-8722
Dreyfus BASIC Muni MM Portfolio	k	3.69	3.60	48	(800) 782-6620
Evergreen Municipal MMF/Cl A		3.69	3.53	36	(800) 690-1593
Nations T-E Fund/Investor B	k	3.69	3.52	26	(800) 321-7854
Schwab Municipal MF/Value Adv Cl	k	3.69	3.60	45	(800) 435-4000
Zurich Tax-Free Money Fund		3.69	3.63	33	(888) 523-4140
Fidelity Municipal MMF		3.63	3.52	27	(800) 544-8888
Northern Municipal MMF	k	3.61	3.50	42	(800) 595-9111
Boston 1784 Tax Free MMF		3.54	3.48	48	(800) 252-1784
JP Morgan Tax-Exempt MMF		3.52	3.46	20	(800) 521-5411
CMA Tax-Exempt Money Fund		3.51	3.35	40	(800) 262-4636
Heritage Cash Trust Muni MMF		3.51	3.41	25	(813) 573-3800
Great Hall Tax-Free MMF		3.47	3.32	44	(800) 934-6674
Smith Barney Municipal MMF		3.47	3.40	43	(800) 451-2010
T Rowe Price Tax-Exempt MF		3.47	3.41	61	(800) 638-5660
Schwab Municipal MF/Sweep Cl	k	3.46	3.38	45	(800) 435-4000
Centennial Tax-Exempt Trust		3.45	3.29	54	(800) 525-7048
Chase Vista T-F MMF/Vista	k	3.45	3.35	47	(800) 348-4782
Federated/T-F Instr Tr/Invmt Cl	k	3.45	3.30	45	(800) 341-7400
Municipal Cash Series II	k	3.45	3.28	45	(800) 245-0242
Waterhouse Inv Cash Mgmt/Muni		3.45	3.24	16	(800) 934-4410
Prudential/Command T-F Fund		3.44	3.35	68	(800) 222-4321
Rembrandt T-E MMF/Common Cl	k	3.44	3.38	35	(800) 443-4725
SSgA Tax-Free MMF/Cl A		3.44	3.29	20	(800) 647-7327
Cash Equivalent Fund/T-E Port		3.43	3.33	29	(800) 231-8568
CitiFunds Funds T-F Reserves	k	3.43	3.32	59	(800) 331-1792
Harris Insight Tax-Exempt MMF/Cl A	k	3.37	3.31	35	(800) 982-8782
Scudder Tax-Free Money Fund	k	3.37	3.28	34	(800) 225-2470
The Rodney Square T-E Fund		3.37	3.29	38	(800) 336-9970
Dreyfus Municipal MMF		3.36	3.29	49	(800) 782-6620
Excelsior S-T T-E Money Fund	k	3.36	3.34	48	(800) 446-1012
Victory Tax-Free MMF	k	3.35	3.25	48	(800) 362-5365
Dean Witter/Active Assets T-F Tr		3.34	3.28	35	(800) 869-3863
PaineWebber RMA Tax-Free Fund		3.34	3.28	38	(800) 762-1000
BT Alex Brown Cash Res/T-F		3.33	3.25	31	(800) 553-8080

k = waiving some or all expenses.
Source: IBC's *Money Fund Report*, a service of IBC Financial Data, Inc, of Ashland, Mass.
On the Web at http://www.ibcdata.com.

STATE SPECIFIC TAX-FREE MONEY FUNDS
as of 5/7/98

FUND	NOTE	7-DAY	30-DAY	AVG. MAT.	PHONE
Calvert T-F Reserves/CA MMP	k	3.91	3.72	22	(800) 368-2748
Vanguard PA Tax-Free/MMP		3.88	3.76	26	(800) 662-7447
USAA Tax Exempt CA MMF		3.80	3.67	33	(800) 382-8722
Fidelity Spartan FL Muni MMF		3.75	3.60	33	(800) 544-8888
Vanguard OH Tax-Free/MMP		3.74	3.67	53	(800) 662-7447
Fidelity Spartan PA Muni MMF		3.73	3.61	23	(800) 544-8888
Salomon Bros NY Muni MMF/Cl O		3.71	3.57	38	(800) 725-6666
Vanguard CA Tax-Free/MMP		3.69	3.59	39	(800) 662-7447
Benham CA Tax-Free MMF		3.63	3.50	26	(800) 472-3389
Vanguard NJ Tax-Free/MMP		3.62	3.51	58	(800) 662-7447
Vanguard NY Tax-Free MMP		3.59	3.53	52	(800) 662-7447
Fidelity OH Municipal MMF		3.58	3.48	38	(800) 544-8888
Fidelity Spartan CA Muni MMF		3.57	3.44	35	(800) 544-8888
Nuveen CA Tax-Free/MMP		3.57	3.49	23	(800) 621-7227
Fidelity Spartan NY Muni MMF		3.56	3.46	40	(800) 544-8888
Northern CA Municipal MMF		3.52	3.40	32	(800) 595-9111
Schwab CA Muni MF/Value Adv	k	3.51	3.37	33	(800) 435-4000
Fidelity MI Municipal MMF		3.50	3.38	21	(800) 544-8888
Fidelity Spartan NJ Muni MMF		3.50	3.35	68	(800) 544-8888
Fidelity Spartan MA Muni MMF		3.48	3.36	64	(800) 544-8888
Dreyfus BASIC NY Muni MMF		3.46	3.36	48	(800) 645-6561
Fidelity NY Municipal MMF		3.45	3.33	39	(800) 544-8888
Pacific Hrzn CA T-E MMF/PacHrzn Shr		3.45	3.30	31	(800) 332-3863
CMA AZ Municipal Money Fund		3.42	3.27	27	(800) 262-4636
Fidelity CT Municipal MMF		3.42	3.29	48	(800) 544-8888
CMA MA Municipal Money Fund		3.41	3.25	28	(800) 262-4636
CMA MI Municipal Money Fund		3.38	3.26	29	(800) 262-4636
CMA OH Municipal Money Fund		3.38	3.29	43	(800) 262-4636
Federated/MN Muni Cash Tr/Cash Ser	k	3.37	3.23	50	(800) 341-7400
Fidelity CA Municipal MMF	k	3.37	3.25	33	(800) 544-8888
CitiFunds NY Tax-Free Reserves	k	3.36	3.27	50	(800) 331-1792
Fidelity NJ Municipal MMF		3.35	3.20	71	(800) 544-8888
Fidelity MA Municipal MMF		3.34	3.23	59	(800) 544-8888
Schwab NY Muni MF/Sweep Cl	k	3.34	3.25	43	(800) 266-5623
Smith Barney Muni Fund NY MMP/A		3.33	3.24	42	(800) 451-2010
Chase Vista NY T-F MMF/Vista	k	3.32	3.24	37	(800) 348-4782
CMA CA Municipal Money Fund		3.31	3.18	42	(800) 262-4636
CMA PA Municipal Money Fund		3.31	3.23	40	(800) 262-4636
Federated/OH Muni Cash Tr/Cash II	k	3.31	3.19	52	(800) 341-7400
Schwab CA Muni MF/Sweep Shrs		3.30	3.17	33	(800) 435-4000

k = waiving some or all expenses.
Source: IBC's *Money Fund Report*, a service of IBC Financial Data, Inc, of Ashland, Mass.
On the Web at http://www.ibcdata.com.

The Least You Need to Know

➤ Money market funds are the least risky mutual funds.

➤ Money market funds generally allow check writing, but be aware that there may be a minimum check amount.

➤ You can park money in a money market fund and then switch into other funds with a toll-free call to your fund group.

➤ Money market funds are not FDIC-insured.

➤ Money market funds typically pay higher yields than bank money market accounts or interest checking accounts.

Chapter 12

Bonding: Investing with Bond Funds

In This Chapter

➤ Who should invest in a bond fund?

➤ How do bond funds differ from bonds?

➤ The unique risks of bond funds and how to reduce 'em

➤ Managing your bond funds when bond prices fall

Why would anybody want or need a bond mutual fund? After all, you already learned about the dangers of changing bond prices in Chapter 3, "Investing: Your Options, Your Risks, Your Rewards." The price of the bond fund goes down when interest rates rise, and it goes up when interest rates fall. If you invest in a bond fund, you have to be comfortable watching the value of your principal fluctuate.

Despite that, many investors plunk their money into bond funds: Nearly two thirds of all mutual fund assets are in bond mutual funds or money market funds. The reason? Investors in bond funds get regular income with less risk than with stock funds.

In this chapter, you'll learn whether you're better off buying a bond mutual fund or an individual bond itself. Although these guys are in the same family, they are completely different animals. There are different risks and rewards to each. Read on, and you'll learn some low-risk ways to make money from a bond mutual fund.

Who Should Have a Bond Fund?

Now we're getting into the investment big-time. Remember that bond prices fluctuate with changes in interest rates. Invest in a bond fund, and you're investing in a riskier investment than a money market fund. In exchange, you get the longer-term potential of greater income and earnings.

Before you even consider investing in a bond mutual fund (or any of the other mutual funds we're going to talk about in this chapter and beyond, for that matter) you must re-examine your investment goals.

Review the game plan you worked out in Chapter 2, "Mutual Funds: To Own or Not to Own?" listing your time horizons. Then, peek at the results of your risk tolerance quiz in Chapter 6, "Which Funds Are Right for You?" Remember, you want money in a bond fund only if you can stomach seeing your original investment or principal fluctuate. Your bond mutual fund investment also should be just one facet of your long-range plan.

There are good reasons to invest in a bond mutual fund that could pay off handsomely down the road. First, you need to nail down whether these reasons fit your own personal needs and game plan. Let's look at some of the investors who might be good candidates for a bond fund investment.

Are You a Retiree?

Bond mutual funds are particularly attractive for retirees or those who need regular income for living expenses. They typically pay regular income, generally monthly. In fact, our very own Mom Lavine has a U.S. Treasury securities bond fund. She gets about $400 monthly from the fund—more than she would ever get from a CD. Mom Lavine loves this investment because it combines advantages of both bond critters and mutual funds, all of which we discussed in Chapter 3. (Remember?) With a mutual fund, you can do the following:

➤ **Invest as little as $500 to $1,000 to get started.** Stand alone bond funds can require minimum investments as high as $25,000! Most require a $1,000 to $5,000 initial investment.

➤ **Get professional management.** Our Mom sure would hate to pick out each individual bond investment on her own.

➤ **Become an owner of many investments.** Mom Lavine, for example, is well diversified with her bond fund. It won't be the end of the world if one bond in her fund does poorly. In addition, she doesn't have to worry about the U.S. government going out of business.

➤ **Switch funds or get cash with just a toll-free phone call to your fund group.** Mom Lavine knows that if she needs the cash, she can get it quickly.

If you need monthly income to live on, bond funds might be your cup of tea. It's easier to manage your money when you have checks coming in at the beginning of each month. By contrast, when you invest in individual bonds, you get paid only every six months— so you'd better have plenty of cash in your checking account.

Do You Want to Diversify?

Bond funds are great for diversifying your investments. You don't want to put 100 percent of your money in the stock market because you can't tolerate the idea of losing a large chunk of your precious cash if Wall Street suddenly goes south. At least, that's the way we look at it! Because bond funds don't always move in the same direction as stock funds, a bond fund might perform well if a stock fund loses.

Are You in a High-Income Tax Bracket?

Tax-free bond funds are great for wealthier taxpayers in the 28 to 39.6 percent tax brackets. Because you avoid paying taxes, you can sometimes profit more in tax-free bond fund investments than in higher-risk taxable investments. Chapter 13, "Choosing the Right Bond Fund," explores tax-free bond funds in more depth and discusses who should own them.

Bond Funds versus Bonds

There are several major differences between investing in a single bond and investing in a bond fund. In fact, these differences are so significant it pays to think twice before determining which you really want.

Bonds Are Safer

When a bond is *held to maturity*, it is kept for the entire term. Then, the bond issuer pays the investor back his or her *principal*, which is the original investment. You might be pretty surprised to hear this, but an investment in a U.S. Treasury bond that is held to maturity is actually less risky than an investment in a bond mutual fund. With a bond, the U.S. Treasury promises to pay your interest and repay your principal at the end of the term. That's a guarantee from the nation's top creditor!

You get no such principal guarantee with a mutual bond fund (even one that contains U.S. Treasury bonds). Unlike Treasury bonds themselves, Treasury bond mutual funds have no specific terms to maturity. The fund manager is always buying new bonds to replenish those that mature. As a result, the bond fund itself never matures.

It works the same way with corporate bond funds, too (as you will learn later in the chapter). Corporate bonds have an extra layer of risk compared to Treasury bonds. When you invest in a corporate bond fund, you are investing in a corporation, not the U.S.

government, and you run the risk that the corporation's business will sour. If business gets bad, the company may have a tough time repaying the principal or paying interest on its bonds.

Also recall that bond prices move in opposite directions of interest rates. When interest rates rise, bonds prices fall. A bond mutual fund investor who sells at the wrong time can take a licking.

News You Can Use

Unlike a bond fund, a bond has a specific term to maturity and guarantees you'll get your principal back at the end of the term or when the bond is called. A bond fund carries no such guarantee because the fund manager is always buying and selling bonds. On the other hand, bond funds pay interest monthly, but most bonds pay interest every six months.

Many bond funds come with checkbooks. If you need instant cash, you can write checks against your bond fund account, as if it were a regular bank checking account. It's generally best to avoid using the checks, however. Once you cash one, you're actually selling shares of your fund and could be required to pay taxes on any profits. Plus, you'll need to keep good records of the prices of each sale as well as the different selling dates in case of any tax questions.

Bonds Are Free

There's another good reason for selecting bonds over bond funds. You have no expenses when you buy a Treasury bond. You can buy a bond at no charge from the nearest Federal Reserve Bank or by calling the Bureau of Public Debt (202-874-4000). With a bond fund, you will pay an ongoing management fee. There also might be a load, or commission. In addition, you could shell out a 12b-1 fee for sales and marketing expenses. (see Chapter 7, "The Cost of Investing," for an explanation of costs and fees.)

Of course, not all bonds are free of fees either. Although Uncle Sam cuts you a break on that score, you do get zapped if you buy a corporate or municipal bond from a broker. Then, you pay a commission that is already taken out of the price you pay for the bond.

Bond Funds Are Reliable

The great thing about bond mutual funds is that they pay investors periodic interest income from the bonds in which they invest. Remember, bonds are loans to governments or corporations. The bond issuer, who is the borrower, agrees to pay the bondholder, or lender, interest on the loan and repay the lender on a specific date.

Many bond issuers guarantee the loan with collateral. Collateral is an asset that a company pledges to give its bondholders if the company defaults on its debt obligations. Bond fund portfolio managers look for this collateral when they invest in bonds. This way, if the company issuing the bond goes under, a mutual fund likely gets something to resell to make back some of the losses.

Chapter 13 discusses the different kinds of bond funds and their investments in more detail.

> **Hot Tip!**
> Bond funds generally pay higher yields than long-term federally insured bank CDs. Why? With a bank CD, you're guaranteed to get your original investment back at maturity. With a bond fund, you're not. The bond fund pays you more interest for taking on more risk.

Other Differences to Consider

When a company calls in a bond, it gives investors back their principal before the bond is due to mature.

There are other issues to look at when considering to invest in individual bonds or bond funds:

➤ Municipal and corporate bonds can be called after a period of years (typically 10). You might invest thinking you will earn high stated rates of interest for 20 years, only to learn that the bond issuer is redeeming the bonds after 10 years when interest rates have declined. You get your principal back, but you're forced to reinvest the money at lower rates. This is referred to as *call risk*.

➤ If you buy corporate or municipal bonds, you should own at least 10 to 20 securities in case 1 or 2 bonds decline in price as a result of bad news about the bond issuer. This means you probably need at least $50,000 to invest in individual corporate or municipal bond funds to diversify properly.

➤ Individual bonds pay higher rates of interest than bond funds. Why? There are no annual expenses deducted from individual bonds. By contrast, you pay an annual management fee, possibly a 12b-1 fee, and operational expenses for corporate or municipal bond funds.

Low-Risk Ways to Pad Your Pocket

Here are three strategies that could boost your total return from bond funds while limiting some of the risk associated with them:

1. If you are a low-risk-minded investor who is used to investing in CDs and money funds, you may be able to earn 1 percent more income by investing in short-term bond funds, which you learned a little about in Chapter 4, "Mutual Funds for Everyone," but will explore further in Chapter 13. These funds have longer average

maturities than money funds—typically up to 3 years, compared with a money market fund average maturity of 90 days. You can earn 6.5 percent in a short-term bond fund, compared with 5.5 percent in a money fund or one-year CD during the beginning of 1997. Don't forget, however, by extending your maturity, you are accepting a bit more risk.

2. Bond fund investors can make more money with little more risk by investing in U.S. government GNMA bond funds, rather than funds that invest directly in U.S. Treasury bonds. GNMA bonds, which you'll learn more about in the next chapter, are backed by the "full faith and credit" of Uncle Sam against default.

3. Choose corporate bond funds that invest in highly secure bonds rated single A to triple A by Standard & Poor's and Moody's. In 1998, corporate bond funds investing in highly secure bonds, based on SEC yields, earned 6.5 to 7 percent interest income. (Of course, your total return can vary based on interest rates and business conditions.)

Bond Risks—and How to Reduce 'Em!

Unfortunately, there's no free lunch when you invest in bond funds. Before you invest in a bond mutual fund, it is important to do your homework so that you don't get burned by this investment. Here's what to watch:

➤ A company that issues a bond to your mutual fund could default on its interest and principal payments.

Solution: Stick with bond funds that invest only in the strongest companies and governments. Fortunately, two major companies, Standard & Poor's and Moody's, rate bond issuers' strength.

> **Money Matters**
> As a general rule of thumb, the higher the yield on a bond fund, the greater the risk that you could lose money. You don't get something for nothing! Invest in a bond fund that yields more than 10 percent today and you might pay for it later. The fund manager could be gambling on risky bonds.

➤ Bonds rated single A to triple A are lowest in risk, as illustrated in Table 12.1. Anything below that, and you could run into trouble. Bond funds that invest in below A rated securities pay higher yields because there is a greater risk that the companies could default on their interest or principal payments.

➤ As you learned in Chapter 3, when interest rates rise, bond prices fall. (Unfortunately, many investors learned this the hard way when interest rates shot up in 1994.) The longer the maturity of the bond, the greater the risk of a price decline. Chapter 13 shows how much the price of your bond fund changes when interest rates change.

Solution: Limit your losses by investing in short- or intermediate-term bond funds. The shorter the term, the lower your risk.

➤ The steady income from your bond fund may not be enough down the road to cover the rising prices of groceries, gas, utilities, and clothes.

Solution: Invest regularly in your bond fund. You buy more shares when bond rates are higher, so you get more income over the years.

Table 12.1   Bond Credit Ratings

Standard & Poor's	Moody's	Meaning
AAA	Aaa	Highest quality bonds. Unquestioned credit quality.
AA	Aa	High quality, but slightly more risk than triple bond issuers.
A	A	Strong, but issuers don't have the financial strength of triple or double A rated issuers.
BBB	Baa	Medium-grade bonds. Short-term financial strength of issuer is good, but there could be long-term risks.
BB to B	Ba to B	Speculative bonds. Risk that debts may not be repaid.
CCC to C	Caa to C	Danger of default is high.
D	—	Highest degree of uncertainty with respect to payments of interest and repayment of principal.

When you are just starting out in the world of bond funds, it's best to stick with those with the lowest risk—funds that invest in U.S. government securities or those that invest in bonds rated triple A to single A by Standard & Poor's and Moody's. That way, you can sleep at night.

Once you get used to bond funds, you can stick your neck out just a little bit. But do it like a turtle. Some bond funds keep an average credit rating of AA or A. That means they invest some of the money in bonds with lower credit ratings of BBB, BB, and B. You will earn a higher yield from these funds with little risk because overall, the bond funds own high-quality bonds from the most creditworthy issuers.

Hot Tip!
You typically don't make as much in bond funds as you do in stock funds, so the fees you pay on the fund will be taking a bigger bite out of your earnings!

You also can invest in junk bond funds. These funds own bonds rated BBB or BB and below. You'll earn yields of as high as 10 percent. But remember, you could lose. In the early 1990s when the economy turned sour, some junk bond funds declined 20 percent in value.

What to Do When Interest Rates Rise

It was rapidly rising interest rates that caused many bond fund investors to lose 5 to 8 percent on their investments in 1994. Does that mean that the next time interest rates shoot up, you should sell?

Nope with a capital N. There are several ways to cut your losses on your bond fund in times of higher interest rates. You may have to do some fund switching to protect yourself, but it's not all that complicated. Here are just a few ideas:

1. **Just calmly sit tight, reinvest your bond fund distributions, and wait for interest rates to drop—which they eventually will.** Interest rates go up and down all the time. Even if interest rates rise over the shorter term, you should profit over the long term.

2. **Invest in a money market fund to play it safe.** Then every month, take money out of the money market fund and put it into an intermediate- or long-term bond fund. You'll earn higher yields, but you don't have to worry about losing a bundle if you invest a big chunk of money in a bond fund.

3. **Diversify your fixed-income investments.** Invest in federally insured CDs, Treasury bills, and bonds, as well as bond and money market funds.

4. **Ladder your bond funds.** Don't invest in just one bond fund. Put money in bond funds that have different average maturities. Invest in a money market fund, short-term bond fund, intermediate-term bond fund, and long-term bond fund. You'll earn high yields, but with less risk than putting all your money in one long-term bond fund. Chapter 13 discusses the average maturity of bonds owned by short-term, intermediate-term, and long-term bond funds.

Hot Tip!
If the bonds in your bond fund are issued by the U.S. Treasury or U.S. government, don't worry too much about your risk; those agencies aren't going under any time soon. You still could lose big, however, if interest rates rise or inflation escalates.

Particularly when rates are in a free-fall, it gets more and more tempting to go for the bond funds with bigger yields. Bond funds, however, are perhaps the trickiest of mutual funds to understand. Although they tend to be less risky than other types of mutual funds, you need to make certain that a bond fund rather than a bond itself or a lower-risk money fund truly fits your needs.

Then, brace yourself for principal fluctuations to come.

The Least You Need to Know

➤ Invest in bond funds for regular income.

➤ You get monthly income from bond funds; individual bonds typically pay interest income every six months.

➤ Reduce your risk of losing money by putting money in shorter-term bond funds that invest in either U.S. government securities or highly secure corporate bonds rated single A to triple A.

➤ Make regular investments in a bond fund to combat inflation. When inflation heats up, interest rates rise. By investing regularly, you can earn higher yields to keep pace with inflation.

Choosing the Right Bond Fund

> ## In This Chapter
>
> ➤ Picking a bond fund that's right for you
>
> ➤ Can you save taxes with bond funds?
>
> ➤ Avoiding the biggest mistakes with bond funds

You now know that bond mutual funds are great for providing regular monthly income. They're convenient. They're also less risky than many stock mutual funds, so it may be a good idea to have one in your hip pocket.

In this chapter, you'll learn how to tell a good bond mutual fund from a bad one—and how to stay clear of the high-risk bond funds. You'll see how much of an impact rising interest rates can have on the value of your investment, and you'll find out how to make sure you're getting the best deal you possibly can.

How Long Is Your Bond Fund?

Here's the long and short of investing in bond funds, so to speak. As you learned in Chapter 3, "Investing: Your Options, Your Risks, Your Rewards," there are bond funds that invest for the short, intermediate, and long term in U.S. government bonds or notes, corporate bonds, foreign securities, and tax-free municipal bonds.

In general, the higher-yielding bond funds in each category—in other words, the funds that pay the most—typically invest a larger percentage of their assets in corporate or foreign bonds and notes. The lower-yielding funds in each category generally invest more heavily in U.S. Treasury or government agency bonds or notes. You learn more about these different categories of bond funds later in this chapter.

It's important to understand how the average maturity of your bond fund can affect your total return.

Instant Gratification: Short-Term Funds

Short-term bond funds generally own a portfolio of bonds with an average maturity of one to five years. This doesn't mean they invest only in bonds with those terms. They can own some bonds that mature in 5, 10, or 20 years, or they can invest in cash or money market instruments that mature in 90 days or less. Add everything up, however, and the average maturity of a short-term bond fund is one to five years.

Short-term bond funds generally provide a less risky bond fund investment—one that will not show large increases or declines in total return. The total return of short-term bond funds is less vulnerable to changes in interest rates than longer-term bond funds. Plus, short-term bond funds generally pay higher yields than CDs or money funds. That makes them a good short-term parking place for your money.

If interest rates rise or fall 1 percent, a $1,000 investment in a short-term bond fund drops or goes up in value 3 to 4 percent.

The Middle of the Road: Intermediate-Term Funds

The average bond owned by an intermediate-term bond fund matures in 5 to 10 years. The total return, however, is more volatile on intermediate-term bond funds than it is on short-term bond funds. If interest rates rise or fall 1 percent, the total return of an intermediate-term bond fund rises or falls about 6 percent.

News You Can Use

Surprisingly, Ibbotson Associates research shows that intermediate-term bonds have provided about the same total returns as long-term bonds with significantly less risk. It might seem as though long-term bonds provide a greater total return because they pay higher interest rates than short- or intermediate-term bonds. However, over the last 51 years, long-term bonds grew at an average annual total return of just over 5 percent. What's more, the number of down years (when the total return declined into negative territory) was 16. The average total return during those down years was –3 percent, and the worst one-year return was –9.2 percent.

By contrast, intermediate-term bonds grew at a slightly higher average annual total return of 6 percent. The number of down years was just 5. The average decline in total return was 1 percent, and the worst one-year total return was –1.3 percent.

Intermediate-term bond funds are ideal investments for individuals with a moderate tolerance for risk. Typically, with an intermediate-term bond fund, you receive about 85 percent of the interest income that you would receive from long-term bond funds; however, intermediate-term bond funds have less volatile total returns. That makes intermediate-term bond funds a good long-term investment for those who want income or modest growth in the value of their investment over the longer term. They can be used as a lower-risk way to save for a child's college education, a down payment on a house, or retirement.

The Long View: Long-Term Funds

Long-term bond funds invest in bonds with an average maturity of 10 to 20 years. Long-term bond funds tend to pay the highest interest rates, but their total returns are more volatile. The total return on long-term bond funds can be +12 or –12 percent when interest rates rise or fall 1 percent. As a result, long-term bond funds are best suited for investors with a high tolerance for risk. The bond funds can be used as a source of retirement income or for a long-term saving plan or to help you diversify your investments.

The Long and Short of It

Should you invest in a short-, intermediate-, or long-term bond fund?

As you know, you earn higher yields with longer-term bond funds. Of course, there's a trade-off. When interest rates rise, longer-term bond funds drop more in value. Here is how the value of a $1,000 investment changes if interest rates change 1 percent. As you can see, if interest rates rise 1 percent, the value of your $1,000 investment in a short-term fund drops only $38, but a long-term bond fund drops 94 smack-a-roos:

Type	Rates Rise 1%	Rates Fall 1%
Short-term	$962	$1,040
Intermediate-term	$938	$1,067
Long-term	$906	$1,112

As a rule of thumb, short-term bond funds are less risky than longer-term bond funds. Follow these rules:

➤ Invest in a short-term bond fund if you are investing for two years or less.

➤ Invest intermediate-term if you are investing for 10 years or less or if you want to play it safe with your principal and still get decent income from your fund over your lifetime.

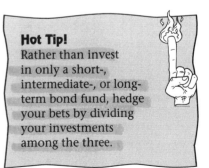

Hot Tip!
Rather than invest in only a short-, intermediate-, or long-term bond fund, hedge your bets by dividing your investments among the three.

➤ Invest in long-term bond funds if you want higher income and you can tolerate seeing the value of your principal drop 10 percent or more in any given year.

How Do You Choose?

Don't worry, troops. Choosing a bond fund is not an impossible task. In fact, it's kind of like buying detergent, which we all manage to do on a regular basis, right? There are detergents for cold water and detergents for hot water. You use some for towels and sheets, and others are for delicate fabrics. Wash your underwear with the wrong kind of detergent, and you wind up scratching yourself all day.

Fortunately, we've already given you the basics to avoid scratching yourself with bond funds. You already know these facts:

➤ Bond funds issued by the U.S. Treasury or government agencies are the least risky. You have the backing of the U.S. government against default.

➤ For low risk, any bonds in your corporate bond fund should be rated single A to triple A by Standard & Poor's and Moody's. These funds own bonds issued by the most creditworthy companies.

➤ The longer the average maturity of the bonds in your fund, the greater the risk. For lower risk, invest in short-term or intermediate-term bond funds.

➤ Invest regularly in your bond fund to combat inflation. Then when inflation heats up and bond rates rise, you can invest to take advantage of the situation.

Your Safest Bets

It's time to nail down your choices even further. If low risk is as much of an issue for you as it is for us, we suggest that you look at your fund's investment objective. Then, limit your bond fund selection to the types described in the next sections.

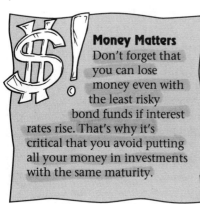

Money Matters
Don't forget that you can lose money even with the least risky bond funds if interest rates rise. That's why it's critical that you avoid putting all your money in investments with the same maturity.

U.S. Treasury Bond Funds

Treasury bond funds, like the one Mom Lavine has, invest in U.S. Treasury bonds and notes. They come in three primary sizes:

➤ Short-term Treasury bond funds invest in T-bonds that mature in three to five years.

➤ Intermediate-term funds invest in Treasury bonds maturing in 6 to 10 years.

➤ Long-term funds invest in 20- and 30-year T-bonds.

However, there's now a newer type of Treasury bond to consider. You know how we keep harping on the importance of earning enough money to beat inflation or the rising prices of your important needs? The U.S. Treasury Department has come up with a bond designed to do just that. They are called *Treasury Inflation Protection Securities,* or TIPS for short. TIPS yield just 3.6 percent—not the greatest, but these bonds come with a nice kicker: Bond principal is supposed to increase in value, based on a specific formula, along with inflation.

The downside to these bonds is that if there is no inflation, the yield you get on TIPS often is less than you would get on a fixed-rate Treasury bond with a comparable maturity.

If you are interested in learning more about this kind of bond, the PIMCO Group of Funds and American Century Benham Group of Funds both offer bond funds that invest in TIPS.

Zero Coupon Treasury Bond Funds

Treasury bond funds also have a distant cousin, known as *zero coupon Treasury-bond funds.* The difference is that instead of getting monthly income from these mutual funds, you collect accumulated income and principal at the bond's maturity. However, if these funds are outside a retirement plan, you must still pay federal income taxes on the interest annually, even though it has not been received. With these funds, you can determine exactly how much you'll earn by a certain date.

Money Matters
Zero coupon bonds and bond funds are more volatile than other types of bonds and bond funds. Brokerage firms actually manufacture these bonds by splitting Treasury bonds and selling the interest and principal as separate securities.

The Benham Group of Funds and the Scudder Group of Funds both have zero coupon bond funds.

U.S. Government/Mortgage Bond Funds

U.S. government/mortgage bond funds are ranked next lowest on the risk list, but investors in these bonds have one extra-special risk to deal with that they don't have with U.S. Treasury bond funds. U.S. government/mortgage bond funds invest in longer-term U.S. government agency bonds, which are primarily used to finance home mortgages. They pay about 1 to 1.5 percent more than pure Treasury-bond funds because virtually any creditor—even a government agency—is riskier than the U.S. Treasury.

These mortgage bond funds are particularly attractive to those living on fixed incomes because the federal guarantee makes them low risk. They're tricky little devils, however, because they're different from traditional bond funds that pay you monthly income based on their yield.

If you've ever paid off a mortgage, you know that monthly payments on mortgages include more than just interest payments, right? They also include principal. As a result, a mortgage bond fund, which owns the mortgage bonds, distributes the interest income to shareholders. It takes the principal portion of the payments and reinvests it.

That sounds great on the surface—but it can be a killer when interest rates fall and homeowners refinance, paying off their entire mortgages! Then, the mortgage bond fund gets more principal returned faster than expected. The fund manager is forced to reinvest the principal at lower rates.

Guess who's the final recipient of those lower rates? That's right—you, the shareholder.

High-Quality Corporate Bond Funds

High-quality corporate bond funds buy bonds issued by the nation's financially strongest companies. There are a variety of high-quality corporate bond funds from which to pick. Short-term, intermediate-term, and long-term bond funds are available from most mutual fund families. Typically, these funds yield about 2 percent more than comparable U.S. Treasury bond funds.

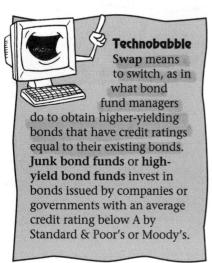

Technobabble

Swap means to switch, as in what bond fund managers do to obtain higher-yielding bonds that have credit ratings equal to their existing bonds. **Junk bond funds** or **high-yield bond funds** invest in bonds issued by companies or governments with an average credit rating below A by Standard & Poor's or Moody's.

Any corporate bond fund represented as high quality must invest at least 65 percent of its assets in investment-grade bonds. Investment-grade bonds are rated A to triple A by Standard & Poor's and Moody's. The rest can be invested in cash, U.S. government securities, lower credit-rated bonds (usually rated BBB to BB), and overseas bonds.

Corporate bond fund managers have a number of ways they can earn higher returns or reduce risk. Depending on their outlook for interest rates, they can invest in short-, intermediate-, and long-term bonds. They often look for mispriced bonds from issuers expected to get an upgrade in their credit ratings—from A to AA, for example. Often, they will swap bonds or switch to higher-yielding bonds that have the same credit ratings as their existing bonds.

Insured Municipal Bond Funds

Municipal bond funds invest in bonds whose interest is paid by cities, counties, states, toll roads, schools, water projects, and hospitals. The interest income from municipal bonds is tax-free and the bonds are insured against default by large private insurance companies, such as the American Municipal Bond Assurance Corp. (AMBAC) and the Municipal Bond Insurance Association (MBIA).

These insurance companies, incidentally, don't insure just any municipal bond. The state or city issuing the bond has to be economically strong and have a lot of tax revenue. Typically, insured municipal bond funds yield between one-quarter to one-half of one percent less than uninsured municipal bond funds. Why? The bond issuers have to pay for the insurance coverage, so they pay less interest.

However, insured municipal bond funds often outperform uninsured bond funds based on total return—price gains plus the yield. The reason for such performance is the strong demand for these bonds, which results in higher prices. Protection against defaults makes insured municipal bonds more attractive to investors.

How good is the bond insurance? The insurance companies conduct a worst-case scenario before they insure any issuer. According to Standard & Poor's and brokerage firms' evaluations, the default rate on insured municipal bonds has been less than one-half of one percent over the past 20 years. Insurance companies have made good on the losses.

Uninsured High-Quality Municipal Bond Funds

Uninsured high-quality municipal bond funds also invest in the least risky municipal bonds, rated single A to triple A. They're just not insured. In addition, some municipal bond funds limit investments to a single state if you want to escape state taxes.

News You Can Use

Invest in municipal bond funds only if you're in a high-tax bracket (28 percent or greater). You can tell whether these funds are worth it by doing a little math.

Subtract your tax bracket from 1. Then, divide that number into the municipal bond fund's yield. That gives you the taxable equivalent yield on your municipal bond funds. If the taxable equivalent yield is higher on the municipal bond fund than on the taxable bond fund, you've got a good deal.

For example, suppose you're in the 31 percent tax bracket and the municipal bond fund yields 6 percent:

$1 - .31 = .69$

$6 \div .69 = 8.7$ taxable equivalent yield

Comparable taxable bond funds yield 7.5 percent, so the municipal bond fund is a better deal.

Go International: International Bond Funds

There are all types of international bond funds, with varying degrees of risk. Once you get into international bond funds, however, you add one extra element of risk to the whole mutual fund bond proposition. Fund managers must convert U.S. dollars into foreign currency to buy the bonds. Therefore, if the value of the dollar rises against foreign currencies, the value of your investment can drop. True, you can earn higher yields and make bigger profits in funds that invest in some of these critters, but they're not for beginners. Nor do you want to sock all your money in them.

Given that caveat, the international bond funds considered least risky invest in bonds issued by foreign governments worldwide. Others invest in governments and large multinational corporate bonds. Global or world funds may also own U.S. bonds. All these types of mutual funds are among the least risky of the international bond funds. The fund managers diversify not only by country but also by corporate bond issuers and the industries of the companies.

Some bond funds invest in Latin American bonds and other emerging markets. These are high-risk investments because these countries may be politically or economically unstable.

As in the U.S., you can tell a well-managed international bond fund by focusing on total return as well as yield. You don't want to invest in a high-yielding international fund only to find the market value of your investment declining. You want to see that the fund is managing its investments properly. That means international bond fund managers try to limit losses when interest rates rise and bond prices fall. If they believe interest rates are rising in one country, they may invest in another, where rates are expected to decline. They may reduce the average maturity of the fund to cushion the blow of rising interest rates in some countries.

The world's economies don't move the same way American bond markets do. There's a good chance that when rates are low in the U.S., they are higher elsewhere. That's why a well-diversified international bond fund that invests in government or high-quality corporate bonds can be a good deal. You might consider keeping a small part of your bond fund holdings in a well-managed bond fund that invests worldwide.

Three of the best-rated international bond funds over the past five years, according to Morningstar Inc., include

➤ Compass International Bond Fund, now called BlackRock International Bond Fund (888-426-6727)

➤ Payden & Rygel Global Fixed Income (800-572-9336)

➤ Warburg Pincus Global Fixed Income (800-369-2728)

Remember, however, when you invest in international bonds, you face an extra layer of risk. That's why it's a good idea to keep only a small part of your bond fund holdings in these types of funds.

How to Pick a Bond Fund

You have to do your homework when you invest in bond funds:

➤ Read the bond fund's prospectus before you invest to be sure the fund's investment objectives match your own.

➤ Ask yourself why you want to invest in this fund:

Do you need the interest income to live on?

Do you want to diversify your investments—hedge your stock fund investments by owning a bond fund?

Do you want to use a bond fund as a temporary place to park your money until a better investment comes along?

How long do you expect to invest?

➤ Decide whether you want to invest in short-, intermediate-, or long-term bond funds.

➤ Compare similar bond funds' charges. Use the following Bond Fund Worksheet to help out:

What's the load or commission?

What is the management fee?

Is there a 12b-1 fee?

What's the expense ratio, or percentage of assets taken out to cover expenses?

➤ What does the fund yield compared with other funds? You can check various bond fund reports like the one illustrated next to compare.

➤ Look at the fund's *total return* over at least three years. You don't want to own a high-yielding fund only to discover the total value of your investment is declining. You want consistent returns, not wild price swings.

➤ Check the credit ratings of the fund's holdings, which are listed in the fund's prospectus and quarterly reports.

Bond Fund Picking Worksheet

Fund	Yield	Load	12b-1 Fees	Management Fee	Expense Ratio	Term--S,I,L

Use this worksheet to compare different bond funds.

Mistakes to Avoid

There's a lot of material to digest when considering a bond mutual fund. If you decide to go that route, don't make the following costly errors. You'll save a lot of heartache—and money:

➤ Chasing after high-yield funds without understanding the risks.

➤ Investing in long-term bond funds when you only want to park your money for less than a year.

➤ Investing in a tax-free municipal bond fund if you're not in a high-tax bracket.

➤ Paying more than 1 percent annually in expenses for your bond fund. The average bond fund expenses run just under 1 percent a year. Be sure to check the prospectus.

➤ Investing in municipal bond funds in an IRA or other retirement account. Your IRA is already in a tax-deferred retirement savings account. It makes no sense to put something that is tax-free into a tax-deferred investment.

➤ Using your bond fund as a checking account. Most bond funds come with check-books, but each time you write a check, you are selling shares and you could be paying taxes on your profits.

High-Risk Funds to Avoid

High yields might be your objective, but they can also spell big trouble, particularly in an economic downturn. In the last recession, in 1990, at least 20 percent of junk bond issuers defaulted. The following types of bond funds should be tackled by only the most sophisticated investors:

➤ **Junk bond funds** in mid-year 1998 were yielding 8 percent to 9 percent. It's no wonder. Junk bond funds, also known as *high-yield bond funds*, invest in companies with poorer credit ratings. The bonds are rated below A by Standard & Poor's and Moody's. With these funds, there's a greater chance you won't get back your principal and interest.

➤ **Convertible bond funds** invest in bonds that can be converted into stock. You increase your risk when you invest in these funds because you lose if either the bond or stock markets do lousy.

➤ **Uninsured high-yield municipal bond funds** earn the highest tax-free yields. The funds invest in states or municipalities with lower credit ratings. You may run into trouble with these funds. In 1994, when Orange County, California, defaulted on some of its tax-free bonds, some funds were stuck with uninsured Orange County bonds that matured at the end of the year. Fortunately, the bond funds that owned insured Orange County bonds did not have to worry.

159

TOP YIELDING FUNDS BY CATEGORY

12 Month Yield as of 1/31/98

General Bd - Investment Grade

Fund	Yield %
Preferred Fixed Income Fund	10.10
MAS High Yield Secs Adv	8.00
Croft-Leominster Income	7.70
State Street Strategic Income S	7.70
Phoenix Duff&Phelps Inst Mgd Bd X	7.40

General Bd - Long

Fund	Yield %
Salomon Brothers Strategic Bd O	9.10
Salomon Brothers Strategic Bd A	8.50
Salomon Brothers Strategic Bd B	8.20
Salomon Brothers Strategic Bd C	8.20
GE S&S Long Term Bond	6.50

General Mortgage

Fund	Yield %
Countrywide U.S. Govt Secs	9.90
MAS Mortgage-Backed Secs Instl	8.10
AMF USG Mortgage Securities	7.70
AMF Intermediate Mortgage Secs	7.30
Baird Adjustable Rate Income	7.20

Global Income

Fund	Yield %
Sierra Tr Sh-Term Glb Govt A	13.80
Sierra Tr Sh-Term Glb Govt B	13.50
Alliance Multi-Market Strategy A	13.00
Alliance Multi-Market Strategy B	12.70
Alliance Multi-Market Strategy C	12.70

Municipal - High Yield

Fund	Yield %
Davis Tax-Free High Income A	6.30
Heartland High Yield Muni Bd	6.20
Prudential Muni-High Yield Z	6.00
MFS Municipal High Income Fd A	6.00
Van Kampen Amer Cap H/Y Muni A	5.90

Municipal - Insured

Fund	Yield %
Vanguard Muni-Insd Long-Term	5.30
Vanguard PA Tax Free Insd LT	5.20
Franklin Insured Tax-Free Inc I	5.20
Nuveen NY Insured Muni Bond R	5.10
Nuveen MA Insured Muni Bond R	5.10

Municipal - Single State

Fund	Yield %
Dupree KY Tax Free Income	6.40
Dupree TN Tax-Free Income	6.30
Dupree NC Tax Free Income	6.20
Aquila Hawaiian Tax Free Trust Y	5.90
Aquila Tax-Free Tr of Arizona Y	5.90

U.S. Government/Agency

Fund	Yield %
RBB Fd-Government Securities	9.80
Parkston Govt Income Inst	7.60
Lord Abbett Invt Tr-U.S. Govt B	7.40
Lord Abbett Invt Tr-U.S. Govt A	7.40
Lord Abbett Invt Tr-U.S. Govt C	7.40

U.S. Government - Short & Interm

Fund	Yield %
Fidelity Spartan Ltd Mat Govt	6.90
Delaware Grp - Ltd Term Govt Inst	6.90
Oppenheimer Limited Term Govt A	6.70
Dupree Interm Government Bond	6.70
Marketvest Interm U.S. Gov Bond	6.60

U.S. Treasury

Fund	Yield %
Dreyfus 100% UST Interm Term	7.10
Sierra Tr Target Maturity 2002 A	6.60
Eclipse Ultra Short Term Income	6.40
Dreyfus 100% UST Sh-Term Fund	6.30
Flag Investors Tot Return UST B	6.10

Convertible

Fund	Yield %
Reserve Convertible Securities A	5.00
Value Line Convertible Fund	4.60
Smith Barney Inc-Convertible Y	4.50
Franklin Convertible Securities I	4.20
Vanguard Convertible Fund	4.20

Corporate - High Yield

Fund	Yield %
Janus Fd Inc-High Yield Bond	12.50
Morgan Stanley High Yield A	12.10
Dreyfus High Yield Securities	11.00
Touchstone Income Opportunity A	10.80
Touchstone Income Opportunity C	10.60

Emerging Market Income

Fund	Yield %
Morgan Grenfell Emerging Mkts Fix	11.80
Fidelity New Markets Income	10.60
Federated Intl High Income A	10.40
Phoenix Emerging Markets Bond A	10.20
Phoenix Emerging Markets Bond B	10.20

General Bd - Short & Interm

Fund	Yield %
Standish Fd-Fixed Income Fund	7.20
MainStay Sh-Term Bond Inst Fd	7.10
Nicholas-Appelgage Sh Intm F/Inc I	7.10
MAS Domestic Fix Inc Instl	7.00
MainStay Sh-Term Bond Inst Serv	6.80

Multi-Sector Bond

Fund	Yield %
Janus Fd Inc-Flexible Income	8.30
Federated Strategic Income Fund F	8.30
MFS Strategic Income Fund A	8.20
MFS Strategic Income Fund C	8.20
Oppenheimer Strat Income Fd A	8.20

Municipal - National

Fund	Yield %
Lebenthal Taxable Municipal Bond	6.30
CGM American Tax Free Fund	5.90
USAA Tax Exempt-Long Term	5.50
Smith Barney Managed Munis Y	5.40
Franklin Federal Tax-Free Inc I	5.40

U.S. Government - Long

Fund	Yield %
Delaware Grp-U.S. Government Inst	7.10
Fundamental U.S. Govt Strat Inc	6.90
Delaware Grp-U.S. Government A	6.50
Schwab Total Bd Market Index	6.20
Delaware Grp-U.S. Government C	6.10

Source: CDA/Wiesenberger Mutual Funds Update

The Least You Need to Know

➤ For safety, invest in U.S. Treasury bond funds, U.S. government securities bond funds, and high-grade corporate and municipal bond funds. Avoid junk bond funds, convertible bond funds, and international bond funds.

➤ Short-term bond funds lose less money than longer-term bond funds when interest rates rise.

➤ Longer-term bond funds pay higher yields.

➤ Invest in the least risky and highest-yielding bond fund that charges the least amount of expenses.

Chapter 14

Building Your Wealth with Stock Funds

In This Chapter

➤ Why do stock funds grow in value?

➤ The different types of stock funds

➤ The best-rated stock funds

➤ Building your wealth for the long term

With this chapter, you're headed into the big stakes. Of all the major types of mutual fund investments, stock mutual funds can make you the most money the fastest. They also can lose the most equally as fast.

This chapter discusses how stock mutual funds work. You'll learn about each category of stock fund and how it is best used. You'll also get a dose of the best long-term performers in each category—plus you'll find out what to stay away from in considering stock mutual funds.

Stock mutual funds, we admit, are not for the faint-hearted. When used as part of a long-term diversified plan, however, they can provide a significant hedge against inflation and play a key role in building your wealth.

Stock Funds Are Long-Term Affairs

Buy a stock mutual fund, typically for as little as $1,000, and you are starting to take a completely active role in the American dream.

When you invest in a stock fund, you become a partial owner of not one, but many businesses. Of course, you need a certain mentality to own a business, and it's a good idea to refer to the risk tolerance quiz in Chapter 6, "Which Funds Are Right for You?," to see exactly how much of that stuff you have. With a stock mutual fund, you need to be prepared to take the lumps as well as the good times that come not only with the stocks in your fund, but also with the economy and the stock market in general.

Two features of stock funds make the associated risks more palatable. For one, your up-front investment in a stock fund can be very small. For another, the fact that you own not one, but several businesses in a stock mutual fund makes a more diversified investment mix.

To get an idea of how a stock mutual fund can quietly build wealth, let's peek in on Comfortably Retired Ralph. When Ralph was in his early 30s in 1959, he started investing in a stock mutual fund. In those days, there were few no-load mutual funds around. A mutual fund salesman went from door to door to pitch funds.

The salesman, Vinny, talked Ralph into investing $100 a month in a blue-chip common stock fund. Ralph had been dabbling in stocks for several years at the time, so he knew how stocks worked. This time, Ralph was looking for something he could buy and hold and forget about until he retired. He settled on the Rainbow Growth Fund, suggested by Vinny.

Everything went well until 1961. The Rainbow Growth Fund was up almost 30 percent over the first 2 years. Then wham! The economy turned sour. The economy went into a recession and the Rainbow Growth Fund lost 14 percent. Ralph's wife, Eleanore, wanted him to sell, but Ralph refused. He was stubborn.

Fortunately, the Rainbow Growth Fund had some smooth sailing after that. The fund made back its losses—and more. The total return on the fund was 19 percent in the fourth year. Then boom! In 1973 and 1974, the value of Ralph's stash plummeted 45 percent. Those were bad years for the economy and the stock market.

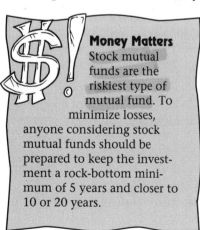

Money Matters
Stock mutual funds are the riskiest type of mutual fund. To minimize losses, anyone considering stock mutual funds should be prepared to keep the investment a rock-bottom minimum of 5 years and closer to 10 or 20 years.

Did Ralph sell? No. He hung in there, although it was an incredibly tough decision. Eleanore even threatened to get a divorce at one point. Ralph just kept pumping $100 a month into his stock fund. The move turned out to be a good one. By the time Ralph retired at age 66 in 1994, his $100-a-month mutual fund investment was worth $481,000. His investment grew at an annual average total return of 11.8 percent.

Now, Comfortably Retired Ralph always has a smile on his face. He and Eleanore retired to Boca Raton, Florida, several years ago. They have their Social Security, other income, and a nice mutual fund nest egg. The mutual fund's stash pays them more than $2,400 a month. The investment continues to grow. Ralph did pretty darned good. (The Rainbow

Growth Fund that Ralph invested in actually is a fictitious fund, but its performance is based on the historical return on the average diversified stock fund, according to Lipper Analytical Services, Summit, NJ.)

Of course, past performance is no indication of future results. Nevertheless, Ralph's story gives you a good idea of how a stock fund can do if you invest for the long term. Invest in a stock fund for the short haul, however, and you can lose big-time.

Is the Risk of Losing Money Worth the Return?

Ralph kept his Rainbow Growth Fund through the rough periods. Whenever the stock market loses more than 15 percent, it's usually called a *bear market.* There have been a number of bear markets over the years, but in most cases, the stock market bounced back after about a year. Then, *bull markets* occur when the stock market moves higher for a couple of years running.

Ralph could have bailed out in 1973 or 1974, when the stock market hit the worst bear market since the Great Depression. Many of his friends did. They sold and took their losses. In fact, some swore off mutual funds forever. However, those with the courage to stay put, like Ralph, made their losses back—and more. Over the past 20 years since the bear market of 1973–74, the average stock fund gained 15 percent annually.

Stock funds tend to outperform other investments long-term largely because ownership in corporations is one of the best ways to make money. During periods of economic prosperity, business profits. As a result, owners of the companies profit.

Technobabble
When the stock market loses more than 15 percent, it's a **bear market.** When the stock market moves higher for two or more years straight, it's a **bull market.**

The ABC Pen Company, for example, is having a great year. It can sell its pens for $2 each instead of the $1.59 it charged last year. Meanwhile, it costs no more to produce and sell the pens. The owners of the company are happy because the stock they bought at $10 a share now sells for $14 a share. That's how both stocks and stock mutual funds grow in value.

Over the long term, stocks have outperformed all other types of investments, such as bonds and CDs. Of course, there have been dips along the way—as Comfortably Retired Ralph discovered. That happens during an economic recession. Businesses start to lose money and people get laid off.

How Stocks Grow

Let's get back to Comfortably Retired Ralph. He gave up short-term losses in return for long-term gains when he socked away money in the Rainbow Growth Fund. Ralph started putting it away in 1959. The average stock fund gained 11 percent annually over the past 36 years until he retired. Wow! A $1,000 investment grew to a whopping $481,000.

Now don't think when you invest in a stock fund, you will earn 11 percent a year. The highest you would have made from the average stock fund over the past three decades was +37.3 percent in any one year. The worst was –24.3 percent, according to Lipper Analytical Services. Year after year, it will be a bumpy ride. Remember Ralph, however. He traded a string of good years for just a few bad ones.

Is the risk worth the return? It sure is if you have a game plan, know why you are investing, and do it for a long time. There are different kinds of stock funds—some more risky than others. (Chapter 6 helped you match up your risk comfort level with the right funds.) If you are not prepared to invest for an absolute minimum of 5 years—and to lower the risk, 10 to 20 years—you should stick with less risky money funds and short-term bond funds.

News You Can Use

What do stock fund portfolio managers look for in a company before they invest? No two fund managers think alike. However, they make their decisions based on a number of factors:

➤ Most professional portfolio managers talk to a company's management to discuss the firm's business plans and goals. The manager wants to know what the company has up its sleeve in regard to research, development, and marketing, as well as how financial problems are solved.

➤ Fund managers look at a company's financial statement for gems of information about financial strength and profitability. They may want to own companies whose profits have been rising over the past couple of years, or they may spot stocks selling at very low prices in relation to their future earnings potential.

➤ Fund managers may look at a company's industry to evaluate how it will do in the future. For example, when the economy is picking up steam, employment is high and people spend money. Then, leisure, entertainment, and airline stocks do well. People tend to buy houses when interest rates decline. Then, home-building stocks do well. By contrast, when a recession is looming, businesses serving basic necessities, such as utilities and food manufacturers, tend to do well.

➤ Some fund managers look at trends. They buy stocks that are showing strong upward price trends. They sell based on downward price trends.

News You Can Use

Stock funds are one of the best ways to protect your money from the ravages of inflation. The price of goods and services rose at about 3.5 percent a year since 1959. Stock funds, on average, grew at an annual average total return of 11 percent. Therefore, less 3.5 percent inflation a year, stock funds grew at an annual average total return of 7.5 percent. If you invested in stock funds during those years, you were protected from rising prices.

For Aggressive Investors Only

Although stock funds in general are riskier than bond funds and money funds, there are different categories of stock funds, and some are riskier than others. You can curb your risk a bit based on the type of stock fund you select. Keep in mind that the more conservative your fund, the fewer price swings you'll have—and those price swings can be up as well as down. The next sections present the most aggressive categories of stock funds, which can bring you the greatest returns as well as the greatest losses.

Aggressive Stock Funds

Recall from Chapter 3, "Investing: Your Options, Your Risks, Your Rewards," that aggressive stock funds invest in small, medium, and large companies. The typical aggressive stock fund buys and sells stocks for quick and (you hope) big profits. The fund managers may use speculative tactics to boost returns.

Most aggressive stock funds own stocks for about six months and trade them frequently. Why? The managers look for opportunities to buy low and sell high. They like to trade stocks often for rapid profits (or to cut losses).

The typical aggressive stock fund owns companies whose sales and profits are growing more than 20 percent a year. You will see familiar names such as Microsoft, Dell Computer, and Office Depot, as well as smaller technology companies, in the portfolios of many of these funds.

Hot Tip!

When you look at the portfolio holdings of an aggressive stock fund in the financial reports, keep in mind that because turnover is so rapid, the fund may no longer own some of these securities.

Aggressive growth funds invest in smaller companies that are pumping their profits back into their businesses instead of paying shareholders dividends. The funds focus on growth in the share price of the stocks they hold. What little dividends the shareholders of the funds would receive are paid out quarterly. However, any capital gains for the profits on the sale of stocks are paid to shareholders at the end of the year.

The best-rated aggressive stock funds frequently have the capability of buying hot stocks early and getting out with a tidy profit. Table 14.1 shows you some of the top-rated aggressive growth funds as of this writing.

Table 14.1 Top-Performing Aggressive Growth Funds, Average Annual Total Return, 10 Years Ending in January 31, 1998

Fund	Average Total Return %
AIM Aggressive Growth	21.2
J. Hancock Special Equities A	20.4
AIM Constellation	20.4
Robertson Stephens Emerging Growth	19.1
PIMCO Opportunity Fund C	19.1
Putnam Voyager	19.1
Managers Special Equity	18.7
INVESCO Dynamics	18.7
Principal Mid-Cap	18.1
First Eagle Fund of American	18.1

Source: CDA/Wiesenberger Mutual Funds Update

Small Company Stock Funds

Small company stock funds own little acorns that can grow into oak trees. These funds buy new companies or smaller companies that plow all their profits back into their businesses. These companies may have annual revenues of several hundred million dollars a year. (By contrast, blue-chip companies pull in several billion dollars in revenue per year.) Most small stock fund portfolio managers use the growth stock investment style. They invest in companies whose earnings are growing at a rapid clip, such as Peoplesoft, a human resources software manufacturer; Tracor, which makes electrical software; and Cisco Systems, which makes computer networks. Many of these companies, but not all, are in the technology business.

Some small company funds invest in undervalued stocks—overlooked companies that should register strong profits in the future. The fund managers buy and hold stocks such as ABM Industries, a building maintenance company; A.C. Nielsen, a media ratings service; and Scan-Optics, which produces optical technology, for the longer term. These fund managers look for gems. They buy early and wait for the companies to do well. Then, they profit when others invest.

Most small company stock funds tend to buy and hold stocks for a few years. Funds such as the Acorn Fund, which has grown at an 18 percent annual rate over the past 20 years, buy and hold attractive new companies for 3 to 5 years. The fund managers need time to see the companies prosper.

The typical small company stock fund owns its securities longer than aggressive stock funds. Why? Sometimes it takes a while for a small company to show growing business profits, which stimulates the demand for the firm's stock. Just like aggressive growth funds, however, small company funds pay little if any dividends to the fund's shareholders. You are more likely to see annual distributions of capital gains from small company stock funds.

You also can go for a wild ride when you invest in a small company stock fund. Small company stocks perform in streaks. They may do well for three or four years running. Then, they die before things pick up again. That's why you have to invest in them for the longer term. According to Morningstar, the average small company stock fund gained 50 percent in 1991 but lost 10 percent the year before.

There's a fine line between aggressive growth stock funds and small company stock funds. Small company stock funds tend to be less volatile than aggressive stock funds because the fund managers want to own small companies, watch them grow, and sell them at a profit when they are bigger outfits.

Table 14.2 Top-Performing Small Company Stock Funds, Average Annual Total Return, 10 Years Ending January 31, 1998

Fund	Average Total Return %
Kaufman Fund	25.9
Skyline Special Equities-I	21.7
American Century 20th Century Giftrust	20.4
Delaware Group Trend Fund A	19.7
Alger Small Cap Portfolio B	19.4
Van Kampen American Cap Emerging Growth	19.1
Barron Asset	19.1
Babson Enterprise Fund I	17.8
Berger Small Cap Value	16.1
Ariel Growth	16.0
Alliance Quasar	15.7

Source: CDA/Wiesenberger Mutual Funds Update

News You Can Use

How do you pick a stock fund? When shopping for a stock fund, look for the following:

➤ Compare a fund's year-by-year performance. Avoid funds with wide swings in annual returns. Invest in funds with the most consistent year-by-year returns.

➤ Compare a fund's annual average returns over at least a three- to five-year period.

➤ Compare how the fund did in bad years such as 1981, 1984, 1987, 1990, and 1994. You want the fund that loses the least amount of money.

➤ Check the fund's prospectus and annual report to be sure the investment objective of the fund is in line with the type of stocks it owns.

➤ Check the fund's prospectus for the fund's expense ratio and loads. You want the fund with the lowest expenses and the best track record so that you will earn more money.

Growth Funds

Growth stock funds are typically a little different from aggressive growth and small company stock funds. Growth funds stick with proven companies that have a solid track record of sales and profits. These funds invest in larger, well-established, well-managed companies—brand-name companies such as Coca-Cola, Disney, General Motors, and General Electric. These companies like to plow their profits back into the company so that they can improve and produce more popular products. In addition to investing in brand-name companies, many growth funds may own a small stake in small companies and overseas stocks.

Some growth funds like to buy and hold undervalued stock for a few years. These funds are characterized by low portfolio turnover, so you are likely to see some of the same stocks in your growth fund's portfolio for a couple of years running. By contrast, other growth funds turn over the stocks they own more than once a year. These funds look for rapid profits from the sale of securities.

Because growth funds invest in larger, more established companies, you're likely to receive some quarterly dividend income from the funds. You are also more likely to receive annual capital gains distributions from growth funds if they sold stocks at a profit during the year.

According to Lipper Analytical Services, Fidelity Magellan Fund was one of the best growth funds in recent history—up at an annual average total return of 19.3 percent over the past 15 years.

Nevertheless, growth funds are still aggressive investments. Today, the fund is so large that it only does as well as the average growth stock fund. Over the past 3 years, Magellan grew at an annual rate of 26.8 percent. By contrast, the average growth fund gained 28.5 percent. The year before, when we had an economic recession, it lost 5 percent.

Table 14.3 Top-Performing Growth Funds, Average Annual Total Return, 10 Years Ending January 31, 1998

Fund	Average Total Return %
Fidelity Advisor Equity Growth I	22.8
American Century-20th Century Ultra	22.4
MFS Emerging Growth	22.3
Fidelity Contrafund	22.2
Janus 20 Fund	21.5
CGM Capital Development	21.5
FPA Capital	21.3
AIM Value Fund	20.1
Brandywine Fund	20.5
Alliance Growth Fund	19.8

Source: CDA/Wiesenberger Mutual Funds Update

For Conservative Investors Only

Some funds are designed for more conservative investors. They are willing to risk their principal a little in exchange for greater long-term profits but can't bear the thought of large losses in their portfolios. The next sections discuss these funds.

Growth and Income Funds

All those sexy stories you hear at parties about the hot stock fund that doubled its money in two years are lies. If they're not lies, they're likely to be lies by the time you plunk down your hard-earned money. Once you're willing to wager, the fund will promptly lose 20 percent! Face it. When the little guys get wind of a sizzling mutual fund, it's generally too late. If you want to invest your money wisely, and if you own just one fund, it should be a growth and income fund.

A growth and income fund is a great investment for moderate investors. (Refer to your risk tolerance quiz in Chapter 6.) The objective of this type of fund is long-term growth of your money plus income. Growth and income funds can achieve this goal because they invest in blue-chip stocks—American companies that have stood the test of time. You'll frequently see well-known companies such as Gillette, Pepsi, Coca-Cola, Colgate-Palmolive, Anheuser Bush, Kellogg, and Wal-Mart in the portfolios of growth and income funds. Sure, they may lose some money when there's a recession, but their profits keep rising almost every year. They pass on 50 to 60 percent of their profits to their shareholders through stock dividends.

The secret of growth and income investing is reinvesting the income you get from these blue-chip companies. If these businesses continue to grow and profit, so will your investment in them.

You don't get as big a bang for your buck from growth and income funds as you would from more aggressive stock funds, but you do get a steadier investment. The income from the fund cushions some of the losses when the value of the fund declines. For example, in 1991, the average growth and income funds gained 27 percent. Aggressive stock funds gained almost twice as much. In 1990, growth and income funds lost 4 percent, and aggressive growth funds lost more than 8 percent, according to Morningstar.

Table 14.4 Top-Performing Growth and Income Funds, Average Annual Total Return, 10 Years Ending January 31, 1998

Fund	Average Annual Return %
Vista Growth & Income	24.0
Fidelity Growth & Income	19.2
SAFECO Equity Fund	19.0
Dreyfus Disciplined Stock Fund	18.4
FAM Value	18.0
Van Kampen American Cap Exchange	17.9
MFS Mass Investors Trust	17.8
Vanguard Growth & Income Portfolio	17.8
Nationwide Fund	17.7
Evergreen Growth & Income	17.3

Source: CDA/Wiesenberger Mutual Funds Update

News You Can Use

Some of the best-performing mutual funds over the past 50 years have been growth and income funds, such as Investment Company of America (800-421-9900), Affiliated Fund (800-426-1130), Seligman Common Stock Fund (800-221-2450), Fidelity Fund (800-544-8888), Massachusetts Investors Trust (800-343-2829), State Street Investment Fund (800-882-0052), Putnam Investors (800-225-1581), United Income (800-366-5465), and Safeco Equity Fund (800-426-6730). As you will see in Appendix C, "Authors' Picks: Mutual Funds That Have Withstood the Test of Time," you earn solid returns for years to come with these funds.

Equity Income Funds

Equity income funds are second cousins to growth and income funds. The difference is that equity income funds emphasize more income than growth. The fund managers invest in large companies that typically pay out more of their profits to their shareholders compared with other companies. You will see a lot of telephone and oil company stocks in the portfolios of equity income funds. You'll also see some of the same stocks that growth and income funds own.

Table 14.5 Top-Performing Equity Income Funds, Average Annual Total Return, 10 Years Ending in January 31, 1998

Fund	Annual Return %
INVESCO Industrial Income Fund	16.6
United Income Fund	16.4
Federated Equity Income Fund	16.2
T. Rowe Price Equity Income Fund	16.1
One Group Income-Equity Fund	15.9
Fidelity Equity Income Fund	15.9
Smith Barney Income-Permanent Total Return	15.8
Prudential Equity Income	15.2
Managers Income Equity	15.2
USAA Income	14.8

Source: CDA/Wiesenberger Mutual Funds Update

For Very Conservative Investors Only

Are you worried you will lose a lot of money in a stock fund? You might consider low-risk alternatives, such as balanced funds and income funds.

Balanced funds typically own just 50 to 60 percent of the fund in blue-chip stocks. The rest is invested in government and high-grade corporate bonds. Historically, balanced funds earn about 80 percent of what a stock fund makes, but balanced funds lose half as much money when the economy sours. If your stock fund is down 8 percent, chances are that your balanced fund is down just 4 percent. Fair trade-off!

Asset allocation funds are balanced funds that invest in a greater variety of stocks and bonds than the typical balanced fund. An asset allocation fund may split its stock investments among U.S. and foreign companies, as well as large and small company stocks. On the bond side, it might own U.S. government, corporate, and foreign government bonds. Unlike a typical balanced fund, which generally splits investments relatively equally between stocks and bonds, asset allocation fund managers act according to their own analyses of the markets.

Income funds are funds tilted toward income and low risk. They yield almost as much as bonds because they usually invest in a combination of government and corporate bonds, preferred stock, and utility and blue-chip stocks. These funds are ideal for those who live on a fixed income or who want a slightly riskier alternative to bank CDs. These funds pay higher yields than all other kinds of stock funds.

News You Can Use

Two of the most tried and true balanced funds are Fidelity Puritan Fund (800-544-8888) and Vanguard's Wellington Fund (800-662-7447). A more aggressive balanced fund to consider is the CGM Mutual Fund (800-345-4048). All three funds carry top ratings by Morningstar. Best-rated asset allocation funds include SoGen International (800-334-2143) and USAA Investment Cornerstone (800-382-8722).

Boosting Your Returns Overseas

The U.S. stock market isn't the only game in town. There are stock markets throughout the world. Many foreign corporations are as profitable as their U.S. counterparts. In addition, economies in Asia, the Pacific Basin, and Latin America are growing faster than ours. There are a lot of investment opportunities abroad. That's why it's a good idea to consider investing in a well-managed mutual fund that invests overseas.

There's no free lunch, however, when you invest in mutual funds that invest overseas. About one third of the increase or decrease in the total return of international stock funds can be attributed to the changing value of the dollar. (You learn more about foreign currency risk later in this chapter.) In addition, you face other risks when you invest overseas, such as the impact of a political or economic crisis on the country's stock market.

Despite the pitfalls, it could pay to invest in a well-managed fund that invests overseas if you want to diversify your portfolio.

In Chapter 13, "Choosing the Right Bond Fund," you learned about international bond funds, which are good for diversification. It's even more important to have some kind of international stock fund. Why? Two thirds of the world's companies exist outside the good old USA. Over the past 10 years ending in 1997, foreign funds grew at an 11.6 percent annual average total return. By contrast, the average U.S. stock fund gained 15.4 percent annually, according to Morningstar.

As with international bond funds, international stock funds come in all shapes and sizes. Some funds invest in blue-chip stocks around the world. Nestlé Group, Canon, Hitachi, and Bayer are common holdings in such funds. Others invest in small company stocks worldwide.

Funds that invest worldwide are often called *global funds*. Some funds invest only in European, Latin American, or Asian companies. Others invest in single countries, such as Japan.

Table 14.6 Top-Performing International Foreign Stock Funds, Average Annual Total Return, 10 Years Ending January 31, 1998

Fund	Annual Return %
GAM International Fund	18.2
Harbor-Fund International	18.0
Ivy Fund International	14.5
Templeton Foreign	13.4
Templeton Foreign I	13.6
Scudder International	11.2
Managers International Equity	11.6
Smith Barney International Equity	10.5
Vanguard International Growth Portfolio	9.7
Nations International Growth	8.9

Source: CDA/Wiesenberger Mutual Funds Update

A Yen for Investing

You learned about some of the foreign currency risk involved in investing internationally in Chapter 13. Fund managers have to change all their U.S. dollars into foreign money, such as the Japanese yen or German mark, before they can buy overseas stocks. Sometimes, U.S. money is exchanged at a rate worse than it was when you put up your dollars to buy it. Even after the fund buys overseas stocks, the exchange rate between U.S. dollars and foreign dollars can fluctuate, affecting the value of your fund.

Money Matters
Unless you are a sophisticated investor, avoid funds that invest in a single country. They are not diversified and you are investing in only one country's financial market, so you can lose big-time. A political crisis, government coup, or change in the value of the country's currency can hurt your fund's performance. To avoid these headaches, stick with well-diversified funds that invest worldwide.

Fortunately, fund managers take steps to protect themselves from foreign currency risk. Nevertheless, here's a taste of how this foreign currency risk can affect an international fund:

➤ The value of your fund may drop if the foreign currency declines in value against the U.S. dollar.

➤ The value of your fund can rise if the foreign currency increases in value against the U.S. dollar.

There are extra risks when you invest overseas. At this writing, the Asian markets had lost 50 percent due to economic problems and weak currencies. That's why it's important to put your money in a well-diversified international fund that invests worldwide.

The Least You Need to Know

➤ You invest in stock mutual funds for long-term growth.

➤ Aggressive growth funds buy and sell all types of stocks for profits.

➤ Small company stock funds invest in companies that the portfolio manager expects will grow into profitable larger corporations.

➤ Growth and income funds invest in blue-chip stocks.

➤ Minimize the risk with balanced funds. They own both stocks and bonds.

Chapter 15

Mutual Funds for Special Situations

> **In This Chapter**
>
> ➤ Risks and rewards of funds that sell at bargain prices
>
> ➤ The funds that invest in specific businesses
>
> ➤ Hedging your investments against inflation
>
> ➤ Investing with a conscience

Got a hankering for something a bit different from the run-of-the-mill stock or bond fund? This chapter delves into even more mutual funds options that are available to those investors who are looking for even greater challenges.

For example, you can buy funds for 80 or 90 cents on the dollar. Some high-risk funds promise unbelievable profits because they invest in one type of industry. Do you have strong moral and ethical feelings about how companies do business? You have still other funds to pick! This chapter examines specialized mutual funds for all kinds of investors.

Closed-End Funds

Know how you can't pass up those President's Day sales? You can buy all those clothes and shoes with Italian names cheaply. Last year, for example, one of us (guess who?) picked up a pair of $200 Ferragamo shoes for $80. One of us, although not necessarily the other, was mighty proud of that find.

Sometimes, you can also buy certain types of investments on sale. They don't have sexy European names, nor are they big box office draws, but they can be far more worthwhile than a pair of fancy shoes or a hot ticket. They go by names such as Baker Fentress, Tri-Continental, Gabelli Equity Trust, and Royce Value. Read on to learn more about these good, but overlooked, investments.

A Different Breed of Mutual Fund

Up to this point, the funds you have been reading about are open-end funds. They have no limit in the number of shares that investors can buy and sell.

Some other animals known as *closed-end funds* are technically not mutual funds, although they are frequently classified as such. These are also called *closed-end investment companies* and *publicly traded funds*. So that you don't get them mixed up with open-end mutual funds, we will refer to closed-end funds as closed-end investment companies.

Technobabble
Closed-end funds are investment companies that sell a fixed number of shares which are traded on the stock exchange. Mutual funds are **open-end funds**, which means that there is no limit to the number of shares that investors can buy and sell.

Closed-end investment companies, although similar to mutual funds, are not mutual funds. Mutual funds are open-ended because they continually offer new shares for sale to the investment public. By contrast, closed-end investment companies issue a limited number of shares and do not redeem them. Instead, closed-end shares are traded in the securities markets, with supply and demand determining the price. The closed-end investment company's shares of stock are traded on the securities exchange just like the stock of a corporation.

The closed-end investment company's business is managing a portfolio of securities. Different companies have different investment strategies and goals:

➤ Some may invest in stocks, bonds, overseas securities, or a combination of securities.

➤ Some are diversified among many different companies; others concentrate on a specific industry or group of industries.

➤ Some invest in single countries of the world, such as Japan; others invest in regions of the world, such as Europe.

➤ Some closed-end investment companies invest in Treasury, corporate, and foreign bonds.

➤ High-tax-bracket investors can invest in closed-end investment companies that buy municipal bonds.

➤ Dual-purpose closed-end investment companies issue two classes of shares. The first class of shares is for investors who want income, and the second class of shares is for those who want growth.

You can't buy and sell shares of the closed-end investment company's portfolio. You can only buy or sell the closed-end investment company's stock, which is traded on a stock exchange. The shares of stock easily can be bought or sold through a stockbroker just like any other stock. Closed-end funds work this way:

➤ You own stock in the closed-end investment company that manages a portfolio of securities. You have to buy or sell shares of a closed-end investment company from a stockbroker. Don't forget: You pay the broker a commission for that.

➤ Depending on the investment objective, a closed-end investment company pays its shareholders distributions in the form of interest, dividends, and capital gains based on the earnings of its portfolio of securities.

➤ The investment company charges a management fee that ranges from one-half of one percent to 1.5 percent based on the amount of assets in the portfolio. Share-holders can take the distributions in cash or reinvest them and buy more shares of the closed-end investment company.

➤ Do you want to buy a closed-end fund? There are two prices to examine: the investment company's stock price and the net asset value (NAV) or share price of the closed-end investment company's portfolio of securities.

➤ When a share of stock in the investment company sells for significantly less than the share price of the mutual fund, you might have found a good deal. Voilà!

Buy at 80 to 85 Cents on the Dollar

You can find some real bargains when you invest in closed-end investment companies. For example, suppose you talk to a stockbroker (you also can get the information from the stock tables in the newspaper) and find that the stock of the XYZ closed-end investment company sells for $8 per share.

Then you check the net asset value of the portfolio of securities managed by the closed-end investment company. It's $10 per share. That means it costs you $8 per share of stock to become a shareholder of an investment company with a portfolio of securities that are priced at $10. That's a real bargain! The idea is to buy shares of stock in the closed-end investment company at a discount to the net asset value of the portfolio of securities it manages. That way, you've invested for less than the assets of the investment company are worth. You can buy and hold a well-managed, closed-end investment company for the long haul. Or you might sell your stock at a profit when it rises in price and the discount between the share price of the closed-end investment company and net asset value of the portfolio narrows.

Focusing In on Sector Funds

Recall that *sector funds,* or specialty funds, which you learned about in Chapter 4, "Mutual Funds for Everyone," are not for beginners. When you invest in a sector fund, you're betting on stocks in a specific industry sector, such as technology, banking, chemicals, oil and gas, durable goods, paper products, and so on. If the industry you've invested in hits a sudden downturn, you can lose money with sector funds. You've got to know what you're doing. You have to understand business conditions and anticipate changes in the economy to make money in sector funds.

Several fund groups have a stable of sector funds. With these programs, you typically can switch in and out of different sector funds as investment conditions change. Most are low-load or no-load. Fund groups with such programs include Fidelity Investments (800-544-6666), the INVESCO Group of Funds (800-525-8085), and Vanguard Group of Funds (800-662-7447).

Hot Tip!
Considering sector funds? It could pay to subscribe to a newsletter that tracks sector funds, such as *The Sector Funds Newsletter* (619-748-0805).

Investing in sector funds can be like riding a roller coaster. For example, Fidelity Select Air Transportation fund's total return was 31 percent in 1993. However, in 1994 when the economy slowed and people cut back on travel, the fund lost 22 percent in total return.

Those who make investment decisions at a turtle's pace should probably forget sector funds. To be successful, you have to use sophisticated investment tactics and buy or sell quickly. Otherwise, you can buy a fund only to find its price sink like the Titanic. Here are some examples of key trends that influence sector funds:

➤ When the economy starts to churn, stocks of industries such as heavy metals, machinery, and chemicals tend to rise in anticipation of demand for manufactured goods.

➤ When the economy is strong but starting to slow down, foods, consumer products, and health care stocks do well because investors favor steadier businesses.

➤ In an economic recession, stocks in the auto and construction businesses tend to do well in anticipation of an economic recovery.

Utility Stocks for Mom and Pop

As you learned in Chapter 4, *utility stock funds* are lower-risk sector funds. No matter how bad it gets, everyone uses electricity, gas, water, and the like. Retirees like utility stock funds because they get monthly income. (Individual utility stocks, by contrast, mail dividend checks quarterly.) Most utility stock funds own a large number of electric utility companies, as well as telephone and other communication companies.

Utility stock funds invest in all kinds of utility companies, which are cash cow businesses. Over the past 10 years ending in 1997, the average utility stock fund gained 12.5 percent annually. Half the gain came from income and half from the price appreciation of the funds.

Heavy Metals and Real Estate

Precious metals funds, which invest in gold mining stocks, and real estate stock funds are also popular. These funds perform well when inflation heats up. In 1978, when inflation was unbearable and prices were rising at more than 12 percent annually, share prices of precious metals funds soared. (There also have been bad times for these funds. The average precious metals fund lost 23 percent in 1990.)

The best bets in precious metals funds, according to Morningstar, Inc., are U.S. Fidelity Select American Gold, INVESCO Strategic Gold, and IDS Precious Metals. All outperformed the average precious metals fund, which gained just one half of one percent (.5) percent annually over the past five years. Precious metals funds are the riskiest type of mutual funds.

Real estate stock funds also perform well in times of inflation. Compared with precious metals funds, real estate stock funds don't give you as big a bang for your buck, but you also lose less when the economy sours. The best real estate stock fund over 5 years ending in 1997, according to Morningstar, is Cohen & Steers Realty Shares. It grew 19.1 percent annually.

A Healthy Choice

Everyone buys drugs and needs health care. That's why investment advisers often recommend that you keep part of your mutual fund holdings in funds that exclusively invest in health care stocks. Over the past 15 years, health care funds have grown at a whopping annual rate of 19 percent ending in 1997. With medical breakthroughs, such as Viagra, a breast cancer cure, and a cancer cure either in the works or in production, health care stocks are likely to keep rising.

However, sector funds that invest in health care stocks are not a sure thing. If you happened to invest in the worst-performing health care funds in 1991, 1992, and 1993, you would have lost a total of 44 percent of your hard-earned money, according to Morningstar.

Money Matters
When interest rates rise, utility stock funds can lose money because investors flock to high-interest bonds. In 1994, when both short- and long-term interest rates rose, utility stocks lost 8 percent. Even with utility stocks, the type of sector fund with the least risk, you need to be prepared to ride out all sorts of weather.

Hot Tip!
As a rule of thumb, you can keep about 5 percent of your mutual fund investments in a real estate or precious metals fund as a hedge against inflation. You can lose at least 20 percent in these funds in any given year, however. That's why it pays to invest only a small amount. Let it sit. Then, when inflation heats up, these funds should gain.

Near term, the outlook for sector funds that invest in health care stocks is clouded. As the health care industry becomes market driven, analysts say, uncertainties abound; profit margins are under pressure in some sectors and the threat of government regulations could dampen earnings. But there are also opportunities.

Among many other developments, managed care is coming to the huge Medicare population. The Food and Drug Administration is accelerating the process for approving new drugs. There are new treatments for diabetes, heart disease, and cancer, as well as new biotechnology products on the horizon. In addition, the aging of the U.S. population bodes well for health care companies.

Two of the highest-rated health care funds at year-end 1997 were the Fidelity Select Health Care Fund and Vanguard Specialized Health Care, which stick with rock-solid large company health care stocks, according to Morningstar. They invest in the most profitable drug, hospital, service, and technology companies.

The Fidelity Select Health Care Fund, up more than 28 percent annually over the past 3 years ending in 1997, invests solely in large company health stocks. The companies are growing earnings at 22 percent annually. As a result, the fund typically is a play on large company drug stocks. These companies are expected to lead the way to greater growth in the industry.

However, the fund shies away from HMOs and hospitals, which must deal heavily with Medicare. Largest holdings include American Home Products, Bristol-Myers Squibb, and Merck.

The Vanguard Specialized Health Care, up 29 percent annually over the past 3 years ending in 1997, also invests in large company health care stocks. However, it attempts to buy undervalued companies rather than companies with fast-growing earnings. Largest holdings include Warner-Lambert, Pharmacia & Upjohn, Abbott Laboratories, McKesson Corp., and Allergan Inc.

An up-and-coming fund: The Warburg Pincus Health Science Fund was up 27 percent in 1997. The fund invests in health care companies that are growing their earnings at a faster clip than they have in the past. The fund owns only 50 stocks in fast-growing large and small companies. So there is more upside potential with this fund when biotechnology firms become successful. Pat Widner, the manager of the fund, likes drug stores because he thinks that these companies will benefit from rising prescription prices and over-the-counter drug use. Rite-Aid, a drug store chain, is the fund's largest holding. Others include CVS and Walgreen Co.

Funds for Pure Hearts

Do you have strong feelings about gun control and the arms industry, the environment, pollution, or how workers are treated? *Socially responsible funds* do not invest in any old companies. These funds have super-strict investment rules. Social funds specifically scout for companies in the alternative energy business or those committed to staying out of the arms or nuclear energy business. They want to invest in companies with great employee benefits. They like firms that don't discriminate against women, minorities, or other groups. They do not invest in tobacco companies, the gambling businesses, or alcohol.

Socially responsible mutual funds have come of age. Ten years ago, about $250 billion was invested in companies that were free of South African business ties or that were not involved in defense, nuclear power, tobacco, alcohol, gambling, or environmentally unfriendly cyclical industries. Today, institutions and individuals invest more than $700 billion in socially responsible corporations. There are now more than 40 socially responsible mutual funds with more than $4 billion in assets.

Money Matters
Socially responsible means different things to different people. If you have a specific reason for investing in a socially responsible fund, read the prospectus to make certain that the fund meets your own personal "socially responsible" objective. Don't forget to scan the list of investments in the quarterly or annual report to make certain that none of the companies conflict with your beliefs.

Socially responsible mutual funds still tend to be smaller than other types of funds, and they tend not to be tracked by all readily accessible services. To check on the performance of a socially responsible fund, you can visit the Social Investment Forum at http//www.socialinvest.org. Don't expect to hit a home run when you invest in socially responsible stock funds, either. These types of funds tend to track the market averages.

Investing for the good isn't a bad idea. One reason major socially responsible funds have done so well over the past few years is that they invest in companies with excellent employee relations. When the boss treats his or her workers well, they feel better about getting up in the morning and punching the time clock. Productivity increases; as a result, more goods are produced at a lower cost. So the company is more profitable. Many socially responsible companies such as Quaker Oats, Wal-Mart, Coca-Cola, Hewlett-Packard, and Intel have great employee benefits and flex time and give employees some say in how the firm is managed.

Socially responsible investors tend to be conservative. We are told that a lot of churches and religious groups invest in these funds. Some great brand-name companies, however, such as Wal-Mart, Coca-Cola, and Hewlett-Packard, are on the buy list of many socially responsible stock funds.

News You Can Use

Socially conscious funds have performed well over the past 5 years ending in 1997 because their fund managers took advantage of lower stock prices in 1993, when the market dropped more than 10 percent. They bought socially responsible companies with good employee relations that were growing earnings more that 15 percent annually. Some of the companies they invested in included Thermo Electron, which manufactures environmental instruments and biomedical equipment; Columbia/HCA Health Care Corporation, the world's largest health care services company; and Merck, one of the world's largest drug companies.

The moves paid off. Some of the most popular socially responsible funds have grown 20 percent annually over the past 5 years.

Great Funds for the Ethical Investors

You can pick from several socially responsible funds. Some invest in large companies; others go after cheap stocks or smaller firms in the alternative energy business. The following are some examples of socially responsible funds:

➤ **Domini Social Equity Fund (800-762-6814).** This fund, designed for growth and income, invests in a basket of socially responsible companies that make up the Social Stock Index. Over the past 5 years, the fund has grown at an 18.95 percent average annual total return.

➤ **Dreyfus Third Century Fund (800-645-6561).** This fund invests for growth. Over the past 10 years, it has grown at a respectable 16.18 percent average annual total return.

➤ **Parnassus (800-999-3505).** This fund invests for growth and may own large, midsize, and small company stocks. Over the past 10 years, the fund has grown at an annual average total return of 14.8 percent.

➤ **Pax World (800-767-1729).** This is a balanced fund that invests in Treasury bonds and large company stocks. Over the past 10 years, the fund has grown at a 10 percent average annual total return.

➤ **New Alternatives (800-423-8383).** This is a small company stock fund that invests in companies involved in alternative energy businesses. Over the past 10 years, the fund has grown at a 12.98 percent average annual total return.

The Least You Need to Know

➤ A closed-end fund can be a real bargain when the share price is less than the NAV (net asset value).

➤ Most sector funds are risky investments. Investing in them can be like riding a roller coaster.

➤ Utility stock funds are low-risk sector funds considered attractive by those who need regular monthly income. Even utility stock funds can lose money when rates rise.

➤ Precious metals and real estate stock funds perform well during periods of high inflation.

Part 4
Quick and Easy Investment Plans

Picking a mutual fund to buy, unfortunately, is not the end of the line when it comes to investing. You need to keep on top of your fund's performance. Is it up or down as much as similar funds? Is it a dud?

If you're like most of us, you don't have time to manage your investments. It's no wonder! How can you possibly stay on top of all the wheeling and dealing on Wall Street when you have to work full time and raise a family?

Mutual funds help make it easy to invest. This part of the book makes it even easier. You'll learn easy ways to evaluate your mutual fund's performance, and you'll find out tried and true strategies you can use to get the best mileage out of your investments with the least amount of time and worry.

How Ya Doing?

Even though you've probably selected the right mutual funds for yourself by now, you're not quite finished with the exercise of setting up your investment portfolio. At least once a year—better yet, every three to six months—you want to be sure your mutual funds are doing what they say they're supposed to do: make you money.

This chapter reviews ways to monitor your mutual fund performance. You'll learn how to evaluate how your fund is doing and whether you should sell your old fund and buy a new one.

Your Mutual Fund Check-Up

You've got a couple of funds. Now what? With a car, you get an oil change about every four months. Once a year, you take it in for a tune-up. Mutual funds are no different. You probably should give your funds a financial check-up at least every three months.

Check on them daily and you'll drive yourself bonkers. On the other hand, you don't want to be an ostrich. If you bury your head in the sand and forget about your fund, much can change. A portfolio manager's hot hands can turn into ice cubes. Or you could suddenly discover that your fund manager has retired from your fund to write a best-selling book!

If you've done your homework and invested in funds with good long-term track records, you probably can rest assured that your funds will grow in value over the years. You might not own the number one fund for the year, but based on your investment comfort level, it's enough if your funds lose less in down markets and do well compared with similar funds over 3-year, 5-year, and 10-year periods.

There are almost 7,000 mutual funds. The odds of investing in next year's top-performing fund are equivalent to your chances of winning the Kentucky Derby. Remember, however, with mutual funds, just because you didn't cash in a winning ticket doesn't mean you forfeit bragging rights.

Every three months, when you do your check-up, it's best to compare your funds' returns with similar funds. Look at the average annual total return of the entire group of funds over the last three months, one year, three years, and five years.

The best place to look is in *The Wall Street Journal*, *Investor's Business Daily*, or *Barrons*. These publications list the return on the S&P 500 and the Lehman Brothers Bond Index and the average return on mutual funds based on their investment objectives.

Here is another option: Most public libraries have either Morningstar, Value Line Mutual Fund Survey, or CDA/Wiesenberger Mutual Funds Update. These services are the most comprehensive sources of information on mutual funds. They list performance year-by-year and annual average total returns for 1 through 10 years. These reports also tell how the fund ranks when compared with similar funds.

Here's what to do once you've looked up the information:

1. Ask yourself, "What was my fund's total return this year-to-date compared with the total returns on similar funds and the fund group average?" Compare the average annual total returns on your fund to similar funds and the peer group average over the past one-year, three-year, or five-year periods.

2. You also can compare your funds' total returns to the market averages this year-to-date and over one-, three-, or five-year periods. The S&P 500 is an index that shows the performance of a large group of stocks in the United States.

   If you have an international stock fund, you can compare it to the Europe, Australia, Far East Index (EAFE), which tracks stocks listed on major world stock exchanges.

   You can compare how your fund or funds performed based on total return to the Lehman Brothers Long-Term Bond and Treasury Bond Indexes. These indexes tell you how the bond market is performing so that you can compare how your funds stack up against the performance of the bond market.

190

3. Subtract the total return on your fund from the average peer groups' return (often listed under a heading such as "Investment Objective Averages" in a separate area). You also can subtract the return from the market averages. If the difference is positive, your fund is doing better than other funds. If it's negative, you're doing worse.

You can use the following Fund Performance Worksheet to compare funds.

Let's take the Janus Fund, a no-load growth fund. Assume you owned the fund for five years. Over the past five years ending in December 1997, the Janus Fund racked up an annual average total return of 15.8 percent, according to Morningstar. The S&P 500 had a 20.3 percent annual average total return, and the average growth fund had a 16.2 percent annual average total return over the same period. Over the past five years, the Janus Fund earned 4.5 percentage points annually less than the stock market average and .45 percentage points less than the average growth stock fund.

> **Hot Tip!**
> Have a computer? You can buy software that keeps track of your investments. Quicken (520-295-3220) and Kiplinger's Simply Money (800-225-5524) will keep tabs on how your mutual funds perform.

Fund Performance Worksheet			
Your Fund	Your Fund's Total Return %	Peer Group or Other Funds' Return % (Subtract from Your Fund's Return %)	Difference

Create a worksheet like this one to compare your fund's performance with the performance for similar funds.

That doesn't look so hot. But most mutual funds failed to outperform the market averages during the past five years. There are a couple of reasons for this. The S&P 500 merely is a benchmark—not a mutual fund. So unlike a mutual fund, the S&P 500 does not subtract expenses, which, of course, would cut its return. It also has no manager. Mutual fund managers typically keep some money in cash waiting for buying opportunities when the stock market declines. This lowers the return of a stock fund in a rising market—which we've experienced for the last several years. As a result, mutual funds simply haven't caught up with the unmanaged benchmark.

Does this mean you should sell the Janus Fund because it lagged behind? No. During the first two-and-one-half months of 1997, the Janus Fund is up 13 percent, whereas the market is up 11 percent. Fund manager James Craig put the fund's money to work in some attractive, undervalued, large company European growth stocks last year. Now the fund is reaping the benefits.

It's important to look at how a fund fared against its peers over the long haul. Even over five years, a good fund can fall slightly behind. But then it rebounds when its stock selections start doing well. Sometimes it can take three to five years for things to happen, so don't give up the ship.

The Janus Fund has ranked in the top 40 percent of funds in its class; it has done better than 60 percent of all other growth stock funds over the past year. That means it's a good choice. Good enough! Of course on the flip side, you know your stock or bond funds are doing particularly well when they beat their market averages. Don't forget with your fund, you're paying management fees, and some of your fund's holdings are kept in cash. Indexes, such as the S&P 500, don't reflect these factors.

How Does Your Fund Stack Up?

You also can check newspapers, magazines, or even the fund's financial reports for information on how your fund compares funds with the same investment objectives over several time periods. Chapter 10, "Opening Your Mutual Fund Account," discusses the annual, semiannual, or quarterly financial reports shareholders receive from their funds. Look for how your fund stacks up against funds with the same investment objective and market averages, such as the S&P 500.

Depending upon which publication you pick up, the fund's ranking may be expressed either as a number or coded percentile. A numerical ranking provides a number showing how the fund did in relation to other funds or funds with the same investment objective. The percentile ranking explains in which percentile of funds your fund ranks. Listings may compare your fund with all mutual funds. They also can compare your fund to funds with the same investment objective. A fund with a percentile ranking of 5 means its performance ranks in the top 5 percent of its category.

You don't need to buy the paper every day—just when you perform your quarterly and annual reviews. *The Wall Street Journal,* for example, lists fund performance and ranks funds by investment objectives based on Lipper Analytical Services data. On Fridays, you'll see the total return and ranking for one year, three years, and five years, so you can get a clear picture of how a fund stacks up against its peers over different periods of time. See Table 16.1 for an example of the *Journal's* rating system.

Table 16.1 The Wall Street Journal's Fund Rankings: What They Mean

Rank	Group Ranking Based on Investment Objective
A	Top 20 percent
B	Next 20 percent
C	Middle 20 percent
D	Bottom 20 percent

Investor's Business Daily takes a different approach, which is equally useful (see Table 16.2). Funds are ranked based on total return against all other funds over the past three years. It's always a good idea to see how a particular fund stacks up against all other funds. This information may help you decide whether to invest in a fund that's doing better than other funds over the past few years. If you're a bottom-fisher, the rankings may help you spot funds that have lagged behind other funds but could rebound and register higher total returns in the future.

Table 16.2 Investor's Business Daily Fund Rankings: What They Mean

Rank	Ranking Compared with All Funds
A+	Top 5 percent
A	Top 10 percent
A–	Top 15 percent
B+	Top 20 percent
B	Top 25 percent
B–	Top 30 percent
C+	Top 35 percent
C	Top 40 percent
C–	Top 45 percent
D+	Top 50 percent
D	Top 60 percent
D–	Top 70 percent
E	Below 70 percent

News You Can Use

You need to check a couple of other items besides performance. Look at your fund's latest financial report or call the fund group and get information about major changes in the fund's holdings—such as a large company stock fund that loads up on small company stocks.

If you own a bond fund, check to see whether there have been any major changes, such as a change in the average bond ratings of the fund's holdings or a change in the average maturity of the fund. If a bond fund's average credit rating has dropped, the fund manager could be taking on more risk to earn higher returns.

Why Do Funds Lose Steam?

Why would a fund with a good long-term track record suddenly fall behind? Its stock-picking style may be out of favor. Growth fund managers may lag behind because bargain-priced undervalued stocks are in favor. By contrast, a couple of years down the road, growth stocks, which tend to show 25 percent to 30 percent annual earnings growth, may be in, and undervalued stocks may be out.

Funds that have too much money in cash instead of stocks may trail the overall stock market and stock funds that are fully invested in a bull market. The fund's manager may have misjudged the direction of the stock market and kept money in cash as a safe haven. As a result, the manager may have just 70 percent to 80 percent of the fund's holdings invested in stocks when the market moves higher.

Plain old lousy stock picks are another reason a fund may do poorly. The fund manager's evaluation of a company, an industry, or the economy could be off the mark. Bad timing can also be a factor. The companies a fund owns could look good on paper, but the darned stock price doesn't move. For some unexplained reason, there could be more sellers than buyers of the stocks the fund happens to own.

Your fund could be down because the overall stock or bond market is down. The performance of most funds is highly linked to the return on the market. If the stock market is down, there is a good chance your fund lost some money, too.

Markets may fall because of a high or increasing rate of inflation, high or rising interest rates, or declining or stagnating corporate profits. Other reasons include political instability or international conflicts, high unemployment, or a tight money policy by the Federal Reserve. Does this mean you should dump your fund? No. You must look at several factors before you decide when to sell.

When to Sell Your Funds

When should you sell your fund? Give it at least three years before you decide to dump it; stock returns tend to move in cycles.

It definitely could be time to make a change if your fund underperforms similar funds over at least a five-year period. You also should consider changing funds under the following conditions:

➤ Your fund manager has a good track record and then leaves.

➤ The fund changes its investment objective.

➤ The fund merges with another fund that has a mediocre track record.

➤ Your own financial condition or tolerance for risk has changed.

There is no hard and fast rule on when to sell a fund. Much depends upon your own situation, so before you sell, look at all these factors. Of course, if your financial condition changes—say you suddenly need cash in a few months—you don't want to run the risk of losing money in a stock fund. You might want to park your money in a money fund.

If your fund manager leaves, it could pay to take a close look at the new manager first. Maybe he or she already has a good track record. See how the fund performs compared to similar funds before you sell.

Is there a big change in the investment objective of the fund? You might sell it if it becomes riskier. If it's just a slight change, however, you might want to sit on it a while and see how the fund performs first.

Evaluating Your Fund Picks

What if you own several different types of funds? You have to look at the total return on your investment and compare it to a similar type of benchmark.

Suppose that you have 50 percent of the investment in a growth stock fund that registers a total return of 10 percent for the year and 50 percent in a bond fund that has a total return of 6 percent for the year. Figure your investment's total return for the year by following these steps:

1. Multiply .50 times 10 percent, the total return on your growth stock fund for the year. That equals 5 percent.

2. Multiply .50 times 6 percent, the total return of your bond fund for the year. That equals 3 percent.

3. Add the total returns that represent the growth fund and bond fund's share of your portfolio: 5 percent plus 3 percent equals 8 percent.

This represents a weighted average total return on your entire portfolio. Now you have to compare that to a couple of benchmarks. In our example, one useful comparison in this instance might be to compute your return if you were to have 50 percent invested in the S&P 500 and 50 percent invested in the Lehman Brothers Aggregate Bond Index.

Suppose the S&P 500 total return for the year was 9.5 percent and the Lehman Brothers Bond Index total return was 5.8 percent. Fifty percent of 9.5 percent equals 4.75 percent. Fifty percent of 5.8 percent equals 2.9 percent. The combined total return (5.8 percent plus 4.75 percent) is 7.65 percent.

To see how your investment mix did against the market averages, subtract 7.65 percent, the combined total return of the market averages, from 8 percent, the combined total return of your funds. The result is .35 percent.

Your mix of mutual funds gave you some extra return over the appropriate benchmarks, which reflect the market averages. If your mix of funds underperformed the benchmarks by a wide margin, it may be an indication that you might consider selling those funds and finding funds that perform better. You also can use this method to compare the combined total return of your investment mix with similar funds or the fund's investment objective averages.

The Least You Need to Know

➤ Compare your fund's performance with similar funds, the average of funds with the same investment objective, and indexes, such as the S&P 500 index.

➤ If your fund is underperforming by a small margin, give it a chance—at least three years.

➤ Use the mutual fund tables available in the newspaper or through several reporting services to monitor your fund's performance every three months.

➤ Sell if your fund underperforms similar funds over three to five years.

Chapter 17

Getting Rich a Little at a Time: Dollar Cost Averaging

In This Chapter

➤ The importance of investing regularly

➤ Starting a savings program

➤ Buy low and sell high

➤ The best funds for dollar cost averaging

Well, people, you have a choice. You can read the paper daily, sweat out all the market's hiccups, and sell when you think your mutual fund's share price has peaked. Unfortunately, most of us don't know when that's actually going to happen, so there's a good chance you will miss some big profits this way.

Your other option is to just sit tight and play it cool. This chapter focuses on one investment strategy that enables you to do just that. The trick is to invest a certain amount of money regularly. This way, some of your cash is invested when share prices are high, and some is invested when share prices are low. The gurus have a fancy name for this style of investing: *dollar cost averaging.*

With dollar cost averaging, you can build your wealth in a systematic, level-headed manner. You don't have to watch every single move the market makes. You don't need an MBA or Ph.D., either. This chapter discusses the pluses and minuses of dollar cost averaging, which is one of the simplest ways to invest. This is the kind of investment strategy you can use for at least 5 to 10 years.

A Piggy Bank for Grown-Ups

One member of this writing team once enjoyed a bonus weekend in Disney World—and it wasn't by winning a contest. It was the result of periodically dumping the pennies, quarters, and dimes from a bulging purse into an empty one-gallon plastic water jug for a full year. Then, on a quiet holiday weekend, the change was systematically wrapped and counted. It wound up being close to $100—enough for a hotel room for one night!

Dollar cost averaging works kind of like that, but in a slightly more disciplined way. The results, for those who keep it up for several years, are apt to be even more impressive.

With dollar cost averaging, you invest a certain amount ($50 or $100, for example) every month into the mutual fund of your choice. Whether you're saving for your child's future education, a vacation home, or your retirement, this is a low-risk way to invest. When you fill out your mutual fund application form, you check the box that indicates you want your earnings to be reinvested automatically. When you do that, your earnings also buy more shares of your fund each month.

With dollar cost averaging, there's no need to worry if the fund's share price drops. When this happens, your regular monthly investment, plus any earnings, purchases new shares of the mutual fund at the lower prices. When you check out the value of your fund a few years later, once the price rises again, you'll be in for a shock—a pleasant one!

Mutual fund families even help you dollar cost average through some of the services they provide. Most have automatic investment savings plans. You can have your money automatically taken out of your checking account and invested in the fund of your choice before you have a chance to miss it.

News You Can Use

The stock market, as measured by the S&P 500 index, has grown at an average annual rate of 12.8 percent over the past 20 years. Those who tried to move between cash and stocks at the right times didn't have much room for error. If they missed the 5 best investment months over the past 240 months, the return on their investments dropped to 9.3 percent. That's why a dollar cost averaging strategy makes more sense than a hit-or-miss approach.

Taking the Guesswork Out of It

Dollar cost averaging takes the guesswork out of investing. When you dollar cost average, you don't have to worry about timing the markets. You are always buying shares. Because you always have money invested, you profit during periods in which a fund's price rises. Other times, the share price may decline. But like a squirrel accumulating nuts for the winter, you are accumulating shares. Then, when the fund's share price rises, your investment is worth more.

Suppose you invest $100 each month in a no-load stock fund (we discussed those in Chapter 16, "How Ya Doing?") that sells at $20 per share. You invest $100 and receive 5 shares. The market changes and the fund's share price drops to $10 per share. You again invest your $100. At $10 per share, you receive 10 shares for your $100.

Let's assume by the next month, the market returns to where it was when you started, and your fund sells at $20 per share. You receive 5 shares for your $100 investment. Table 17.1 shows what your investment looks like.

> **Hot Tip!**
> For a free booklet, "A Guide to Understanding Mutual Funds," complete with a section on dollar cost averaging, write the Investment Company Institute, 1401 H Street, NW, Suite 1200, Washington, DC 20005, or call 202-326-5800.

Table 17.1 How Dollar Cost Averaging Works

Month	Regular Investment	Share Price	Shares Acquired
Month 1	$100	$20	5
Month 2	$100	$10	10
Month 3	$100	$20	5
Total	$300		20

Average Share Cost: $15.00 ($300 divided by 20 shares)
Average Share Price: $16.67

You own 20 shares of the fund in which you invested $300. Your shares are worth more than what you paid. The average purchase price of your shares was $16.67. The average cost was $15.00 because you invested $300 and bought a total of 20 shares.

The idea behind dollar cost averaging is to invest for the long term. You have to invest through thick and thin, sticking with a fund in down markets. If you bail out early, you can be forced to sell shares at a loss.

Test Case: Massachusetts Investors Trust Fund

Let's look at a case based on real stock market performance to see how dollar cost averaging works. Suppose that back in 1924, you began investing $100 a month in the Massachusetts Investors Trust Fund, the first mutual fund ever created. Let's say that you continued to invest from year-end 1924 through year-end 1997—a total of 73 years.

The $100 monthly investment was worth a whopping $16.6 million in 1997, whereas the total amount invested was $2,582,480 over the past 70 years. (Too bad we can't get into a time machine and go back to 1924 and start a saving plan!)

Let's examine how your investment did during the best and worst of times.

You did well during the last half of the roaring 20s. Your $100 monthly investment from year-end 1924 through year-end 1928 was worth a total of $6,016, and you invested $4,800.

As we all know, the stock market fell out of bed and through the floor in October 1929. During the Great Depression, the S&P 500 lost the following amounts in its very worst years based on total return:

-8.4 percent in 1929

-24.9 percent in 1930

-43.3 percent in 1931

-8.2 percent in 1932

-1.4 percent in 1934

-35 percent in 1937

-.4 percent in 1939

-9.8 percent in 1940

There were a few market rallies in the 1930s, but for the most part, everyone lost their shirts. So how did your dollar cost averaging plan fare? Fortunately, you had a cushion. You had been investing $100 a month for 4 years in a rising market. The total value of your investment at the end of 1929 was $9,285.

The fund managers took action to cut losses in the 1930s. They cut back on their stock holdings and stuck with Treasury bonds. You lost money, but not as much as you would have with a 100 percent stake in the S&P 500. Nevertheless, by the end of 1931, the total value of your investment declined to $5,067, representing a whopping 45 percent loss, (including the $100 a month you kicked into the fund in 1930 and 1931).

You had to have a strong stomach to stay in the fund during such rough weather. But because you were dollar cost averaging, you were buying more shares of the fund at much lower prices.

From year-end 1929 through year-end 1931, you bought 605 more shares of the Massachusetts Investors Trust Fund. Plus you reinvested dividends and capital gains. Gradually, you began a comeback. By year-end 1940, you owned a total of 7,181 shares worth $21,605. You invested $19,800 and came out ahead.

Over the 16-year period, which is by far the worst in the history of the stock market, your mutual fund investment grew at an annual rate of just 1.2 percent. That doesn't seem that great compared with today's stellar double-digit stock returns. But making 1.2 percent on your money wasn't anything to sneeze about when you consider that almost everyone in the 1930s was flat broke, out of work, and half starving. Most businesses were bankrupt.

Making 1.2 percent on your money during the Great Depression is like making at least 25 percent today!

Hot Tip!

It pays to invest in a fund with a good long-term track record. For example, Massachusetts Investors Trust, the very first mutual fund, launched in 1924, is still doing well. The fund has grown at a 17.9 percent average annual rate over the past 10 years. By contrast, the average growth and income fund gained 15.2 percent.

The Downside of Dollar Cost Averaging

Dollar cost averaging is simple and effective, but, like anything else, it's not perfect. Our friend Sheldon Jacobs, who publishes the *No-Load Investor Newsletter*, encourages regular investing through dollar cost averaging, but he also issues some warnings.

He says that you should be aware of dollar-cost-averaging limitations. This type of investment strategy may not be for everyone. If you are an aggressive investor who can tolerate a big drop in total return in exchange for long-term growth, you might want to invest a lump sum.

Sheldon points out that dollar cost averaging loses its value over time. If the same amount is invested each month, the money you've accumulated may not go as far as you thought when you consider inflation or the increasing cost of necessities. As a result, he suggests increasing your monthly investment each year (by $25 or $50, for example) to keep up with rising inflation.

Second, no rules tell you when to sell after you've used dollar cost averaging for a number of years. There are no guarantees that the average cost of the fund shares you bought over the years will be less than the market price of the fund when you sell. To make dollar cost averaging work, you have to pick the right time to sell the fund.

Third, if you're just starting out with dollar cost averaging, you might find it hard to invest in a fund at bargain prices. Jacobs says that bull markets last twice as long as bear markets. Most of the time, you'll buy fund shares at higher prices. His solution is to invest twice as much in your fund during bear markets.

Fourth, if you invest a lump sum in a fund, you have more money working for you at the beginning, compared with stashing away a little bit every month. Over the long haul, the lump sum investment grows much more. Of course, if you don't have much money in the first place, dollar cost averaging is better than nothing at all.

Finding the Best Funds

Dollar cost averaging works well with all types of stock funds, ranging from aggressive growth and small company stocks to tried-and-true growth and income funds. It works best with more volatile funds—the ones that drop and then soar in value.

In Chapter 3, "Investing: Your Options, Your Risks, Your Rewards," you learned about the beta value, a mutual fund measure that tells whether a fund is volatile. The higher the beta, the more the fund's price can bounce up and down. If you invest in a fund with a good long-term track record that also sports a beta value of greater than one, you've found a great fund for dollar cost averaging.

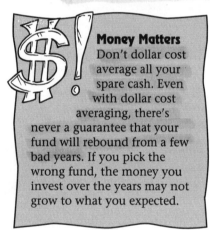

Money Matters
Don't dollar cost average all your spare cash. Even with dollar cost averaging, there's never a guarantee that your fund will rebound from a few bad years. If you pick the wrong fund, the money you invest over the years may not grow to what you expected.

Hot Tip!
The Value Line Mutual Fund Survey is the only rating service that shows dollar-cost-averaging performance on more than 2,000 stock and bond funds. The report is available in most public libraries.

With dollar cost averaging, even Nervous Nellies can cheer when the fund loses money. Why? You're buying more shares of the fund at a lower price. When the fund rebounds, you build up a tidy sum. If you use this tactic over the years, dollar cost averaging will serve you well.

When shopping for a mutual fund to use in a dollar cost averaging investment plan, consider the following:

➤ The ideal dollar-cost-averaging candidate should have outperformed its peers over the long term. You want a fund with a good long-term track record. Look at the fund's annual rate of return over at least a five-year period. Then, look at the fund's return from year to year. You want to invest in funds that have performed as well or better than similar funds over the long term.

➤ The fund should have shown a proven ability to bounce back from bad years such as 1973, 1979, 1981, 1987, 1990, and 1994.

➤ If the fund is part of a no-load mutual fund family, you don't pay brokerage commissions on your investments. You can save a lot.

➤ The fund group should have an automatic investment plan. That way, you can have money automatically taken out of your checking account and invested in your mutual fund.

The Worst Funds

Some funds are better dollar-cost-averaging candidates than others. If you dollar cost average into money funds or shorter-term bond funds, you accumulate money that earns a lower rate of interest. With these kinds of funds, you're saving, not investing. Dollar cost averaging also won't build your wealth as much in a balanced fund or income fund as it will in a growth fund. To make dollar cost averaging work best, you need to invest in more aggressive funds that have the ability to grow.

For those who are nervous about socking away money in an aggressive growth or growth fund, consult Chapter 21, "Loaded for Bear: What to Do When the Stock Market Falls Out of Bed." You'll learn about some low-risk ways to dollar cost average into stock funds to build your retirement nest egg.

What About Bond Funds?

Dollar cost averaging can work with long-term bond funds. When interest rates rise or fall 1 percent, most long-term bond funds can move down or up in value about 10 to 12 percent. Over the past 10 years, long-term bond funds have grown at an annual rate of close to 9 percent. If you invested $12,000 through thick and thin in your bond fund over the past 10 years, your money grew to $18,232. Not bad!

Getting Started with DCA

Even before you start dollar cost averaging, as you learned in Chapter 2, "Mutual Funds: To Own or Not to Own?" you need to make sure that you have money socked away to meet emergencies such as medical bills, a leaky roof, or an unexpected financial crisis. You should put this money in a low-risk investment, such as a savings account or money market fund. You need to establish your goals and determine your investment mix based on your tolerance for risk, as shown in your answers to the quiz in Chapter 6, "Which Funds Are Right for You?"

Dollar cost averaging should begin only after you develop a financial cushion for emergencies and determine that you're willing to take on a little more risk in exchange for building your wealth long term. Then, you can pick a fund for dollar cost averaging.

The first step is to start saving regularly in a passbook savings account until you have $1,000 to make the initial investment required by most funds. After that, you can invest as little as $50 a month. But there is no upper limit on what you can sock away regularly. Once you decide how much you want to invest, you have several ways to go about it:

1. You can write a check and send it to the fund each month. That way, you can increase or decrease your investments as time goes by. You also can skip a payment if you have a financial emergency. What's the drawback to this method? You need the discipline to invest every month.

2. You can sign up for the fund's automatic investment plan, as discussed in Chapter 10, "Opening Your Mutual Fund Account." That way, you don't have to do anything. Investing is handled for you by the fund. If you need to make changes in the amount you want to invest, you can always call the fund. The drawback? You've got to be sure you keep a balance in your checking account large enough to cover your monthly investment. Otherwise, you might find yourself overdrawn and face extra charges for bounced checks. That's a no-no.

3. Special contractual plans are available for dollar cost averaging when you invest in load funds with stockbrokers. Often, the broker will agree to waive the minimum initial investment as long as the investor agrees to certain terms. For example, the investor might agree to make monthly investments for 10 years. In return, the broker will take half of all commissions for 10 years in the first year of your investment. That may sound like a pretty stiff penalty, but investors who agree to these programs are forcing themselves to save for the long term.

4. Contractual plans differ greatly from broker to broker, but many plans come with special features. For example, the commissions may be lower if you make large investments. You might be able to withdraw money and later put it back into the fund without paying a commission, or you might reinvest distributions commission-free. Drawbacks? You're paying a lot in commissions up front, and you're locked into the deal for a specific term.

News You Can Use

Considering dollar cost averaging? This could be the one time to ignore the coward in you. Instead, choose a riskier fund that has a history of recovering strongly, suggests Steve Savage, editor of the Value Line Mutual Fund Survey, New York.

Although a lower-risk fund might be the better choice for someone who's investing a lump sum, that's not the case when it comes to dollar cost averaging. The reason: More volatile stock funds tend to show greater price appreciation when bouncing off their lows.

Take the case of the high-risk CGM Capital Development Fund. Although a $10,000 investment grew to $326,709 over the past 20 years, making it one of the top performing funds, the fund still trailed the low-risk Mutual Shares by $66,000. However, if you factor in a modest additional investment of $100 per month for both funds, CGM soared to $691,647—almost $92,000 ahead of its more conservative peer.

The Least You Need to Know

➤ With dollar cost averaging, you invest every month for the long term.

➤ You can invest as little as $50 a month through a mutual fund's automatic investment program.

➤ Dollar cost averaging takes the guesswork out of investing.

➤ It takes a few years for dollar cost averaging to work. You have to accumulate enough shares to benefit from the growth of the fund.

Chapter 18

The Easy Way to Buy and Sell: Constant Dollar Investing

In This Chapter

➤ Boosting the return on your investments

➤ The truth about buying low and selling high

➤ The funds that give you the best returns

➤ How to avoid large losses in your stock funds

Maybe after reading Chapter 17, "Getting Rich a Little at a Time: Dollar Cost Averaging," you're still not convinced. "Buy low, sell high," was the advice your very first financial advisors, Mom and Dad, probably drummed into your head shortly after you outgrew your diapers. Yet, we already told you the downside of this strategy. How many times have you talked to people who regretted not taking profits from their stock fund before its value went sinking like a ship in a bear market? When things are going great guns, most investors don't want to sell because they think the share price of their fund will go higher. What happens? Of course, the share price plunges. Then, when the fund is headed lower, they start selling shares because they fear it will drop more. Guess what happens? It goes higher, of course.

We keep telling ya: The stock market is a unique animal unto itself. You can't predict what it's going to do. However, by using a couple of easy rules, you might, at least, be able to buy a little lower and sell a little higher. This chapter tells you how.

Simple Rules to Buy and Sell

Constant dollar investing is an easy way to take the guesswork out of deciding when to buy and sell. However, unlike dollar cost averaging, which you learned about in Chapter 17, you can't exactly put this strategy on automatic pilot. You need to take a slightly more active role.

You might also find the constant dollar investment plan a little more conservative than dollar cost averaging. In other words, you might not make quite as much over the long haul with this program. With the constant dollar investment strategy, however, you preserve your stock fund profits while buying more shares at lower prices than you originally paid.

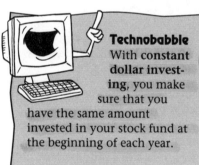

Money Matters
There's no way to predict stock market behavior. Even with the constant dollar investment plan, it's still possible to lose. Be prepared to keep investing while your stock fund is dropping in anticipation of higher returns down the road.

Assuming you have six months' worth of emergency cash in a bank or CD and you're able to tolerate some risk, all you need are a stock fund and a bond or money market fund to get started. You don't even need a lot of money to start the constant dollar investing plan; it's best to begin with $1,000 to $10,000.

The objective of constant dollar investing is simple. You merely keep the value of the stock fund the same as it was on the day you first bought it. You do this by evaluating your funds at least once a year and taking the following steps:

Technobabble
With **constant dollar investing**, you make sure that you have the same amount invested in your stock fund at the beginning of each year.

➤ If your stock fund's total value is worth *more* than when you first bought it, you take the excess cash and deposit it in the bond fund or money market fund.

➤ If your stock fund's total value is worth *less* than when you first bought it, you take money from the bond fund or money fund and deposit it in the stock fund to restore its original value.

By doing this, you always maintain the same amount in your stock fund each year.

The constant dollar investment method gives you an easy-to-use formula that tells you when to take profits and when to invest. It's a good idea to check the total value of your stock fund once a year. If it's up in value at the end of the year, take out your profits. If it's declined in value, kick in more money to bring the investment back to the constant dollar amount you designated when you started the investment plan.

Constant dollar investing works this way: Suppose you start with $1,000 in your stock fund. At the end of every year, your stock fund should be worth $1,000. If you have more than $1,000, take the profits and invest them in your bond or money fund. If you have losses, take an amount equal to those losses from the bond or money fund and redeposit it into the stock fund to restore its value to $1,000.

Suppose your stock fund is up to $1,300 at the end of year one. You take $300 and sock it away in your money fund. Next year, the stock fund drops to a value of $875. You kick in $125 from your money fund and bring the value of the stock fund back to $1,000. In the following year, the fund is up to $1,300. You take the extra $300 and put it back in your money fund.

Constant dollar investing is a viable plan for virtually any investor who feels more comfortable taking profits and hates to see the value of his or her investment decline in a bear market. A constant dollar investor typically is focused on the nearer term than an investor who uses dollar cost averaging. An investor using dollar cost averaging is socking money away for a lifetime through thick and thin.

> **Hot Tip!**
> Constant dollar investing, as well as other investment tactics, works best for tax-deferred retirement savings investments such as IRAs and 401(k) company pension plans. You don't pay taxes on your switches in a retirement plan. If you invest in taxable funds, on the other hand, you may pay from 15 to 39.6 percent of your profits to Uncle Sam.

The Best Funds for Constant Dollar Investing

With constant dollar investing, it's important to open an account either with a no-load mutual fund family or a load fund group that charges no commissions on trades between existing funds. Otherwise, you pay through the nose for switching money between funds. (See Chapter 7, "The Cost of Investing," for a discussion of fund costs and fees.) You have a greater choice of stock funds if you invest with a large fund family.

Next, select the stock fund of your choice. You get the most for your money by investing in an aggressive stock fund or a small company fund, but growth and income funds also work well. Why? You get more growth in the share value of your fund if it invests in stocks rather than bond and money funds.

Select a bond fund or money fund as a place to stash your cash. Money funds are the less risky option because the fund's price, as you learned in Chapter 12, "Bonding: Investing with Bond Funds," stays at $1 a share.

> **Hot Tip!**
> If you plan to use constant dollar investing, find out when your fund family sends statements so that you can plan to adjust your investments around the statement dates. You need your statement information to make the adjustments. Otherwise, you have to keep tabs on the funds yourself.

However, if you want higher income and the possibility of some growth when interest rates fall and bond prices rise, select a bond fund rather than a money fund. Remember, you can lose money even with the least risky bond funds. Recall from Chapter 3, "Investing: Your Options, Your Risks, Your Rewards," and Chapter 13, "Choosing the Right Bond Fund," that bond prices and interest rates move in opposite directions. Also, if you select a mortgage bond fund, your mortgage holders could refinance, forcing your fund manager to make new investments at lower rates.

Money Matters
Avoid low-risk income stock funds and balanced funds for the constant dollar investment plan. You don't get enough of a return to make the tactic worth using.

Also, avoid stock funds that hold a lot of cash. You want your stock fund to be fully invested to reap the maximum profits.

Make sure you choose a stock fund that stays fully invested. You don't want to own a fund whose manager socks away 10 to 20 percent of the portfolio into cash because he or she is nervous about the outlook for stocks. You're already nervous. That's why you're taking profits when your stock fund is up or you're kicking in more when it is down. You don't need to add more money to a fund that has a lot invested in cash.

The best bets are aggressive growth, growth stocks, small company stock, or emerging market mutual funds. You want funds that can zoom so you can take profits. At the same time, you want to invest when their prices are cheap. You might want to consider index funds that invest in a basket of stocks. The funds stay 100 percent invested and their performance tracks the overall market for stocks. Because index funds buy and hold stocks, you get little in the way of year-end capital gains distributions. So you pay less taxes on index funds than an actively managed stock fund.

We think the Vanguard Group of Funds is one of the best places to use the constant dollar method of investing. Vanguard has 20 index funds to choose, ranging from the Index 500 Fund to the Small Cap Fund.

The best combination is to invest in a stock fund with a good long-term track record and a high-yielding money fund.

Whatever you choose, remember to reinvest the stock fund distributions into new shares. That way, you build a larger number of shares to work with.

Getting Started

For the sake of simplicity, suppose you invest $1,000 as your constant dollar amount. Realistically, you should start the investment program with a constant dollar amount of at least $2,000 to $5,000, but for this example, suppose you invest $1,000 and the stock fund is worth $1,500 at year's end. Take $500 out and invest in a money fund. Now, you're back to square one with an investment of $1,000. Say, in the following year, your stock fund is down $100 to $900. You kick in $100 from your money fund to bring the stock fund's value back to a grand.

You can make adjustments every three or six months if you prefer, but one-year intervals provide more time for your money to grow. Over the long term, you take profits when the price dips. On the other hand, if you make adjustments every three or six months, you're assured of taking profits before something serious happens. By taking profits every six months, an investor would have avoided big stock market losses in October 1987 and November 1990.

How Constant Dollar Investing Works

We cranked up our computer and performed a mini-study using Morningstar data to see how constant dollar investing has worked over the years. We suggest that you take the time to set up a worksheet you can use to calculate the values of your constant dollar investment program. Pen or pencil and paper work fine for those of you who don't want to bother with a computer. If you're a mutual fund nut and can set up a program, go for it. It will save time. Either way is fine. Just be sure to take your profits in good years and kick in money in bad years.

Table 18.1 gives an example of how a constant dollar investing strategy could have worked for you. It assumes $1,000 invested in a growth and income fund and $1,000 invested in a money fund that earns 4 percent.

Table 18.1 How Constant Dollar Investing Works

Year Invested	Constant Dollar Amount	End-of-Year Stock Fund Value	End-of-Year Money Fund Value	End-of-Year Total Value
1986	$1,000	$1,160	$1,040	$2,200
1987	$1,000	$1,020	$1,248	$2,268
1988	$1,000	$1,150	$1,319	$2,469
1989	$1,000	$1,240	$1,470	$2,710
1990	$1,000	$950	$1,778	$2,728
1991	$1,000	$1,290	$1,798	$3,088
1992	$1,000	$1,080	$2,172	$3,253
1993	$1,000	$1,110	$2,255	$3,365
1994	$1,000	$980	$2,369	$3,349
1995	$1,000	$1,310	$2,443	$3,757
1996	$1,000	$1,197	$2,563	$3,760
1997	$1,000	$1,243	$2,666	$3,909

The table shows how your money grew based on a hypothetical example, using the total returns of the average growth and income fund and a money fund that registered a hypothetical 4 percent annual average return.

Column 1 lists the year your investment started, 1986. Column 2 lists the constant dollar amount invested in the stock fund, which in this case is $1,000. You want this amount in your stock fund at the beginning of each year. Column 3 lists the end-of-year value of your stock fund, and Column 4 lists the end-of-year value in the money fund. Column 5 lists the end-of-year value of the total investment.

As you can see, for example, in 1986, the $1,000 constant dollar stock fund amount listed in Column 2 grew to $1,160. The money fund grew to $1,040 as listed in Column 4, and the total amount of the combined investment was $2,200 (Column 5). Because the stock fund grew to $1,160, you took $160 out of the fund and invested it in the money fund. In 1987, as shown in Column 2, the constant dollar amount is back to $1,000.

To find out how much you have to take out of your stock fund or add to your stock fund to bring it back to the constant dollar amount, you have to do some figuring. Subtract Column 3, the year-end value of the stock fund from Column 2, the constant dollar amount. If the result is positive, that is the profit you take out of the stock fund and sock away in the money fund. If it's negative, you have to take money out of the money fund and put it in the stock fund.

In the years listed in the table, you would have taken profits in 8 of the 10 years. You would have kicked more money into your fund in 2 of the 10 years. In the years following your losses, 1990 and 1994, your stock fund would have gained 29 percent and 15 percent.

Over the past 12 years ending in 1997, a constant dollar investment plan would have served you well. If you invested $1,000 in a growth and income fund and $1,000 in a money fund that earned 4 percent annually at year-end 1985, your investment would have grown to $3,390 by year-end 1997. This example, however, does not assume taxes have been paid on the trades.

You're not going to get rich quick using constant dollar investing. Of course, keep in mind that past performance is no indication of how constant dollar investing will perform in the future. Nevertheless, a look at the past shows that constant dollar investing works, provided that you invest for at least five years to get results. Even then, if the overall stock market doesn't do that well, neither will your stock fund's constant dollar investment plan.

We have a friend who has been using the constant dollar method of investment for years in his IRA and made out like a bandit. He adjusts it every six months instead of waiting a full year. We guess he can't sit still with his money. Nevertheless, because he makes changes twice a year, he took profits from his growth stock fund just in the nick of time—before the stock market plunged more than 20 percent on October 19, 1987. At the end of 1987, his growth stock fund was down a whopping 25 percent. He then kicked in several thousand dollars.

News You Can Use

Want to put some zip in your stock fund's performance? Consider using value averaging instead of constant dollar investing or dollar cost averaging. With value averaging, the investor makes the value of his or her portfolio increase by a fixed amount periodically.

For example, you might determine you want the value of your investments to increase $300 every three months, but the value of your stock fund increases by more than $300. Take out the extra profits and put them in a money fund. If the stock fund fails to increase $300 in value, you must kick in the difference from your money fund.

Value averaging is a more profitable way to invest compared with dollar cost averaging or the constant dollar investment plan, says Michael Edleson, Ph.D., finance professor at Harvard University and author of *Value Averaging* (International Publishing Corp., Chicago). With value averaging, investors take advantage of relatively short-term declines in their fund's value to invest more money. Then, they take greater profits over the longer term.

Although value averaging can be an attractive way to invest in mutual funds, it has drawbacks. You must spend more time with your investments and keep good records. In a bear market, you must be prepared to kick in a large chunk of money to bring the value of the fund up to the amount the program requires.

The Least You Need to Know

➤ With constant dollar investing, you keep the same amount invested in your stock fund at the beginning of every year.

➤ At the end of the year, take profits in your stock fund and invest it in a money fund.

➤ If you have stock fund losses at the end of the year, take money out of the money fund and invest it in the stock fund.

➤ More aggressive investors can keep a constant dollar amount every six months.

Chapter 19

Keeping an Even Keel: Diversifica- tion and Portfolio Rebalancing

In This Chapter

➤ Getting better returns with less risk

➤ An investment program that takes just an hour a year

➤ When to adjust your investment mix

We live in a paranoid society when it comes to money. The result is that most people oversave and underinvest. They sock too much away in the bank and not enough in stocks or bonds. The reason for this paranoia is that nobody, quite understandably, wants to lose their hard-earned cash. Ironically, years later when that money is really needed to live on, the paranoid people often find that they don't have as much as they'd like. True, they might have succeeded in preserving their principal, but meanwhile, everything they buy costs more. Their low-risk invested money doesn't go quite far enough.

This chapter shows you a low-risk way to invest in mutual funds so that you can avoid this shock later in life. You'll learn how to manage an investment mix that always matches your tolerance for risk. You'll also learn how to combine dollar cost averaging with profit taking to boost the return on your mutual fund investments.

Balancing Your Act

Keeping your investment balanced means diversifying your mutual fund investments by owning different types of mutual funds that invest in different types of assets, such as stocks, bonds, and cash. Stock funds, bond funds, and money funds don't always perform in tandem with each other. If you diversify your mutual fund portfolio, your investment performance should fluctuate less because losses from some investments are offset by gains in others.

For example, if your stock fund's total return has declined, your losses may be offset by the total return on your bond fund and money fund. As a result, you have less risk than if you were to put all the money into one type of investment, such as a stock fund or bond fund.

In addition to lowering your risks, diversification can offer higher total returns than you would expect if you invested in only the most conservative types of mutual funds, such as money funds.

We think diversification makes a lot of sense because no one type of mutual fund performs best in all types of economic conditions. No one can predict which fund will register high total returns in the future. That's why it's important to diversify.

Diversification alone, however, might not be enough to keep you on a steady course. What happens if your stock fund registers high total returns for a couple of years running? You may find you have too much money in stocks based on your tolerance for risk. That's where *portfolio rebalancing* comes into play.

Seventy-year-old Dudley DoRight knows about portfolio rebalancing, although he doesn't necessarily call it that. When his $23,000 CD matured in his IRA 3 years ago, he took a big step and invested in a blue chip stock fund. The rest of his life savings of $12,000 is invested in—you guessed it—a good old-fashioned U.S. Treasury bond that yields about 7 percent and is due to mature in about 15 years.

Dudley DoRight gets a lot of mail and hasn't been watching things very closely. When his last mutual fund statement came in, his eyes bulged! That initial $23,000 he invested in a blue chip stock fund had doubled to a whopping $46,000.

Who would have thought that this diehard CD investor would suddenly have 80 percent of his life savings invested in stocks? Meanwhile, Dudley knows all too well what Sir Isaac Newton once discovered when he got hit on the head with an apple: What goes up must come down. The next bear market could wipe out his sudden windfall. So Dudley started spending a lot of nights tossing and turning.

Eighty percent in stocks just seemed like too much. Dudley visited a local financial planner who had him rebalance his portfolio. He took $23,000 out of his stock fund and put it into a short-term bond fund and income stock fund for the long haul. Ever since, Dudley has been sleeping like a baby.

Rebalancing Your Act

What is rebalancing? Remember playing on the seesaw at the school playground? The idea was to keep the seesaw level. If one kid was too high, the other was too low. The kid on the side closest to the ground had to push up to bring a buddy on the other side down from his or her lofty perch.

Rebalancing your investments works the same way. Sometimes your stock funds shoot up in value and your bond fund or other funds decline in value, so you have to balance things.

In a bull market, such as the one we have had over the past three years, when the average stock fund shot up 26 percent annually in total return, according to Morningstar, you might have found yourself with too much invested in stock funds at the end of the year.

If you get into a bear market, you want to keep your losses to a minimum. It's important to take some of your profits and make some readjustments to your mix of mutual funds at least once a year.

Technobabble
When you **rebalance** your funds, you periodically adjust the mix of your portfolio to keep targeted percentages of your overall investment dollars in each of your funds, based on your risk tolerance.

In Chapter 6, "Which Funds Are Right for You?," you learned your risk tolerance, the types of funds you should invest in, and how to slice your investment pie to get the best returns with the least amount of risk. When you rebalance your funds, you go one step further. You examine your portfolio and make adjustments to ensure your investment mix has remained proportionately the same as when you originally diversified.

For example, suppose you set up your portfolio with 60 percent invested in stock funds and 40 percent in bond funds or money funds. You're earning a decent return, and you are sleeping well at night. What happens if stock prices surge into a bull market? At the end of the year, you look at what your investments are worth and discover that you now have 75 percent of your money in stock funds and only 25 percent in bond funds or money funds.

Whoa! That's too risky.

What do you do? You simply adjust your mix so that you have 60 percent stock funds and 40 percent bond funds again. When you readjust your mix of funds, you sell some shares of your stock fund and invest the profits in the bond funds. That way, you maintain the same percentage of money invested in each stock fund to match your tolerance for risk. You can resume your eight hours of shut-eye every night.

Portfolio rebalancing has some of the same investing characteristics as constant dollar investing, which you learned about in Chapter 18, "The Easy Way to Buy and Sell: Constant Dollar Investing."

What is the difference? With constant dollar investing, you always keep the same amount of money in a stock fund at the beginning of each year. By contrast, with portfolio rebalancing, the value of your investments can go up, but you maintain the <u>same percentage</u> of money that is invested in each fund at the beginning of each year. Both strategies are designed to limit risk; however, portfolio rebalancing is a more aggressive strategy because you will always have more money invested in stock funds each year based on the percentage mix of assets in the portfolio.

The Advantages of Rebalancing

There are several benefits to rebalancing your mutual fund portfolio:

➤ You're keeping track of your investments. Rebalancing your portfolio forces you to check the performance of your funds periodically.

➤ You're maintaining a risk level that's comfortable for you. You have evaluated your tolerance for risk and determined that you are an aggressive, moderate, or conservative investor. As a result, you don't want your mutual fund portfolio to get too far out of line. For example, if you are a conservative investor who is comfortable with a 50 percent investment in a stock fund, you don't want to see the value of the stock fund investment become a major proportion of your portfolio. Then, you'll have too much money at risk.

➤ You're taking profits in funds that are up. You are readjusting the portfolio mix so that it stays in line with your tolerance for risk.

➤ You're buying low and selling high. Similarly, you are taking profits from funds that have increased in share value.

The Disadvantages of Rebalancing

Yes, there really are disadvantages to rebalancing your mutual fund portfolio:

➤ If you rebalance funds outside your retirement plan, you'll pay taxes on your profits. After paying the tax man, your returns may not be that spectacular.

Of course, there are ways to minimize your taxes when you invest outside of a tax-deferred retirement savings account. You can invest in stock funds with low portfolio turnover. These funds do not distribute a lot of capital gains to shareholders because they buy and hold the securities in the portfolio. As a result, shareholders may pay less taxes on fund distributions.

You also can invest in low-dividend-yielding stock funds. These funds primarily invest in small company stocks. Smaller companies plow their profits back into the company and don't pay shareowners dividends. You won't pay much to the tax man if the fund does not earn a lot of dividends.

➤ You could get out of your stock fund too early and miss out on higher returns over the years.

Best Types of Funds to Rebalance

Before you start rebalancing, you first need to make sure you select funds that make a diversified mix of investments. That way when one is down, the other may be up a bit. It all helps. Refer to Chapter 6 for guidelines on the percentages to invest in stock, bond, and money funds. Keep it simple so that it's easier to rebalance your portfolio.

Money Matters
Avoid rebalancing with funds that charge front-end or back-end loads, transaction fees, or redemption fees. Every time you exit the fund, you're stuck paying a fee. You wind up paying your stockbroker or investment company.

To refresh your memory, younger folks who haven't retired yet probably should pick funds among these categories: aggressive growth funds, growth and income funds, international stock funds, and bond or money funds. Retired folks should limit their fund categories largely to growth and income funds, bond funds or a utility stock fund, and money funds. Both groups also might consider a touch of precious metals funds as an inflation hedge.

It's always best to rebalance your portfolio in a tax-deferred investment such as an IRA, the new Roth IRA, 401(k) company pension, or life insurance policy that lets you invest in mutual funds.

Worst Types of Funds

If you plan to rebalance your portfolio, you want to invest in mutual funds that have stated in the prospectus that they are always <u>fully invested in either stocks or bonds.</u> That means the fund has very little money in cash. You also want to avoid funds that state in the prospectus that they can use market timing and move between stocks and cash. Funds like this may have a lot of money invested in cash.

You can check to see how much the fund is invested in cash by reading the prospectus. If it seems like a lot, call the fund group and ask the representative whether the fund historically has taken large cash positions when the portfolio manager is uncertain about the outlook for the financial markets.

If you invest in one of these funds that has a history of holding a lot of cash investments, you can foul up your portfolio rebalancing strategy. Why? Suppose you bring your portfolio back into a 60 percent stock and 40 percent bond mix at the end of the year by moving money out of your bond fund and into your stock fund. Now suppose your stock fund is 30 percent in cash. All you're doing is moving money into an investment with a large cash position. You are not really 60 percent invested in a stock fund and 40 percent invested in a bond fund. That's why its important to own a fund that has an investment philosophy of being fully invested.

Once again, avoid funds with loads, transaction fees, or redemption fees for portfolio rebalancing. If you invest in a front-end loaded fund, you pay commissions every time you add new money into the fund. If a fund has a back-end load or transaction or redemption fee, you pay the piper every time you sell fund shares and rebalance.

Getting Started with Your Investment Plan

Once you determine the percentage of your money to keep in each fund category, the first step is to open accounts with the funds you want to own. It's best to stick with a mutual fund family that has a large number of funds. You also can invest with discount brokerage firms such as Charles Schwab, Fidelity Investments, and Jack White. These brokerage houses have mutual funds from numerous fund families under one roof. However, remember that certain important mutual fund families have refused to make their funds available through these rival brokerage house channels.

Next, set up a log book to track your initial investments and year-end values. Suppose you determine originally to have 20 percent of your investments in each of 5 funds. Your total investment at year-end is worth $5,000, so you must invest $1,000 in each kind of fund.

Finally, tell your fund group or broker how much you want to invest in each fund. If you call before 4 p.m. E.S.T., everything is readjusted the same day. Call later, and adjustments aren't made until the close of business the next day.

Keep a record of all changes. Always compare them with the changes on the mutual fund's confirmation statement, which you should receive in about a week.

How Frequently Do You Do It?

Nervous Nellies can rebalance their investment mixes every three months. Generally, however, it's best to give it 6 to 18 months for a couple of reasons:

➤ If you make frequent changes, you have to pay taxes on your profitable trades unless the funds are in an IRA or other kind of tax-deferred investment.

➤ Make frequent changes, and you could get *whipsawed*. In other words, the funds you're reinvesting might change direction quickly. It's possible to rebalance, take your profits, and reinvest in poorer-performing funds. You could be reinvesting at higher prices than you should.

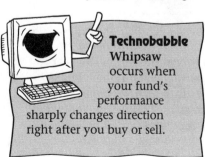

Technobabble
Whipsaw occurs when your fund's performance sharply changes direction right after you buy or sell.

➤ The longer you wait, the less time you have to spend with a calculator figuring out how much to invest in each fund. You want to limit your time as family money manager to one hour a year, if possible.

➤ The longer you wait, the more time your money has to grow. The average bull market lasts about two years. You want to reap the benefits of rising stock prices without feeling as if you're taking on too much risk. One year, history tells us, seems like a nice compromise.

Getting It to Work

Let's look at how rebalancing worked from 1986 through 1997, based on the performance of Morningstar's average growth fund and the average government bond fund. The hypothetical example assumes that distributions are reinvested. Taxes were not taken into consideration.

Suppose you invested $1,500 in a growth fund and $1,000 in a government bond fund at the beginning of 1986. Your mix was 60 percent stocks and 40 percent bonds. You readjusted once a year. (You can use more funds if you want an extra layer of diversification, but let's keep it simple.) See Table 19.1 for an example of how to rebalance your funds, keeping 60 percent of the dollars in growth funds and 40 percent in government bond funds.

The table shows how your money will grow if you rebalance at the end of each year, assuming that 60 percent is invested in a growth fund and 40 percent is invested in a bond fund at the beginning of the following year. Fund distributions are reinvested, but taxes are not taken into consideration. Past performance is no indication of future results. This is a hypothetical example to show you how it works. Your total returns may be different in the future.

Column 1 of the table lists the year-end period of the hypothetical study. Column 2 shows the total value at year-end of the growth fund investment, and Column 3 shows the bond fund's total value at year-end. The last column shows the combined total value of both funds.

At the end of each year, you multiply the combined total value of the portfolio by 60 percent to get the amount you should invest at the beginning of the next year in the growth.

Table 19.1 Rebalancing Your Funds

Year Ending	Total Growth Fund $	Total Bond Fund $	Portfolio Total $
1986	1,725	1,120	2,845
1987	1,758	1,149	2,907
1988	2,005	1,244	3,249
1989	2,476	1,456	3,932
1990	2,241	1,698	3,939
1991	3,237	1,795	5,032
1992	3,260	2,133	5,393

continues

Table 19.1 Continued

Year Ending	Total Growth Fund $	Total Bond Fund $	Portfolio Total $
1993	3,744	2,407	6,151
1994	3,616	2,361	5,977
1995	4,728	2,766	6,777
1996	5,382	2,998	8,380
1997	6,360	3,620	9,980

You did pretty well from 1986 through mid-1995. Your $2,500 investment grew to $6,339 because you kept a mix of 60 percent in a growth fund and 40 percent in a stock fund every year. At every year's end, you totaled up the value of both investments. Then, you put 60 percent of the total into your growth fund and 40 percent in your bond fund.

Stock and bond funds had some pretty good years since 1986. Your stock fund lost 5 percent in 1990 and 2 percent in 1994. The bond fund lost just 4 percent in 1994. In the future, the returns may be different, so don't count on earning the same amount as the example did over the next several years.

Hot Tip!

Be sure to check the confirmation statements sent to you by the fund group after you make your trades. You want to make sure it follows your instructions to a "T."

It's important to note that when your investments were up in the example, you took profits. When they were down, you bought more shares at lower prices. The end result was positive. In 1990, for example, your growth stock fund lost 5 percent, and the bond fund gained 8 percent. At the end of the year, you remixed. As a result, you invested a few bucks more in your growth stock fund at the start of 1991.

Voilà! In 1991, your stock fund gained a whopping 37 percent. Look at what happened by mid-year 1994 following losses in both stocks and bonds in the previous year. Your stock fund lost 2 percent in 1994, but by mid-year 1995, it was up 15 percent.

Your bond fund lost 4 percent in 1994, but by year-end 1995, the fund was up 15.3 percent. The stock and bond markets kept soaring. By the time 1997 came to a close, the stash was worth a total of $9,980.

How do you keep tabs on your funds so you can rebalance? It's easy. At the end of every year, for example, you look at the combined total value of your mutual fund portfolio. Then, you slice the pie appropriately. For example, suppose you keep 70 percent in a stock fund, 20 percent in a bond fund, and 10 percent in a money fund. The total value of your portfolio at the end of the year is $10,000. To rebalance, take 70 percent of $10,000 to get $7,000, or the amount you should have invested in your stock fund. Twenty percent of $10,000 ($2,000) is the amount you should have invested in a bond fund, and 10 percent of $10,000 ($1,000) is the amount you should have invested in a money fund.

Once you have the right amounts for each fund, tell your fund service representative or broker how much you want in each fund. The rep or broker will make the exchanges among the funds to bring you into balance.

News You Can Use

The installment investment strategy is a little more aggressive than portfolio rebalancing. It works this way: Split your investment equally among several well-managed stock and bond mutual funds. They can be domestic, overseas, and large and small company funds. Any new investments are made into the fund that performs the worst. If one stock fund is down, you add money to it after the year has ended. In the next year, if the stock fund is up, you add money to all the other funds that are down.

The Least You Need to Know

➤ Rebalancing means periodically taking profits in winning investments and putting them into your other funds so that you retain the same proportional mix you started with.

➤ Rebalancing is a low-risk way to invest.

➤ It's important to avoid loads, transaction fees, and redemption fees if you want to rebalance.

➤ Rebalancing works best in retirement savings plans because you don't pay taxes on the trades.

Chapter 20

Retirement Savings Strategies for the Faint Hearted

In This Chapter

➤ A low-risk way to increase the value of your retirement savings

➤ The best funds for retirement savings

➤ How to increase your profits and curb your losses

Most of us want to take no chances with our retirement savings. Does that mean retirement savers should put all their retirement savings in the bank? Nope. There's a low-risk way to build your wealth by gradually investing in a stock fund for growth.

This chapter shows you how to use the "Stock Fund Builder" investment plan so you can have more money when you retire. All you need are a well-managed bond fund and a well-managed stock fund, and you're on your way.

Building Slowly but Surely

Cluck! Cluck! Those are the words that best describe most of us when it comes to our retirement savings. Chapter 23, "Saving for Important Life Goals," and Chapter 24, "Care and Feeding of Your 401(k)," explore the different types of retirement plans you can use. But for now, let's focus on a low-risk way to rack up retirement savings profits.

Chances are you've always saved for retirement in a traditional bank account and you're doing fine. You never lost money. You always received a guaranteed return.

Hot Tip!
Low-risk investment strategies, such as the Stock Fund Builder, historically have not beaten stock funds over the long term. But for safety-minded investors, they are a good deal. You can earn more than bank CDs or bonds. Plus, your investment is less risky than keeping 100 percent of your hard-earned bucks in a stock fund.

Technobabble
With the **Stock Fund Builder**, you invest your bond fund's interest income into a stock fund to build your wealth. By investing, for example, in an IRA, you achieve tax deferral, which means you don't pay taxes on the principal you invested or its earnings until you retire.

The trade-off? You probably won't make as much in low-yielding bank accounts as you might with a mutual fund.

In this chapter, you'll learn about one way to grow your nest egg. You'll learn more about the different kinds of retirement savings plans, such as IRAs and 401(k)s. In the meantime, the *Stock Fund Builder* investment strategy, which we are about to discuss, works well in any of those plans—provided that you have at least 10 years until your retirement.

"Stock Fund Builder" is the name we've given to an age-old investment strategy that's been used by pension fund portfolio managers for years. People who manage pension funds often invest in bonds and use the interest income from the bonds as a funding mechanism to invest in stocks. The pension fund managers use bond funds to generate income, which is then dollar cost averaged into stocks. This is a low-risk way to invest because you are investing in the stock market a little bit at a time. You can do the same with a bond fund and a stock fund in your 401(k) company pension plan.

Here's how the Stock Fund Builder works:

1. Open an IRA with a mutual fund family so that you can switch money among funds. It's best to stick with one mutual fund family because you're more likely to be able to reinvest your fund's distributions without paying fees. Every year, you invest your tax-deductible contributions into the fund family's bond fund. Because the investment is in a retirement account, the money also grows tax-deferred. You can invest in a long-term, intermediate-term, or short-term bond fund. Consider this your least risky investment.

2. Reinvest the bond fund's distributions, which include income dividends and capital gains, in the stock fund of your choice rather than back into the bond fund. This is a painless way to invest in stock funds for the long haul.

3. Reinvest your stock fund's distributions into new shares of the stock fund.

4. Every year, invest new retirement plan contributions in your bond fund so that you have even more of your bond fund distributions reinvested in the stock fund. Now, you have a recipe to earn a lot more money than with a low-yield bank IRA account.

You don't have to worry about losing a large chunk of money in a stock market crash. By the time you retire, you'll be surprised at how much you're worth. You're investing a little at a time without adding stock market risk to your original principal.

Of course, your bond fund's share value will rise and fall with changes in interest rates. If interest rates rise, you'll see the share value of your bond fund drop. When interest rates fall, the share value of your bond fund will rise. You have to live with the fluctuating bond fund share values because you are using the bond fund as a funding mechanism for your stock fund, but when rates fall, the share value of the bond fund will rise.

News You Can Use

Here's a twist on the Stock Fund Builder tactic for those who want to put more into stock funds but still are chickens. Invest a lump sum in a stock fund for growth, but rather than reinvest the stock fund's distributions (which include dividends and capital gains) back into the fund, invest them in a money fund or bond fund. This is a lower-risk way to preserve your stock fund's profits. Of course, over the long haul, you make more money reinvesting your distributions into your stock fund. However, more conservative investors may want to sock away that extra money in a less risky place.

No Taxes!

The Stock Fund Builder tactic works best with an IRA, 401(k) company pension plan, or tax-deferred annuity that enables you to invest in mutual funds. You don't pay taxes until you withdraw money from your IRA. Then, you pay ordinary income tax on your withdrawals. Tax deferral of your stock fund dividends and capital gains is an important key toward reaping the maximum profits.

The Roth IRA is even a better deal. If you owned the Roth IRA for five years or more and you are at least 59 1/2 years of age, withdrawals are tax-free. So you really rack up low-risk profits by using the Stock Fund Builder tactic. If you paid taxes on your income, dividends, and mutual funds capital gains, you'd have a lot less money.

Investing in a tax-deferred IRA or tax-free Roth IRA makes a lot of sense. Table 20.1 shows how your money grew tax-deferred compared with the after-tax

Money Matters

Avoid fees when using the Stock Fund Builder! Stay away from loads, bond funds with high expense ratios of more than 1 percent, transaction fees, and redemption fees. Fund expenses take a big bite out of your bond fund's distributions. Look for bond funds with expense ratios of just one-half of one percent. They will leave you with more money to invest in your stock fund.

return at age 65 on the same investment. This is a hypothetical study, assuming that the money grows at an 8 percent annual rate and that $2,000 is invested annually. The first column shows the age you start investing. Column 2 lists what the investment grew to tax-deferred at age 65, and Column 3 lists what the investment grew to at age 65 after taxes.

For example, a person who begins investing $2,000 a year at 8 percent annually when he or she is age 35 will have almost $225,000 in an IRA at age 65. Outside an IRA, the tax bite slices that kitty to just over $160,000. It pays to invest tax-deferred.

Table 20.1 Value of Investment at Age 65

Age at Which You Start Investing	Tax-Deferred Value $	After-Tax Value $
55	$31,291	$27,568
45	$98,846	$75,831
35	$224,692	$160,326

That's a whopping difference of $65,000! Chapter 23 goes into greater detail about how you can save for retirement. For now, however, you can see the advantage of investing in a retirement account and using this investment strategy.

Watch Your IRA Grow

By using the Stock Fund Builder and sweeping interest income from your bond fund into a growth and income fund, you can increase your wealth without much worry.

The following illustration shows how a $10,000 investment grows using this strategy, compared to a straight growth and income fund, from December 31, 1985 through December 31, 1997. This is a hypothetical back-tested example we calculated using Morningstar's data to show you how the strategy works. Keep in mind that past performance is no indication of future results.

The growth and income fund increased to $46,323. That's pretty good. However, could you have tolerated the 20 percent plunge experienced by growth and income funds in the last three months of 1987, the year of the Black Monday stock market crash? The Stock Fund Builder was less risky. You earned almost $36,000—and you didn't have to worry about losing. It's a respectable return, considering that at the beginning of 1987, you didn't have a lot of money invested in your stock fund. Because you invested your bond fund's interest into the stock fund, you were dollar cost averaging and picking up more shares when the stock fund declined.

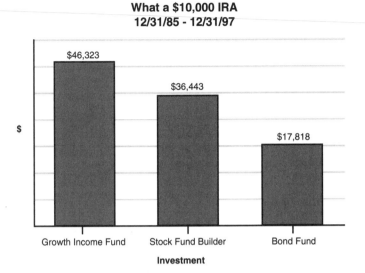

What a $10,000 IRA
12/31/85 - 12/31/97

$46,323

$36,443

$17,818

$

Growth Income Fund   Stock Fund Builder   Bond Fund

Investment

How a $10,000 IRA grew from December 31, 1985 to December 31, 1997.

What if you had left all your money in the bond fund? You would have earned close to $18,000 over the same time frame—$18,000 less than with the Stock Fund Builder.

You can invest a lump sum in a balanced fund that invests about 60 percent in stocks and 40 percent in bonds. However, 60 percent of your money is invested in stocks from the start. That may be too much risk for low-risk-minded investors. The Stock Fund Builder gets you into stocks more slowly, yet you build up a nest egg in the stock fund over the years.

What to Do Later

Over 10 or 20 years, you'll probably have a pile of money in your stock fund by using the Stock Fund Builder. Yet, now you're nearing retirement and you don't want to risk losing what you earned over the years. You have a couple of options:

➤ **Before Retirement.** Stop moving your bond fund earnings into your stock fund. Then, flip back to Chapter 6, "Which Funds Are Right for You?" and zero in on your new investment comfort level. Determine the percentages you want in each fund, based on your new risk tolerance level, and practice portfolio rebalancing, which you learned about in Chapter 19, "Keeping an Even Keel: Diversification and Portfolio Rebalancing."

Hot Tip!
Be sure to invest in stock funds that always stay fully invested in stocks. Otherwise, the Stock Fund Builder investment strategy will not work as well.

229

➤ **After You Retire.** Diversify your money among stocks, bonds, and cash to preserve your wealth and provide retirement income. Chapter 6 discusses the right mix of funds based on your age and tolerance for risk.

Best Funds for Stock Fund Building

Depending on your tolerance for risk, you have a number of fund choices under the Stock Fund Builder. Aggressive investors can use high-yield bond funds and aggressive growth or growth funds. Moderate investors can use high-grade corporate bond funds and growth and income funds. The more conservative should consider a government bond fund and growth and income fund. If you want to add an international component to this tactic, consider a global fund that invests in both U.S. and overseas stocks.

It's best to do business with mutual fund families that have a large variety of well-managed stock and bond funds.

Consider Variable Annuities Automated Program

The Stock Fund Builder works well inside a variable annuity—another tax-deferred investment that we'll discuss further in Chapter 23. If you are a conservative investor but still want the growth that comes along with investing in common stock mutual funds, consider this tactic for your retirement savings.

The Least You Need to Know

➤ With the Stock Fund Builder, you invest in a bond fund or money fund and then invest the fund's interest income in a stock fund.

➤ The Stock Fund Builder works well in a tax-deferred instrument such as an IRA or variable annuity so that you don't pay taxes on your distributions.

➤ You should invest with a mutual fund family that offers a wide variety of stock and bond funds and charges no loads, redemption fees, or fees to transfer.

➤ Even low-risk investment strategies, such as the Stock Fund Builder, historically have not beaten stock funds over the long term.

Part 5
Mutual Fund Investing for Special Situations

By now, we hope you've grasped some of the basics of mutual fund investing. Despite all we've been through together so far, however, all this information is only the tip of the iceberg. Once you make all this money, you have to deal with the tax man. Chapter 22 shows you how to cut your tax bill. Plus, Chapter 21 shows you how to manage your money when the stock or bond market heads south.

Remember all those reasons you wanted to invest? You need money for retirement—and you're confused by the best ways to invest your 401(k) or Roth IRA. See Chapter 24 for the best retirement strategies. You want to finance your child's higher education. Chapter 23 shows you how to help get Junior—financially, at least—through the halls of ivy. You also need to take care of your loved ones when you pass to the above and beyond. See Chapters 25 and 26 for wise advice.

Chapter 21

Loaded for Bear: What to Do When the Stock Market Falls Out of Bed

In This Chapter

➤ Bulls versus bears: what it all means

➤ How to limit your losses

➤ Profiting from market tumbles

➤ Funds that do well when stocks head south

As no doubt you're already well aware, the stock market doesn't always go straight up. Sometimes, it goes straight down and lands with a thud. The Black Monday crash on October 19, 1987, for example, was one scary day that a lot of people would like to forget. The stock market lost 20 percent! Of course, it eventually recovered big time. Nevertheless, that recovery took nearly a year.

Think of the stock market as a balloon filled with different substances at different times. When stock prices soar up, up, and away, the market is behaving like a helium balloon, or, as the Wall Street Big Boys say, we're in a *bull market*. When the stock market plunges, it may be acting more like a lead balloon. That's when people start talking about *bear markets*.

This chapter gives you the hard facts about what to do in a bear market so you can control your fears of this hairy beast. You'll learn how to cut your losses and limit the damage if the market happens to nose-dive while you're invested in it. You'll even find out how to profit from bear markets. Like a boy scout or girl scout, we want you to be prepared and use any market downturns to your advantage.

Running Bear

What is a bear market anyway? A bear market happens when the stock market's value (as measured by market indexes such as the Dow Jones Industrial Average or S&P 500) drops 15 percent. A market stumble—just a 10 percent drop—is referred to as a *correction*. A drop of more than 10 percent starts people talking about a bear market.

Why do stocks sometimes drop in value? Stocks lose money because investors begin to fear the worst from the economy and inflation. Plus, high interest rates scare the heck out of Wall Street.

Technobabble
A **bull market** means that the stock market has been increasing in value for at least one year. When stocks lose 15 percent or more, it's a **bear market**. A **correction** is a 10 percent drop in the stock market. A **crash** is a drop of at least 20 percent that happens in just a few days. **Bulls** are people who think the stock market is headed up. **Bears** are people who think the stock market is headed down.

Historically, you should expect one bad year for every three or four good ones when you invest in a mutual fund. Since the end of World War II, 10 percent price declines in stocks occur an average of every other year. This may be a temporary drop that lasts a couple of weeks to several months followed by a rebound later on. Fourteen times since 1950, stock prices have plunged more than 15 percent.

Investors got whacked pretty badly in some of those bear markets. For example, the average stock fund lost more than 20 percent in those nightmarish last three months of 1987. In 1961 and 1962, stocks lost 29 percent. If you were unlucky enough to have invested in 1973 and 1974, you would have lost 45 percent!

How long must you calmly sit through a bear market? Fortunately, so far, not very long. Since 1926, the average bear market has lasted about a year. After 1950, the average dropped to eight months (and took 13 months to recover). By contrast, the average bull market has lasted about three years.

How to Limit Bear Market Damage

The rest of this chapter shows you several investment strategies you can use to cut the damage when the stock market heads south.

If you get no other message from this book, it should be that history tells us we have to accept the good with the bad when we invest in mutual funds. Unfortunately, the bad is not quite as easy to swallow.

Here are a few golden rules to follow if you're getting jittery:

1. **Know the facts.** Understand realistically what you can expect from a stock fund investment. Over the past 30 years, when the stock market lost at least 15 percent, it took two years to recover. That's happened five times since the 1960s, according to Ibbotson Associates, Chicago. As we said earlier, the average bull market lasts three years.

What can you expect from mutual funds in a worst-case scenario? Based on the past 50 years, a 100 percent investment in stocks grew at an average annual rate of 11.7 percent. Not bad! Of course, you had to accept losses along the way. The average loss was –9.4 percent. The worst one-year loss: –26.5 percent.

2. **If you are losing sleep over your investments, make changes!** The majority of investors who sell mutual funds when the stock market tumbles have invested over their heads. Perhaps they bought a hot growth stock fund because the paper said that it gained 25 percent, and they thought the trend would continue. That's not necessarily so.

Keep your powder dry. Start saving in a money fund. Financial planners often recommend that concerned investors might be better off in a balanced fund that invests in both stocks and bonds. (See Chapter 5, "Is a Fund a Winner or Loser?") One of the best—the Dodge & Cox Balanced Fund, for example—will give you about 85 percent of the return on the S&P 500 with one-third less risk. This fund has grown at a 9 percent annual rate since 1940.

Hot Tip!
Don't invest based on hopes and wishes. Invest because there are sound reasons to put your money in a stock fund or bond fund for the long term. If you feel like you're making a bet on a hot fund, you could lose your shirt.

3. **Don't panic.** Experienced stock fund investors should invest regularly in their stock funds through thick and thin. Over the long term, this strategy pays off. For example, a $100-a-month investment in the Vanguard Index 500 fund over the past 15 years would have grown to almost $61,000. Don't forget. If the stock market drops, you're buying shares at lower prices. So you should be smiling from ear to ear again when the market rebounds.

4. **Cut some of your risk.** Take profits from stock funds and invest in lower-risk bond and money funds. Every year, keep the same percentage mix of stock and bond funds that fits with your investment comfort level.

News You Can Use

Don't think diversification works? The late Bernard Baruch, a Wall Street legend and advisor to President Roosevelt in 1930, lost $18 million in the stock market crash of 1929. That's like losing $400 million today. But he still had $8 million invested in bonds (about $200 million by today's standards). Fortunately, bonds tend to increase in value when stocks tumble. So in 1929, when people were jumping out of Manhattan office buildings, diversification saved Baruch's day!

5. **The older you are, the more you should be concerned about preserving your principal.** On the other hand, those who recently have retired may well live into their 90s, and they also need to make certain their money will hold out. Experts say a 30 percent investment in a stock fund is a good compromise for retirees.

Avoid Accidents

You're asking for trouble if you don't monitor your investments. If you leave your financial statements and reports sitting in their envelopes, your investments could veer dangerously out of control.

Heidi Steiger, managing director at Neuberger & Berman Management, New York, suggests that you avert potential accidents by taking this test. If you answer "no" to any of these scenarios, it could be time for changes:

➤ Do you keep a current running total of your entire portfolio's value?

➤ Do you regularly calculate the percentage of your assets in stocks, bonds, and money funds?

➤ Do you follow your regular plan of splitting up your investments among high- and low-risk mutual funds?

➤ Are you able to name the 10 largest holdings in your stock fund? (If not, you might think you are investing in a high-dividend-yielding fund that invests in blue chip stocks—but you actually might own risky small company stocks.)

➤ Are you aware of each fund's investment objective? In other words, does it invest in small companies or technology or is it a balanced, value, or international fund?

➤ Do you set annual goals to see how much the value of your investment has increased from year to year?

➤ Do you buy stocks or mutual funds without studying brokerage research, annual reports, and prospectuses?

➤ Do you have a selling strategy for your stocks or mutual funds? (If your financial conditions change, a fund underperforms its peers for at least three years, or the fund manager leaves the fund, it might be time to make a clean getaway.)

➤ Do you know how much you pay annually in commissions and fees?

Unfortunately, you can't control interest rates or the markets when it comes to investing. But all of the preceding factors are within your control. Staying on top of your investments can help minimize losses.

"You might be the type of investor that's comfortable with having 40 percent in stock funds and 60 percent in bonds," Steiger warned. But, she added, after one year's stellar returns in the stock market, you could find you have more in stocks than you think.

If that's the case, part of your losses during the next market downturn may well be your own fault.

What Have You Got to Lose?

Bulls are optimists. They think the stock market is headed up. Bears are pessimists. They're willing to swear it's headed down. Although they tend to have opposite views about the direction of the market, they typically agree on one important point: You can lose some hefty money—if you own only one mutual fund and the market goes into a tailspin. If you put 100 percent in an aggressive growth U.S. stock fund, you can lose as much as 20 percent if the market plummets. You can cut your risks dramatically by adding an international stock fund, a bond fund, and money fund.

Here are some statistics that show how much you can expect to lose and gain over the long term based on your investment style. The information is based on the performance of stocks and bonds over the past seven decades, according to Ibbotson Associates, Chicago:

➤ Growth investors: An 80 percent stock and 20 percent bond mix grew at an annual rate of 9.6 percent over the past 70 years. You lost money in one out of every four years.

➤ Balanced growth investors: A 60 percent stock and 40 percent bond mix grew at an 8.6 percent annual rate. You lost money in one out of every five years.

➤ Conservative growth investors: A 40 percent stock, 40 percent bond, and 20 percent cash mix grew at a 7.4 percent annual rate. You lost money in one out of every five years.

➤ Income investors: A 20 percent stock, 60 percent bond, and 20 percent cash mix grew at an annual rate of 6.2 percent. You lost money in one out of every five years.

Keep in mind that these are long-term averages. Plus, the future could be different from the past. However, to approach these results, you should expect to invest in a mutual fund for at least 10 years or longer.

Don't forget, when you are younger, you can invest for growth. So small company, growth, and aggressive growth stock funds make sense. When you retire, experts suggest that you keep about 70 percent in low-risk income investments and a little in blue-chip stocks as well as bonds.

Hot Tip!
For a free brochure on "Strategies for Uncertain Markets," call the John Hancock Funds (800-225-5291).

Stick with Reliable Funds

It's not worth losing a good night's sleep over your mutual funds. If you're looking for low-risk stock funds, we think balanced funds that typically keep 50 to 60 percent of their investments in stocks and the rest in bonds are a good bet. Here are a fistful that have grown at an annual average rate of over 10 percent since 1940. Performance data is according to Morningstar, Inc., Chicago.

➤ Delaware Fund. This balanced fund has grown at an annual rate of over 10 percent since 1940. Over the past ten years, it has grown at an average annual rate of 14.5 percent. It's up 14 percent annually over the past five years. The fund invests in larger companies that are expected to increase their dividends. The fund invests about 40 percent in intermediate-term bonds rated A or above by Standard & Poor's and Moody's. For these reasons, this fund typically pays a higher dividend yield than similar funds. There is a 4.75 percent load.

➤ American Balanced Fund. This balanced fund has grown at an annual rate of more than 10 percent since 1940. Over the past ten years, it has grown at an average annual rate of 13.1 percent. Over the past five years, it's up 14 percent annually. The fund buys undervalued blue-chip stocks and intermediate-term investment grade bonds. There is a 5.75 percent load.

➤ CGM Mutual. This balanced fund has grown at an annual rate of more than 10 percent since 1940. Over the past ten years, it's grown at an annual average rate of 13.9 percent. Over the past five years, the fund has grown at an annual rate of 12.3 percent. Over the past three years, it's grown at an annual rate of 11.4 percent. This is an aggressive balanced fund that can invest up to 75 percent in stocks. The fund looks for undervalued blue chip or smaller company stocks. The fund is no-load.

➤ George Putnam Fund. This balanced fund has grown at an annual rate of over 10 percent since 1940. Over the past ten years, it has grown at an annual average rate of 13.5 percent. Over the past five years, it is up 15 percent. The fund can invest up to 75 percent of its assets in stocks. The fund wants to own undervalued stocks in large companies that should show improved earnings. On the bond side, it invests in higher-yielding corporate bonds. The fund has a 5.75 percent load.

➤ Dodge & Cox Balanced. This balanced fund has grown at an annual rate of around 10 percent since 1940. Over the past ten years, the fund has grown at an average annual rate of 14.1 percent. Over the past five years, it's up 15.6 percent annually. The fund may invest up to 75 percent of assets in stocks. It also invests in longer-term government and investment grade corporate bonds. The fund buys undervalued stocks that have the potential to register strong earnings growth. This is a no-load mutual fund.

➤ Vanguard Wellington. This balanced fund has grown at an annual rate of around 10 percent since 1940. Over the past ten years, the fund has grown at a 14.1 percent average annual rate. Over the past five years, it is up 16.5 percent annually. The fund can invest 60 percent to 70 percent in stocks. The fund invests in undervalued, large company stocks that pay high dividends and should appreciate in value. On the bond side, the fund sticks with government securities and high-grade corporate bonds. The fund is no-load.

Invest to Win, Place, and Show

If you want to protect yourself from a stock market correction of 10 percent or more, buy some bonds or bond funds. Experts were warning that stock prices could decline in 1998 after five years of stellar returns. The average stock fund, for example, has more than doubled in value over the past five years.

Economist Peter Bernstein told Vanguard Group of Funds shareholders in a report not to expect double-digit returns from our stock investments every year. His forecast: Stocks will grow at about an 8 percent annual rate into the near future. So don't expect your stock market mutual funds to do much better. Treasury bonds, he figures, should yield around 6 percent.

"Bonds are an insurance policy," Bernstein says. "Hold bonds to the extent that they will keep you from panicking when the stock market is down."

Financial research by the *No-Load Fund Analyst*, a San Francisco newsletter, shows that since 1950, bonds have cushioned stock market losses. Assuming that you owned 70 percent of your investment in stocks and 30 percent in bonds and held that investment for at least three years: The worst three-year annual return was –5.5 percent. The worst three-year annual return for a 50 percent stock and 50 percent bond mix was –2.4 percent.

Frazier Evans, chief economist of the Colonial Group of Funds, says owning bonds will help cushion any losses in stocks. "Stocks and bonds have declined together only in five of the last 70 years," Evans says. "In almost every year when one dropped, the others rose and made up for the loss. It's the simplest form of diversification."

Evans notes, however, that if interest rates rise this year or next, bond and stock price both could decline. When interest rates rise, bond prices fall.

News You Can Use

Looking for a stock fund that uses strategies to limit downside losses? Tony Sagami, an Austin, Texas money manager, advises conservative investors or those who anticipate a big stock market correction to consider the Gateway Index Plus Fund (800-354-6339). This no-load fund invests in blue-chip stocks that make up the S&P 100 stock index.

Morningstar, Inc. reports that 80 percent of the Gateway Index Plus Fund's holdings are hedged with put options. That means that if the market tumbles, the fund should profit from the fall in stock prices. Morningstar rates the fund as a low-risk stock fund. It is two-thirds less volatile than the blue-chip stock market averages.

The tradeoff: It underperforms the average diversified stock fund. Over the past one, five, and ten years, the Gateway Index Plus Fund has grown at an annual rate of more than 10 percent. Over the same period, the S&P 500 has grown at a 16 percent annual rate.

Other Funds That Rise When Stocks Tumble

Several funds are designed to do well when the stock market tumbles. But be ready to move quickly in and out of these funds. In fact, it could pay to hire a money manager who is used to moving in and out of these specialized funds.

Some of the best money managers in the country who will manage a portfolio of mutual funds worth as little as $15,000 include the following pros:

➤ Hampton Investors, which has registered a 20 percent annual return over the past 12 years ending in November, 1996

➤ Potomac Fund Management, 19.5 percent annual return over the past 17 years

➤ Professional Sector Management, 19 percent over the past 12 years

➤ RTE Asset Management, 16.4 percent over the past 17 years

➤ Cooper Linse Hallman Capital Management, which has racked up a 15 percent annual return over the past six years

To contact these money managers, call AdvisorLink at 800-348-3601. AdvisorLink, for a referral fee paid by the money managers, ranks the best money managers in the business, and gets paid by the advisor for client referrals.

Aggressive investors who use market timing or subscribe to stock-market trend newsletters might consider the Rydex Ursa Fund. This fund engages in short sales, a tactic designed to reap big profits on stock market declines. You can speculate or hedge against losses in your existing stock fund.

You've got to know what you're doing when you invest in this fund. It loses money when the stock market is making money. You should buy it and add it to your investments only when you think there's good reason for the market to head south.

News You Can Use

You've heard of the warning, "Beware the Ides of March?" Some are saying "Beware the Year 2000." Most worldwide computer systems can't properly read that landmark year. Because of our worldwide dependence upon computers, regulators fear this glitch could cause many computer networks to start spewing out wrong information on or before that date.

This problem is of particular concern to financial markets. In fact, some economists predict it could trigger a bear market. However, nobody is certain how widespread, if any, the damage might be.

To protect yourself as an investor, the Securities and Exchange Commission urges you to ask your investment company how it is preparing its computer system for the Year 2000 problem. Find out whether your portfolio accounts will be protected and also whether you will be able to buy or sell shares as usual after January 1.

The Robertson Stephens Contrarian Fund is another stock fund that can make bets on a stock market decline. The fund manager invests for long-term growth most of the time. But when it looks like a possible downturn is coming, the fund will reverse directions and invest to profit when stocks tumble. Over the past year, the fund has lost 29 percent. Over the past three years, it has grown at a 7 percent annual average rate. Other funds to consider include Prudent Bear, Crabbe Huson, Flex Muirfield, and Merriman Asset Allocation.

Making a Few Bucks on a Bear Market

As we always say, when life deals you lemons, make lemonade. By the same token, it pays to make a bear market work for you—not against you.

Here is one bear market strategy, developed by Gerald Perritt, Ph.D., publisher of the *Mutual Fund Letter*. This study was conducted more than 10 years ago. Nevertheless, it shows you how regularly investing during a down market works.

Keep a reserve kitty in cash or a money fund so that you can invest systematically, and use this tactic for at least 10 years:

➤ Invest one-third of your cash in mutual fund shares when the market or your stock mutual fund moves down 10 percent.

➤ Invest half of your cash in more mutual fund shares during a serious bear market when the fund or market drops another 10 percent.

➤ Invest the remaining 17 percent of your cash over the six to eight months that an economic recession may last.

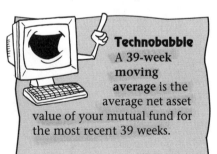

Money Matters
Investing when your fund is heading south? Keep in mind that it could take a year or more before you make back your losses and begin to profit. Past performance is no indication of future return. In other words, no one really knows for sure how long a bear market will last.

The idea behind this strategy is to buy low and sell high. You invest regularly when the fund's share price drops. Temporarily, of course, you have to live with losing some money. But when the fund's price begins to rise, you profit because you bought all these cheap shares.

Perritt back-tested this strategy during several bear markets, followed by the bull market of 1982. His research shows there were 20 buying opportunities from 1950 through 1984 and several more over the past 10 years.

How did this tactic work during some nasty periods in stock market history? From January 1, 1950 through June 1, 1982, a hypothetical study shows that an initial $7,000 investment in the Standard & Poor's 500 Index would have grown to $127,088 by July 1, 1984. In addition, the cash or T-bill account would have contained $16,406. Overall, you would have made $143,494 using this tactic.

Follow the Trends: Moving Averages

If you asked a group of financial advisors how to make money on Wall Street, probably 9 of 10 pros would say you have to buy low and sell high. However, if you asked them to name the right time to trade, most would say that no one can accurately catch the very bottom or top in the financial markets.

Technobabble
A **39-week moving average** is the average net asset value of your mutual fund for the most recent 39 weeks.

Although financial research has proven that no one can time the markets over the long haul with much success, several important indicators can identify future trends in the market and enable investors to avoid large losses in the stock market.

Trend indicators such as the *39-week moving average*—the average share price of a mutual fund over the recent 39 weeks— can facilitate investment decisions to buy, sell, or change the asset mix of an investors portfolio.

Moving averages are one of the major market trend indicators in use today. The philosophy behind the moving average is that if the trend is moving higher, it could go higher. Conversely, if the trend is lower, there's a good chance the market will go lower.

By averaging and plotting weekly prices, for example, for every successive 39-week period, you get an indication of whether the mutual fund stock prices are gaining momentum or the trend line is deteriorating. A stock's price breaking above its moving average is a confirmation of a trend and a buy signal. A stock's price breaking below the moving average is a sell signal.

The experts say that making investment decisions based on a moving average is not a surefire way to profit in the stock market. However, if positive trends are coupled with favorable economic and industry news, investors have a benchmark to help them make some decisions.

Douglas Fabian, publisher of Fabian Investment Resources, Huntington Beach, California, says that 39-week moving averages and trend indicators have been successful investment tools in recent years.

Over the past 15 years ending in 1997, Fabian Investment Resources recommendations to switch out of stock and money market funds has resulted in a 12.3 percent annual return, 13 percent annual return over the past ten years, and 15.4 percent return over the past five years, according to the Hulbert Financial Digest.

By contrast, the S&P 500 grew at a 14.8 percent annual rate over the past 15 years, 14.8 percent rate over the past 10 years, and 16.6 percent rate over the past five years. Although you would have made more money staying 100 percent invested in stocks, switching out of stock funds when the market looked like it was trending down and investing in a money fund was a less risky way to invest.

"Moving averages is a mechanical trend-following investment approach," Fabian says. "If the trend is up, you buy. If the trend is down, you sell. As long as the current prices are above their moving averages, we want to be invested. When the prices fall below their moving averages, we want to invest in money funds."

Over the past 17 years, according to Fabian's Investment Resources newsletter, he's averaged about two trades a year—switching between a basket of stock funds and a money fund. Moving averages, however, are fallible. Fabian got whipsawed in 1988. A *whipsaw* occurs when you move into the market on a buy signal, but prices go lower. A whipsaw also occurs when you move out of a fund on a sell signal, but the fund moves higher.

Should You Use Moving Averages?

If you're the type of investor who can't sit tight and fears losing money in a bear market, then you might consider using a moving average. You can calculate it yourself or you can subscribe to a newsletter with a hot-line service you can call toll-free for investment

243

advice. Two popular sources of information to consider are Fabian Investment Resources (800-950-8765) and Mutual Fund Trends (605-341-1971). Another trend-following newsletter that has you invested safely during bear markets is InvesTech Mutual Fund Advisor (406-862-7777).

Calculating a Moving Average

You can use a shortcut to figure the 39-week moving average of your fund. Let's see how it works the long way first.

To calculate a 39-week moving average, you simply take the average price of 39 weeks of a fund's net asset value (NAV), the funds share price less expenses, listed in the mutual funds tables in your local newspaper. Each week, you add in the new number and subtract out week number 1. That way, you have a moving 39-week average. Then, you compare the recent price to the moving average. If the price is above the average, it's a buy sign. If the price is below the moving average, it's a sell sign. That's a heckuva lot of stuff to keep track of. But here is a shortcut that can help.

Money Matters
Using moving averages to invest in mutual funds can add a comfort level to your investment program because you may avoid large stock market losses—but it's by no means the secret to stock market success. If you jump out of your fund, you may get back in at a higher price than when you left to move into a money fund. Particularly in a sideways or choppy market, you also could get whipsawed. In other words, the market could move opposite from the way the moving average indicates. Plus, if you're not in a retirement fund or annuity, you risk paying taxes on your trades.

A quick way to estimate a 39- or 40-week moving average once per week is to:

1. Take 95 percent of your mutual fund's net asset value for the previous week.
2. Take 5 percent of this week's net asset value.
3. Add the two together to get your moving average point.
4. Plot those points against the most recent week's net asset values of your fund or funds.
5. If the weekly net asset value breaks above the moving average line, it's a buy signal.
6. If the weekly net asset value breaks below the moving average line, it's a sell signal.

It works this way: Say the Flying Walenda's Growth Stock Fund net asset value in the paper this week ending on Friday was $10. Last week, the fund's net asset value or share price was $8. The 39-week moving average is $8 \times .95 = 7.6$ and $10 \times .05 = .5$. So the moving average share price is 8.1 or 7.6 + .5. This week's share price is 10, which is more than 8.1. As a result, the trend is up and it's time to buy.

Say several months later, things turn sour. Your previous week's share price is 14, and this week's is 12. The 39-week moving average is 13.9. Because this week's share price is below the 39-week moving average, it's a sign the market has a low trend. You should consider selling.

Once you have a buy or sell signal, you call your fund group. If it's a buy sign, tell the fund representative to move the money out of your money fund and into your stock fund. Sell signal? Instruct it to move you out of the stock fund and into the money fund.

Keep in mind that you'll have to pay taxes on the trades if the money is not in a tax-deferred retirement account or variable annuity.

Rules of Moving Averages

Here are some tips to help you interpret moving averages:

➤ If the moving average flattens out following a previous decline, or it is advancing and the price of the stock penetrates the average line on the upside, it's a major buy signal.

➤ If the price falls below the moving average price while the average line is still rising, this also is considered a buy sign.

➤ It is considered a buy sign if a mutual fund's price is above the moving average line, is declining toward that line, fails to go through, and starts to turn up again.

➤ If the moving average line flattens out following a previous rise, or it is declining and the price of the mutual fund penetrates that line on the downside, it's a major sell signal.

➤ If the mutual fund's price rises above the moving average while the average line is still falling, it's a sell signal.

➤ It is considered a sell signal if the mutual fund's price is below the moving average, is advancing toward that line, fails to break above the line, and turns down again.

➤ If the mutual fund's price advances too fast above an advancing moving average line, there is likely to be a move back toward the trend line.

The following calculations show you how moving averages work:

A = .95 × last week's fund NAV = _____

B = .05 × this week's fund NAV = _____

A + B = 39-week moving average NAV

If this week's NAV is less than the 39-week moving average, sell.

If this week's NAV is more than the 39-week moving average, buy.

News You Can Use

Are you, like one of us (we won't say which), a math midget? Fortunately, several software programs on the market can calculate moving averages for you. For a complete listing of software programs, pick up a copy of *The Individual Investor's Guide to Computerized Investing*, published by the American Association of Individual Investors, Chicago. For more information, you can call them at 312-280-0170.

A Word about Bond Funds

If you're the type of investor who sticks with bond funds, be careful. Earlier chapters discussed the risk of investing in bonds. The biggest danger is interest rate risk. When interest rates rise, bond prices fall. For example, if interest rates rise 1 percent, the value of your long-term bond fund principal will drop nearly 11 percent. Forget that your bond fund pays an attractive yield of around 6 percent. If rates rise 1 percent, the total return for the year—if everything stays the same—is 11 percent minus 6 percent or 5 percent.

Suppose interest rates rise a whopping 2 percent: The value of your principal will drop about 18 percent, and your total return is —12 percent. Hardly anything to cheer about.

Here are some ways you can hedge your bets with bond funds:

1. The best medicine for bond fund investors is to play it safe. Keep a stash in a money fund. Money funds pay current interest rates, and the share price or net asset value stays at $1. When rates rise, you shouldn't lose principal. Next, spread your money among short-term, intermediate-term, and long-term bond funds. That way, you limit your losses when rates rise.

2. It's always a good idea to invest regularly in your bond funds so that when rates rise, you buy more bond fund shares at a lower price and earn a higher yield. Over five to ten years, it's likely that the average cost of the shares you purchase will be a lot lower than the current market price of your bond funds. If you don't need the interest income from your bond funds, reinvest the income in new shares. This way, you will buy more shares at lower prices when your bond fund drops in value.

3. Don't chase after the highest-yielding long-term bond funds today—at least with money you can't afford to lose. If interest rates rise, the value of your bond fund will decline. That's not what you want from a safe haven.

   The best move: Stock up with short-term bonds or bond funds with maturities from 2 to 10 years. The difference between the 2-year Treasury note and the 30-year Treasury bond is only one-third of one percent. Why take the risk of investing in long-term bonds?

Investing in a 10-year Treasury bond fund, for example, pays you a yield that is 97 percent of a 30-year Treasury bond but with significantly less price risk if interest rates rise.

4. Keep your powder dry. Even though interest rates are headed lower, be careful. The slightest hint of inflation or a stronger-than-expected economy could push interest rates back up again. Hedge your bets. Don't be snowed by all the media talk of growth that's not too fast or not too slow. The bond market is volatile!

Parking some cash in a money fund and waiting for the right opportunity to invest is one way to play the interest rate game. When interest rates are rising, the fund manager normally shortens the maturities on investments so that money can be rolled over quickly at higher rates. You'll earn current market rates, and your share price should stay at $1.

The Least You Need to Know

➤ Balanced funds that invest 60 percent stocks and 40 percent bonds are a lower-risk way to invest.

➤ Bond funds tend to do well when the economy slows down and stocks lose money.

➤ By investing regularly during a bear market, you can profit when things turn around.

➤ Active investors can use a 39-week moving average to gauge trends in the stock market. They also can use a newsletter or hire a money manager to make changes in their mutual fund portfolios.

Chapter 22

Taxes: To Pay or Not to Pay?

In This Chapter

➤ How the IRS taxes your mutual fund earnings

➤ Forms for figuring your taxes

➤ How to calculate taxes when you sell shares

➤ Cutting the tax bite on your mutual funds

You're off and running with your new mutual fund investments—headfirst, you hope, into a bull market. Everything is going great—that is, until you're faced with the sudden realization that it's time to deal with Uncle Sam. Ugh!

You've now come upon one of the sad truths about mutual fund investing. Unfortunately, we all must pay the tax man on our mutual fund earnings. At the beginning of each new year, you're reminded of this fact when you get those funny-looking tax statements from your investment company.

This chapter examines your mutual fund taxes and suggests ways to cut the tax bite. You'll learn what forms you can expect from your investment company and exactly what they tell you about your profits and losses.

Yipes! The Tax Man's Gonna Get Ya!

There's no getting around it, people. Once you start making some bucks in your mutual fund, the IRS wants a piece of it.

You may pay the tax man on three different sources of income from your mutual funds: dividends, capital gains, plus capital gains when you personally sell your fund's shares at a profit.

How do you know what to report on your tax return? You'll pay taxes on the following mutual fund distributions that are listed on the 1099-DIV statement that you receive from your mutual fund every January. Two types of mutual fund distributions are taxed:

➤ **Dividend distributions.** This is income from stock dividends and interest from bonds, net of expenses, that the fund's portfolio has earned during the taxable year. Of course, you do not have to pay taxes on exempt interest dividend income that you made from tax-free municipal bond or money funds.

➤ **Capital gains distributions.** This is the net profit that the fund earns from the sale of the mutual fund portfolio holdings. When a fund sells securities that have risen in value, it takes a profit. Any losses from the sale of securities that have declined in value are subtracted from the profits, however.

If your fund sold securities at a net profit, you pay taxes based on whether they are long- or short-term capital gains distributions. *Short-term gains* are net profits from the sale of securities held for less than 18 months. Short-term capital gains are lumped with dividend income on the tax form you receive from your mutual fund. *Long-term capital gains* are net profits from securities held for 18 months or longer.

You may also pay long- or short-term capital gains taxes if you sell shares of your fund at a net profit. Don't confuse these capital gains from shares of the fund you sold with capital gains distributions paid to you by your mutual fund. The capital gains from the sale of personally sold fund shares is listed in the 1099-B form that you get from your fund along with the 1099-DIV statement.

How is all this money taxed? Retroactive to May 7, 1997, the new tax laws say you'll pay 20 percent on long-term capital gains for investments that you have held for 18 months. (It used to be 28 percent for investments held at least 12 months.) Now if you sell your mutual fund shares before 18 months, you pay ordinary income tax on your profits based on your individual tax rate, which ranges from 15 percent to 39.6 percent.

In January, way before April 15 comes around, you'll begin to get a slew of forms from your mutual fund. Unfortunately, copies are also sent to the IRS. The forms tell both you and your favorite Uncle exactly how much you made on your investments. Here are the forms you might expect from your fund:

➤ **1099-DIV.** This tells you how much you made in dividends and capital gains distributions, except from IRAs or other retirement plans. This little exposé reveals the total distributions you received, broken down for dividend income and capital gains.

➤ **1099-B.** This tells how much you got for selling your fund shares. If you owned the shares for less than 18 months, you pay income taxes on the profits, based on your tax bracket, which can range from 15 percent to 39.6 percent. If you owned the shares for more than 18 months, you pay a maximum of 20 percent capital gains tax on the profits.

➤ **1099-R.** This tells how much income you received from your IRA or other retirement savings plan. It includes any taxes withheld.

➤ **5498.** This form tells how much you contributed to your IRA during the tax year.

We're sorry to be the bearer of bad news, but first, you owe income taxes on your dividend income and capital gains. Retirees also owe tax on distributions they received from their IRAs or pension plan.

Uncle Sam Takes His Cut

You have to pay tax on any fund shares sold at a profit. Of course, if you lose money on the sale, you may be able to write it off on your income taxes. Keep in mind, however, that losses are subject to the $3,000 annual limit for capital losses ($1,500 if married, filing separately).

It's advisable to consult with your accountant or tax attorney before you decide on a method for paying taxes on the sale of your mutual fund shares. There are several ways to pay taxes on the sale of your mutual fund. We'll examine them all in the following sections.

First In, First Out (FIFO)

With the FIFO method, as you sell shares of a fund, you assume that the shares you are selling are the first ones you bought. Their cost basis, therefore, is the cost related to the oldest shares of the fund in your portfolio.

Here's an example. Let's assume that you hold the following 300 shares of a fund: 100 that you bought in January 1993 at $10 a share, 100 that you bought directly or through reinvestment of distributions in January 1994 at $11 a share, and 100 that you bought in January 1995 at $12 a share. Under FIFO, when you sell 100 shares, you assume it's the ones you bought in January 1993 at $10 a share.

Drawback: With this method, you can pay whopping capital gains taxes when you sell fund shares you've owned for a long time. Of course, if your fund's net asset value declined, this is not the case.

Specifying Shares

Under the specific shares method, you designate shares to be sold in advance of the sale. In this way, you can select the highest-cost shares to minimize your tax bite.

Drawbacks: Although you pay the lowest amount of capital gains tax on the sale of fund shares with this method, the IRS requires you to keep accurate records of all your mutual fund transactions over the years. So you must keep much more careful records. If you use this method, be sure that you get a written confirmation from your mutual fund of your instructions to sell specific shares of your fund.

Average Price Per Share

With the average-price-per-share method—the most popular—you figure your profits by first factoring the total cost of all the fund shares you bought and dividing that by the number of shares you bought. This gives you the average cost you paid for all your shares.

Suppose you paid $8,000 for all your shares and you now have 400 shares of the fund. The average cost is $20 a share. If you sold all 400 shares at $22 per share, your capital gain for tax purposes is a $2 per-share gain multiplied by 400 shares. This equals $800. If you sold just 100 shares, you take the same $2 gain and multiply it by 100.

Drawbacks: This is the middle-of-the-road method of figuring taxes due on the sale of fund shares. Unless the value of your shares has decreased, you pay less in taxes than you do under the FIFO method.

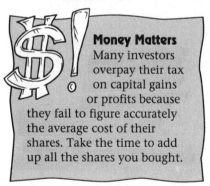

Money Matters
Many investors overpay their tax on capital gains or profits because they fail to figure accurately the average cost of their shares. Take the time to add up all the shares you bought.

However, you might pay more to Uncle Sam than if you had sold specified shares. What do you do if you've been socking away $50 or $100 a month into a mutual fund for years via an automatic investment plan? How do you figure the cost of all those shares?

Fortunately, many mutual fund groups send you a year-end report that lists the average cost of all the shares you've directly purchased or obtained from reinvestment of distributions. Then, you or your accountant can figure any net capital gains based on the sale price of all the fund's shares.

If you don't get a report, you have to calculate the average cost of the fund's shares yourself. Be sure to keep all your mutual fund confirmation statements through the years. Most funds keep records that trace back at least 10 years, in case you are missing some statements.

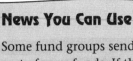

News You Can Use

Some fund groups send you a year-end statement that shows the average cost of your funds. If they don't, you've got to keep good records. If you have any questions about your taxes, you can call the IRS toll-free at 800-TAX-1040 for help. To get tax forms and booklets, call 800-829-3676. Publications to ask for are IRS Publication 564 on mutual fund distributions, IRS Publication 550 on investment income and expenses, and IRS Publication 514 on foreign tax credit for individuals. You also can view IRS publications online at http://www.irs.gov.

Reducing Your Capital Gains Taxes

There's one upbeat note in this otherwise depressing saga of your mutual fund profits and Uncle Sam. You also can write off any losses from the sales of your mutual fund shares on your income taxes.

This gets tricky, particularly if the fund is a good long-term investment and you really want to keep it. To qualify for a tax write-off, you can't repurchase the mutual fund for 31 calendar days after you sell it. If you do, the IRS calls it a *wash sale* and you're dead—tax-benefit-wise, that is. Also remember, as we said before, there is an annual limit on losses you can write off. You can't be a *front-runner* either. In other words, you can't buy any security up to 30 days before the planned tax-loss sale. Violate either rule and you lose your capability of writing off your losses.

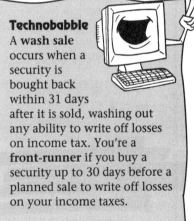

Technobabble
A **wash sale** occurs when a security is bought back within 31 days after it is sold, washing out any ability to write off losses on income tax. You're a **front-runner** if you buy a security up to 30 days before a planned sale to write off losses on your income taxes.

There are several ways to work around these rules:

➤ **Sell the fund shares at a loss, wait 31 days, and buy them back.** The sale at a loss can occur at the close of trading on the last business day of the year, if you want. This way, you realize the loss and can reinvest in your favorite fund 31 days later.

   Disadvantage: The fund's price could rise in 31 days and you might be forced to invest at a higher price than when you sold.

➤ **Buy and then sell.** Buy the same amount of mutual fund shares you already own, wait at least 31 days to avoid the wash-sale rule, and then sell the original holding. You can use this tactic until the end of November. This way, you get to write off your tax loss and still own the fund.

Disadvantage: Because you own more shares, you can be subject to greater losses if the market tumbles.

Money Matters
If you're swapping funds to write off tax losses, make sure the funds you swap are comparable. Otherwise, you can take on more risk than you anticipated.

➤ **Swap funds.** This is a way to avoid the wash-sale rule. Sell your fund and invest in a similar fund that sells at about the same price. You can take the capital loss on your taxes and still have an investment that fits your needs.

Suppose you invest $10,000 in the Putnam High Yield Tax-Free Fund at $14.73 and own 678.72 shares. The fund's net asset value drops to $14.10 by the end of June. Your $10,000 is now worth $9,570. Then you sell the fund for a $430 loss. You reinvest the $9,570 in the T. Rowe Price Tax-Free High Yield fund. You now own 823.58 shares at a net asset value of $11.62. As a result, you've realized a loss, but you still own a tax-free high-yield investment.

More Tax-Saving Tips

The following sections discuss overlooked ways to get a tax break and profit from investing in stock or bond funds.

Loss Carry Forward

Under the tax law, a mutual fund with losses in one year can carry it over until the next year. By selecting funds that have taken advantage of this opportunity, known as a *loss carry forward*, you can save on your own capital gains taxes in the following year. If you invest in a fund with loss carry forward, the subsequent capital gains earned by the fund are offset by the capital losses it carried forward.

To make the most of this opportunity, look for well-managed stock or bond funds that have had a bad year. Ask the fund representative whether the fund is carrying forward any losses. If so, you can invest and get a big tax break. You may not have to pay taxes on any capital gains or profits the fund makes in the coming year!

Avoiding Year-End Investments

Uncle Sam has thrown us yet another curve ball when it comes to enjoying our mutual fund profits. You get hit by this one if you happen to invest at the end of a year. It's generally best to hold off on your holiday resolution to step up investing until after the ball drops in New York's Times Square.

Why? Guess who pays taxes when a mutual fund distributes its capital gains in December? Usted, vous, and you, that's who. You can avoid this killer of holiday cheer by waiting until after a fund's *ex-dividend date* to buy fund shares. The ex-dividend date is a fancy word for the date on which the value of the income or capital gains distribution is deducted from the price of your fund's shares.

This sounds pretty complicated, but you can see how it impacts your taxes by looking at what could happen to an unsuspecting investor. This person invests $5,000 in a growth stock fund at the end of November and becomes the proud owner of 312.5 shares of a fund bought at $16 per share. At the end of December, the investor notices that the fund mysteriously dropped in value by $1 per share.

Upon calling the fund manager, the investor learns it suddenly decided to pay out $1 per share in capital gains that it had been holding in the fund for a year. This investor now owns more shares of the fund, but the value has not changed.

The investor is in for yet another shock when a 1099-DIV arrives the following January, indicating that the investor has $312.50 in capital gains income from the fund. Even though there were no earnings, the investor is forced to pay taxes on capital gains. How can that happen? The investor is no idiot, but he bought the fund at exactly the wrong time—before that so important ex-dividend date. As far as Uncle Sam is concerned, the investor might as well have been a fund shareholder of record for the entire year.

Finding Tax Help

Unfortunately, there's no way to avoid it; tax season will always roll around. Here are a few tips on how to find a good tax preparer who might help you avoid some of these common investment mistakes.

Go to a national tax service if you have a simple return. You'll get a qualified professional to help you; tax preparers typically require a certain amount of coursework. H&R Block, for example, requires 66 hours.

The Better Business Bureau, however, cautions against using storefront tax return preparers who open for business just for the tax season. You run a greater chance of being audited because a seasonal preparer might not be qualified to do your taxes.

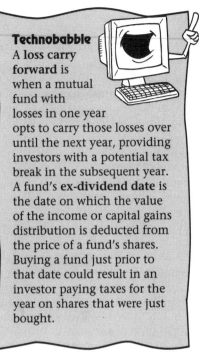

Technobabble
A **loss carry forward** is when a mutual fund with losses in one year opts to carry those losses over until the next year, providing investors with a potential tax break in the subsequent year. A fund's **ex-dividend date** is the date on which the value of the income or capital gains distribution is deducted from the price of a fund's shares. Buying a fund just prior to that date could result in an investor paying taxes for the year on shares that were just bought.

Hot Tip!
You can avoid all the tax hassles that Uncle Sam imposes by keeping your money in a qualified retirement savings account. Your money grows tax-deferred in variable annuities, IRAs, Keoghs, SEP plans, and 401(k) company pension plans until you take your retirement pay. You needn't worry about paying taxes on fund dividends and capital gains distributions or capital gains on the sale of fund shares.

If you are in a high tax bracket, own a business, do a lot of investing, or own property, it's best to seek the help of a Certified Public Accountant (CPA). Better yet: A CPA that's an enrolled agent is approved by the IRS to represent taxpayers in the event of an audit.

Questions to ask a tax preparer before you hire:

➤ How many years of experience do you have preparing income taxes?

➤ How many tax returns do you prepare in a year?

Hot Tip!
Here are two other sources of information regarding hiring tax preparers: Send $2 and a self-addressed envelope to the Council of Better Business Bureaus, 4200 Wilson Blvd., Arlington, VA 22203 for publication 24-226, a booklet, "Tips on Tax Preparers." *The Ernst & Young Tax Guide 1998*, published by John Wiley & Sons, New York, also is an excellent source.

➤ How long will it take you to prepare my tax return? You don't want someone to do your return at the last minute. You don't want your tax return arriving at your doorstep by Express Mail on April 14. You need time to review it.

➤ How do you keep updated on changes in the tax laws?

➤ What is your procedure for checking accuracy?

➤ What are your fees? The more complex the tax return, the higher the fee. Most CPAs charge around $75–$150 an hour for their services.

Then, take two final steps:

➤ Ask for references.

➤ Check with your local IRS office to be sure no complaints have been filed against the tax preparer.

10 Tips on Mutual Fund Taxes

As the Boy Scout's motto says, it's always best to be prepared. Here are several ways to make paying taxes on your mutual funds a less frustrating affair:

1. Not all fund distributions are alike. Make sure that you report dividends from the fund as dividends on your tax return. By contrast, capital gains distributions are reported on another line.

2. Avoid paying taxes twice on your fund distributions. If you reinvest in new shares of the fund, you can add the cost of those reinvested shares to your cost basis when you figure gains and losses on shares that you sell. Fortunately, when you automatically reinvest distributions, the cost of the new shares is listed on your fund's statement. Don't forget to save those monthly statements.

3. Just because you sold fund shares or switched funds doesn't mean you always owe the tax man. You may be able to offset your capital gains with capital losses.

4. Don't buy fund shares right before the fund's ex-dividend date. The ex-dividend date is the date on which the value of the income or capital gains distribution is deducted from the net asset value (NAV) of the fund's shares. The distribution deducted from the share price (NAV) of a fund you just bought is returned to you or reinvested in new shares. However, you'll end up paying taxes on this distribution. That's right: You'll pay taxes on money that you just paid out as part of the purchase price of the shares!

5. Keep good records of all your mutual fund transactions. File all your confirmation statements plus your monthly or quarterly statements. You need the information when you file your income taxes.

6. Watch out for nontaxable distributions from your fund. You don't pay any taxes on the return of your own capital. Form 1099-DIV shows how much in nontaxable distributions comes from your fund.

7. Be sure that your taxpayer identification number is correct when you open a mutual fund account. Otherwise, the mutual fund is required by law to withhold 31 percent of your fund distributions for taxes.

8. Avoid paying double taxes on your international fund's distributions. You are subject to foreign taxes being withheld from your international funds. Be sure you deducted the amount withheld dollar-for-dollar on Uncle Sam's taxes. As mentioned earlier in the chapter, the 1099-DIV lists foreign taxes paid.

9. Don't forget to invest in tax-free bonds and money funds rather than taxable bond funds if you're in a high tax bracket. Individuals with tax rates ranging from 31 to 39.6 percent usually earn higher taxable equivalent yields in municipal bond and money funds than they do in taxable funds.

10. Consider investing in funds that pay "itsy bitsy" dividends and capital gains distributions if you plan to keep the money in a taxable account. The Vanguard Tax-Managed series of funds, the T. Rowe Price Tax-Efficient series of funds, and the USAA Tax-Managed Fund keep taxable distribution to a minimum compared to the average mutual fund.

The Least You Need to Know

➤ You must pay taxes on mutual fund distributions.

➤ You must pay taxes on profitable sales of mutual fund shares.

➤ The investment company sends you forms on the amount you must declare as taxable income.

➤ The average cost method is the most frequently used method to compute taxes on the sale of mutual fund shares.

➤ Take advantage of tax strategies you can use to cut your tax bite. Consult a CPA or tax advisor, if necessary.

Chapter 23

Saving for Important Life Goals

> **In This Chapter**
>
> ➤ Saving for your child's college education
>
> ➤ Calculating how much you need to retire
>
> ➤ The right way to invest for retirement
>
> ➤ The truth about Roth IRAs, SEPs, and other retirement plans

It's tough enough to meet your everyday living expenses. Meanwhile, if you are like most Americans, staring you straight in the face is a double whammy—saving for your child's higher education and your own retirement. Unless you're lucky enough to be born into wealth, or you just happen to pick the right numbers in the lottery, there's only one other way to meet these challenges: Save, Save, Save! Make the wrong investment decisions, or shun the idea of investing altogether, and you could wind up short of money.

This chapter looks at how to save and invest to meet these two important financial commitments in your family's life.

The Cost of a College Education

You've probably already heard the stories. College expenses could double in 10 years. Four years of public college now costs about $38,000 to $45,000. Private schools cost twice that much. And by the time your child is ready for a higher education, assuming costs rise 7 percent annually, four years at a public college could cost almost $120,000.

All this means that you need to save $344 a month over the next 15 years to cover the full cost of a future college education, assuming you can earn 8 percent annually from that investment.

Suppose your Little Lord or Lady Fauntleroy wants to attend an Ivy League school? You'll have to save $677 a month earning 8 percent to pay for an estimated $238,000 for four years.

Table 23.1 shows how much you'll have to save if your child begins college in 2000, 2005, or 2010. This table assumes that college costs are rising 7 percent annually and your investments earn 8 percent annually.

Table 23.1 College Costs and How Much to Save

Year Beginning College	Public Cost	Monthly Savings	Private Cost	Monthly Savings
2000	$65,000	$885	$130,000	$1,770
2005	$91,000	$498	$182,000	$995
2010	$119,000	$344	$234,000	$677

How Much Do You Need to Save?

All this might sound a little intimidating, but actually, it merely involves a little planning. Take a few minutes and fill out the following College Costs Worksheet. Answer each question to find out how much you must save to cover the full cost for one year of college. Once you calculate how much you need to save to cover one year of college, multiply that number by four to get the amount you need to cover four years.

News You Can Use

Overwhelmed by the thought of paying for college? Don't let it get to you. You may not need to save 100 percent of the cost of a four-year college education. For families who make between $20,000 and $60,000 a year, financial aid might pay for 20 to 99 percent of the cost of college, depending on your income and your family's net worth and whether your child attends a public or private school. About 25 to 30 percent of the cost of college is covered by financial aid, reports the Department of Labor.

Other sources of aid include bank loans, home equity loans, and life insurance loans against cash value policies. In addition, your child may receive a scholarship, their grandparents may give them money, and they may work part-time and contribute to the education kitty. By the time you figure in all those options, you may need to save only 50 percent or less of the total cost.

COLLEGE COSTS WORKSHEET

Fill in the blanks

1. Enter your child's age. _____
2. Enter the number of years before your child enters college. _____
3. Enter the annual cost of college from table 1. $_____
4. Multiply #3 by an inflation factor selected in table 2. _____
5. This equals your child's future annual college cost. $_____
6. Multiply #5 by 2 for a two-year college or by 4 for a 4-year school. _____
7. Your child's estimated total future college cost. _____
8. Select from table 3 the investment factor for the investment return you expect to achieve (after taxes). _____
9. Multiply the amount in #7 by #8 (the investment factor). This is the amount you need to set aside each year to fund your child's education. Divide this amount by 12 to achieve the monthly figure; by 52 for the weekly amount.

YEARLY SAVINGS NEEDED = $_____
MONTHLY SAVINGS = $_____
WEEKLY SAVINGS = $_____

TABLE 1: ANNUAL COLLEGE COSTS
(Based on 7% inflation rate/year)

ENTRANCE DATE	PUBLIC	PRIVATE
1992	$9,007	$19,350
1993	$9,638	$20,704
1994	$10,313	$22,154
1995	$11,034	$23,704
1996	$11,807	$25,364
1997	$12,633	$27,139
1998	$13,518	$29,039
1999	$14,464	$31,072
2000	$15,476	$33,247
2001	$16,560	$35,574
2002	$17,719	$38,064
2003	$18,959	$40,729
2004	$20,287	$43,580
2005	$21,707	$46,630
2006	$23,226	$49,894
2007	$24,852	$53,387
2008	$26,592	$57,124
2009	$28,453	$61,123

TABLE 2: COLLEGE COST INFLATION FACTORS

YEARS TO START OF COLLEGE	INFLATION FACTOR			
	4%	6%	8%	10%
1	1.04	1.06	1.08	1.10
2	1.08	1.12	1.17	1.21
3	1.12	1.19	1.26	1.33
4	1.17	1.26	1.36	1.45
5	1.22	1.34	1.47	1.61
6	1.27	1.42	1.59	1.77
7	1.32	1.50	1.71	1.95
8	1.37	1.59	1.85	2.14
9	1.42	1.69	2.00	2.36
10	1.48	1.79	2.16	2.59
11	1.54	1.90	2.33	2.85
12	1.60	2.01	2.52	3.14
13	1.67	2.13	2.72	3.45
14	1.73	2.26	2.94	3.80
15	1.80	2.40	3.17	4.18
16	1.87	2.54	3.43	4.59
17	1.95	2.69	3.70	5.05
18	2.03	2.85	4.00	5.56

TABLE 3: ESTIMATED INVESTMENT RETURNS

YEARS TO START OF COLLEGE	INVESTMENT RETURN, AFTER TAXES OF:		
	4%	6%	8%
1	.981	.971	.962
2	.481	.471	.463
3	.314	.305	.296
4	.231	.222	.213
5	.181	.172	.164
6	.148	.139	.131
7	.124	.116	.108
8	.106	.098	.090
9	.093	.085	.077
10	.082	.074	.066
11	.073	.065	.058
12	.065	.058	.051
13	.059	.051	.045
14	.054	.046	.040
15	.049	.042	.035
16	.045	.038	.032
17	.041	.034	.029
18	.038	.031	.026

Source: Alan Lavine. Printed with permission of Consumers Digest.

Building a College Savings Kitty

Once you've got a fix on how much you need for college savings, you can invest to reach your goal. As you learned in earlier chapters, the more time you have, the more you should invest in stock funds. You can invest 100 percent in aggressive stock funds to save for your child's future education. As your child approaches college age, though, it's generally best to go with the low risk and invest in fixed-income funds. Four or five years before your child enters the halls of ivy, it's best to keep about 60 percent of the stash in intermediate and Short-Term bond funds. CDs, Treasury securities, and money funds are also good investments to protect your profits. The rest may be invested in a growth and income fund or balanced fund.

Table 23.2 provides some examples of how you might allocate your mutual fund dollars, depending on your child's age. The table shows you the historical annual average total return on stocks as an estimate of what you may expect to earn in aggressive stock or growth stock funds. Remember, there are no guarantees. But on average, this is the kind of return these funds have generated.

Table 23.2 Mutual Fund Investments for College

Type of Fund	Child's Age	Risk You Can Tolerate
Aggressive or Growth Funds	1-12	High
Comments: These funds invest in growth stocks. Expect to average 10 to 12 percent total return per year, earning between -11 and +31 percent per year (a typical range). After age 12, substitute growth and income or balanced funds.		
High Yield Bond Funds	1-8	High
Comments: These yield 8.50 percent, but are risky. Put only a small portion of college savings in this type of fund. They have an interest rate and credit risk. Parents in high tax brackets can consider municipal bond funds.		
High Grade Corporate Bond Funds	1-18	Moderate
Comments: Funds invest in A to AAA rated bonds. The yield is 6.50 percent to 7 percent as of this writing. There is an interest rate risk. Parents in high tax brackets can consider municipal bond funds.		
Short-Term Bond Funds	1-18	Low
Comments: Funds invest in U.S. Treasury and corporate bonds. They are less risky than long-term bonds, but yield between 5.50 percent and 6.50 percent as of this writing. Parents in high tax brackets can consider municipal bond funds.		
Money Funds	1-18	Low
Comments: Funds invest in Short-Term money market instruments. They yield 5.2 percent as of this writing. Parents in high tax brackets can consider tax-free money funds.		

Source: Alan Lavine. Printed with permission of Consumers Digest.

Once you establish your college investment plan, it's up to you to change to more conservative funds as the child nears college age. You can avoid this burden with special college savings plans offered by Fidelity Investments College Savings Plan (800-544-8888) and American Century Investments College Investment Program (800-345-2021). With these programs, you use dollar cost averaging (see Chapter 17, "Getting Rich a Little at a Time: Dollar Cost Averaging") in one of the fund group's stock funds. Then, money is automatically moved into the fixed-income fund of your choice when your child nears college age. One hundred percent is invested in a lower-risk money fund or bond fund when your child is ready to enter school.

News You Can Use

One thing you don't need when you're investing for your child's college education is more taxes! There are a couple of ways, besides investing in tax-free bond funds or money funds, to reduce the tax bite of saving for your child. Probably the easiest and most common method is merely to put the investment in your child's name.

It's generally best to set up a custodial account with a financial institution using the Uniform Gift To Minors Act (UGM) or the Uniform Transfer To Minors Act (UTMA). Grandparents also may give the child money for college using this tactic. The IRS allows an annual gift of $10,000 per adult without charging gift taxes.

However, if you take this route, the money becomes the child's when he or she turns 18, or whatever age your state considers adulthood. There are several free sources of information on saving for college that may help you get started:

9 Tips for College Savers, published by Neuberger & Berman Management Inc., 800-877-9700.

The Federal Student Aid Information Center, 800-433-3243.

"The College Planning Kit," T. Rowe Price Investment Services, 800-225-5132.

Relief from Uncle Sam

Several long-standing government loan programs can help you afford a college education. These include Perkins, Stafford and Pell Grants, and Plus Loans.

With the more recently passed Taxpayer Relief Act of 1997, you can deduct student loan interest, up to $2,500 per year for the first five years of repayment.

You can also get a maximum $1,500 Hope Scholarship tax credit in your child's freshman and sophomore years for a child who spent at least $2,000. You can credit up to 100 percent of child's educational costs to $1,000, 50 percent for the next $1,000 in costs.

In the child's junior and senior year, though, credits shrink. A "Lifetime Learning" tax credit, available to students in degree and non-degree programs, is capped at $1,000 annually, increasing to $2,000 annually in the year 2003.

The Lifetime Learning credit is calculated at 20 percent of your educational expenses up to $5,000 ($10,000 beginning in the year 2003). All credits are phased out for joint filers with adjusted gross income starting at $80,000 and for single taxpayers with adjusted gross incomes starting at $40,000. Parents are prohibited from taking both the Hope credit or the Lifetime credit in one year. For more information on the tax rules call the IRS at 800-829-1040.

Hot Tip!
Financial planners suggest saving to pay for at least half the cost of college. The balance can be financed through college financial aid and scholarships and student loans from good old Uncle Sam.

You also can get a tax deduction for the contribution into a prepaid tuition plan, as long as your child goes to a public institution.

One more big break: The Taxpayer Relief Act of 1997 permits parents to make non-deductible contributions of $500 per year per child under 18 into an educational IRA. The funds can be withdrawn for higher educational expenses tax-free.

Start Saving for Retirement Now

Now that you've gotten your college savings plans under way, you probably want to start working on your own retirement. Most of us have to work past age 65 to be able to retire. Don't expect things to get any cheaper by that time, either. In fact, just the opposite is likely to happen. If inflation grows 3.5 percent a year, $60 worth of groceries today should cost $120 in 20 years.

Money Matters
Don't jump the gun and start dumping all your money into a retirement account before first evaluating your insurance needs. You might need disability insurance to protect your income in the event you become ill or injured. Your family also may need permanent income protection in the event of an untimely death.

"I don't have to worry because I pay Social Security out of my paycheck," you say. Unfortunately, no one knows for sure what's going to happen to Social Security by the time the baby boomers head south to Florida to live out their golden years. At this writing, discussions were under way in Washington for major revisions to Social Security due to concerns it could run out of cash in the near future. You might have to work longer, and/or Congress might be cutting back on Social Security benefits over the next couple of decades.

Today, Social Security replaces about one-third of a worker's income. Unfortunately, you probably need about 70 to 80 percent of your annual current income when you retire to maintain your standard of living.

Build Your Own Pot of Gold

Although the government might be talking about cuts in Social Security on the one hand, it is giving money back with the other. While you can't necessarily bank on Social Security, you can put money into an IRA or other type of retirement savings account to build a worry-free retirement.

The best thing about retirement savings accounts, such as IRAs, is that contributions may be tax-deductible or ultimately withdrawn tax-free, depending upon the plan you select. If you have no other pension plan, or, if you earn below a certain income level, you might be able to save twice on a traditional IRA: first, by paying less in taxes to Uncle Sam, and secondly, by deferring taxes on your IRA earnings until you retire.

If you can't make tax-deductible contributions to your IRA because you have a company pension plan and a high salary, it still makes sense to have an IRA. The $2,000 a year in the IRA grows tax-deferred until you take distributions at age 70-1/2. In the following section, you'll learn about the income limits for IRA tax deductions.

Your Personal Retirement Fund: IRAs

With an IRA, you control your investments. You can invest IRA money into your choice of bank CDs and savings accounts, stocks, bonds, mutual funds, and American Eagle gold coins. Before you consider any of these investments, check with your bank, broker, or investment company to make certain they have the capability of setting up your desired investment as an IRA. Because many financial services providers view IRAs as long-term relationships with their customers, it's possible some might require less to open an account if it's being used as an IRA.

Fortunately, Uncle Sam allows any taxpayer who has earned income but doesn't contribute to a company pension plan to make tax-deductible contributions to an IRA. Single taxpayers can put $2,000 annually into an IRA and get a dollar-for-dollar deduction on their income taxes. Married couples that file joint returns can salt away a maximum tax-deductible contribution of $4,000.

However, the deduction is phased out or eliminated entirely, based on income, for taxpayers who already have a pension plan. The phaseout, which in 1998 starts at $30,000 for individuals and $50,000 for married couples, was slated to increase until they reach $50,000 for singles by the year 2005, $80,000 for married couples in 2007.

News You Can Use

With an IRA, you actually control your investments, but you'll be socked with a 10 percent penalty if you withdraw before age 59 1/2—unless the withdrawal meets one of these conditions:

➤ It is used for higher education.

➤ It is made for first-time home purchases.

➤ You are unemployed and need the money to pay for health insurance. That penalty is over and above any withdrawal penalties or termination fees the financial institution might set on your IRA.

How The New Roth IRA Works

These days, everyone is talking about the Roth IRA. Like the IRA, the new Roth IRA also lets you invest up to $2,000 a year. But unlike the original IRA, you can't deduct your contribution from income taxes. The good news, though, is that with a Roth IRA, you can withdraw tax-free if you've maintained it for at least five years and you withdraw under one of these conditions:

Hot Tip!
If your spouse has a pension plan through a job and you don't, don't despair. You still can qualify for a tax-deductible IRA.

➤ You've turned 59 1/2;

➤ in the event of death or disability;

➤ or for a first-time home purchase.

Plus, unlike the original IRA, the Roth IRA does not require you to start taking withdrawals at age 70 1/2.

Eligibility for the Roth IRA starts to phase out for individuals earning adjusted gross incomes of $95,000 and couples with adjusted gross incomes of $150,000.

Should You Switch to a Roth IRA?

Transfer your old IRA into a new Roth IRA in 1998 exclusively, and the IRS cuts you a little break. While you'll get zapped with taxes on the withdrawals from your old IRA, you get to spread out that damage over a four-year period. To qualify for this little break, you must have an adjusted gross income under $100,000 in the 1998 tax year.

Most of us make a lot less than 100 grand a year. So in 1998, we qualify to switch our regular IRA to a Roth. Should you? Sit down with your accountant and crunch the numbers. But the general rules are:

➤ If you're in a low tax bracket now, and expect to be in a high tax bracket when you retire, the Roth IRA makes sense.

➤ If you're in a high tax bracket now and expect to be in a low tax bracket when you retire, or you don't know what your tax bracket may be, it could pay to stick it out in your old original IRA.

➤ The younger you are, the more it pays to convert your old IRA to a Roth and pay the taxes over the next four years.

Assuming your mutual fund investments earn over 7 percent until the day you retire, you should make out just fine. Even if you're in your 50s and 60s, you can do it. Of course the older you are, the more you probably have in your IRA. So the more taxes you're apt to owe if you convert to the new Roth IRA.

News You Can Use

Say you have a $50,000 IRA and are in the 28 percent tax bracket. You would owe the IRS a total of $14,000 when you switch IRAs. But say you invest your Roth IRA in a mutual fund that grows 7 percent annually, you would need five years to make up the $14,000 you paid the taxman. You would need an extra 2 years to make back the lost earnings on the $14,000 you shelled out to the IRS.

If you can afford to pay the whopping taxes for switching to the Roth IRA, it might make sense for several reasons.

➤ All of the mutual fund earnings in your Roth IRA grow tax free.

➤ You don't have to start taking distributions from your Roth IRA at age 70 1/2 like you must do with a regular IRA. You can leave the money in your Roth until you pass on.

➤ You can put money into the Roth when you are older than 70 1/2, which is the age cut-off for the original IRA.

➤ When you die, the Roth IRA goes to your heirs free and clear of income taxes (although the IRS is expected to ultimately put a limit on your heirs' tax-free ride).

Hot Tip!
The Strong Group of Funds at http://www.strong-funds.com and The Vanguard Group of Funds at http://www.vanguard.com have online analyzers to help you figure out the benefits of the Roth IRA. For $9.95, you can buy a more comprehensive "Roth Analyzer Software" from T. Rowe Price at 800-225-5132.

For the Self-Employed: SEPs

A *Simplified Employee Pension Plan* (SEP) is an expanded IRA for the self-employed. As with IRAs, SEP plan holders can invest in bank accounts, stocks, bonds, and mutual funds and deduct their contributions on their taxes. If you own your own business, you can sock away more into a SEP than an IRA. Your employees also have the option of saving through the SEP plan.

This plan is called simplified because it's easy to set up. You fill out a form similar to that for an IRA. As with IRAs, you control the investing. Each year, you can contribute up to 13.0435 percent of net earnings or $30,000, whichever is less, into this tax-deferred retirement savings plan. Unlike an IRA, all contributions to a SEP-IRA are tax-deductible.

Keogh Plans

A Keogh is a more flexible retirement plan for the self-employed than a SEP. You can contribute more to a Keogh than either a SEP or an IRA. Depending on how it is set up, you can contribute 25 percent of your income annually to a maximum of $30,000. As with other retirement plans, Keogh contributions are tax-deductible. A Keogh can be set up as a profit-sharing plan or a plan that pays a specified income after you retire.

To start a Keogh, though, you may have to hire a lawyer to file a written plan with the IRS. There also is a lot of record keeping to do. Annual IRS forms must be filled out, and the IRS requires a lengthy report every three years. Most mutual fund companies provide a standard IRS-approved Keogh plan.

401(k), 403(b), and 457 Plans

These are all known as salary reduction pension plans because your taxable wages are reduced by your contribution so you have less wages to report to the IRS. The 401(k) plans typically are used by people employed in private industry. The 403(b)s are used by those who work for nonprofit organizations, and 457s are for state and municipal employees. Depending on the plan, workers usually agree to put up to 10 percent of their wages into their mutual fund pension plan investments. Employers also are permitted to make matching contributions. Typically, employers pay from 25¢ to $1 for every $1 a worker invests.

See Chapter 24, "Care and Feeding of Your 401(k)" for more on your 401(k) plan.

Variable Annuities

A *variable annuity* is a tax-deferred investment you have under contract with an insurance company. You either invest a lump sum or make regular payments into an annuity. Then you typically can invest in a wide variety of mutual funds including both United States and international stock funds or bond funds, as well as money funds and a fixed-rate account. When you retire, you can take a lump sum distribution and pay taxes on your accumulated earnings or you can receive monthly payments from the insurance company for your lifetime. If you opt for lifetime payments, any remaining assets in the annuity go to the insurance company upon your death—unless special provisions are made. However, you also can opt to set up the annuity so that your beneficiaries receive the balance in your account when you die. (You'll learn more important stuff about this in Chapter 25, "Making Your Money Last as Long as You Do.")

Technobabble
A **variable annuity** is a form of insurance that lets you invest in a selection of mutual funds. When you retire, it can pay you periodic income for as long as you live.

There are other advantages to variable annuities. For one thing, your estate doesn't need to go through a legal process called *probate* before you can pass the money on to your heirs when you die.

Another added attraction: You get insurance coverage in the form of a death benefit guarantee. When you die, the insurance company agrees to pay your heirs your principal or market value, whichever is greater.

Like investing in a mutual fund family, you can switch among investments as market conditions or your needs change. What's attractive about investing in variable annuities is that your money grows tax-free until you are required by the insurance company to take payments at age 80 to 85. By contrast, with a traditional IRA, withdrawals must begin at age 70 1/2. Plus, when you do withdraw, you only pay taxes on your earnings in the variable annuity over the years—your principal or the original amounts you invested.

As with an IRA, there is a 10 percent penalty on variable annuities if you withdraw before age 59 1/2. But unlike the IRA, which taxes everything you take out of it, a variable annuity only requires you to pay income tax on the earnings.

Insurance companies are apt to make up for this little advantage, however. With a variable annuity, you'll typically pay a back-end surrender charge, levied by the insurance company, if you withdraw within, say, seven years.

> **Hot Tip!**
> Most variable annuities sock it to you with 2.25 percent in annual charges. However fund groups such as Vanguard, Scudder, T.Rowe Price, USAA, Ameritas, Fidelity Investments and Charles Schwab have variable annuities that cost half as much.

Your Own Tax Shelter

In almost all of the retirement programs we've mentioned, even if your investments are not tax-exempt, you always have the advantage of tax deferment. In other words, your retirement account is your very own tax shelter. The savings that tax deferment brings is staggering. For example: Suppose you're in the 28 percent tax bracket and you put $2,000 annually in a tax-deferred account for 20 years and earn 8 percent annually. You end up with $98,846.

If you save the money outside an IRA in a taxable investment, you have just $54,598. That's a big difference!

> **Hot Tip!**
> Call the IRS for free publications on retirement savings rules (800-829-1040). Ask for publication number 560, Retirement Plans For the Self-Employed, and 590, Individual Retirement Arrangements.

How Much Do You Need for Retirement?

Once the rest of your financial house is in top shape, you must figure out how much income you'll need when you retire. As mentioned earlier, you'll probably need about 70 to 80 percent of your current annual income after you retire. That may sound like you're taking a pay cut, but nearly 25 percent of your wages goes to job-related expenses. You'd be surprised how much you spend to look sharp and feel sharp!

Of course, you'll also have to consider your current age and how far away you are from retirement. Add to your current income less 50 percent an inflation factor for each year away from retirement you are.

The Savings Gap

What you might run up against is a gap between your Social Security income and what your pension will pay. It's important to make that up somewhere. Social Security doesn't cover that much. As of 1997, the maximum amount a wage earner at age 65 could receive monthly was $1,326. A widow or widower got the same. If, however, you began to withdraw your money early at age 62 to age 64-1/2, you got a lot less. The most a 62 year-old wage earner could get from Social Security was $1,061 a month. A widow or widower got $751.

> **Hot Tip!**
> It's a good idea to obtain an advance estimate of your benefits by calling the Social Security Administration at 800-772-1213. You also can get a copy at your local Social Security office.

To have an extra $100,000 at retirement, assuming the investment grows at an annual rate of 8 percent, you should save $575 a month over 10 years, $307 a month over 15 years, or $219 a month over 20 years.

Achieving Your Goals

Mutual funds can help you reach your retirement goals. The plan is to have 70 to 80 percent of your current income when you retire. Social Security will pick up some of that. Here are a couple of benchmarks to give you an idea of how much you need and how much you must save. This assumes your retirement savings earns 8 percent and pays you 8 percent annually when you retire.

➤ If you currently make $30,000 a year, you need to accumulate $225,000 in a retirement kitty earning 8 percent a year to pay you $22,500 annually when you reach age 65. Over the next 20 years, if you earn 8 percent annually, you must save $4,917 a year to reach that goal.

➤ If you make $50,000 a year, you need to amass $374,000 to provide you with an annual income of $37,500. Over the next 20 years, you have to save $8,173 a year.

➤ If you currently make $70,000 a year, it will take $523,000 to reach your target annual income of $52,500. Over the next 20 years, you have to save $11,429 a year.

What to Invest In

The longer you have to invest, the more you should invest in stock funds. When you approach and hit retirement, however, you need to save your money.

➤ If you're just starting out in the work world, go for the gusto. You'll be investing for 25 to 30 years, so put 100 percent of your investment dollars in stock funds. Split it up among a small company stock fund, growth and income fund or growth fund, and an international fund.

➤ When you are in your peak earning years and have about 15 years to retirement, you need to think in terms of lower risk. A stock market plunge could put a serious dent in your nest egg, and it may take a longer time to recover. Keep a mix of about 60 percent in a stock fund and 40 percent in a bond fund. On the stock side, invest in a growth fund, growth and income fund, and international fund. On the bond side, split your investments among an intermediate-term bond fund and a money fund.

➤ When you hit those retirement years, keep about 30 percent in a well-managed growth and income fund or growth fund and an international growth and income fund. Invest 55 percent in an income fund that pays high dividend yields and a bond fund. The rest should be invested in a money fund in case you need the cash.

The Least You Need to Know

➤ The earlier you invest, the better. The longer you have to invest, the more you should invest in stock funds; the less time you have, the more you should invest in lower-risk bond and money funds.

➤ The closer you are to retirement, reduce the money you have in stock funds and increase the money you have in bond and money funds.

➤ Financial aid may cover more than 50 percent of college expense.

➤ To make up for the shortfall between what your savings will be worth when you retire and the money you need, start investing now.

Care and Feeding of Your 401(k)

It might be tough to get excited about something called a 401(k). Now, a 280ZX is another story! You'd much rather tell your friends that you put a big chunk of change into your 280ZX, wouldn't you?

You might answer differently, however, if you see what putting your money into a 401(k) could do for you in 30 years—particularly if you know how to manage this type of retirement plan. Although your 280ZX is likely to be in the junkyard by then, your 401(k), if managed properly, can help you retire in style.

This chapter looks at how 401(k) company pension plans work. You'll learn how to invest in one and what to do with this retirement plan once you've finally hung up your spikes.

What Is a 401(k)?

Because the overwhelming majority of Fortune 500 companies and an ever-increasing number of smaller companies now have 401(k) plans, there's a good chance your employer may offer one. What is this animal?

A 401(k) plan—creatively named after an incredibly exciting paragraph in the Internal Revenue Code—is a type of pension plan. In other words, it's a stash of money you sock away for your retirement. It's also known as a salary reduction pension plan because your taxable wages are slashed by the amount you fork over into the plan. All this is terrific! With a 401(k), you get to report less of your wages to the IRS. As we always say, anything you can do so that Uncle Sam takes less of your income is cause for applause.

401(k)s have a few other advantages. For one thing, the money you invest grows, tax-deferred, until you retire. Yet another bonus: Most large companies actually are willing to contribute to your retirement plan at a rate of 25¢ to $1 for each $1 you contribute. Skeptical? Don't be. As you might suspect, there's good reason for this good-heartedness. Your employer gets a tax deduction for contributing to your plan, which, it hopes, also will inspire you to work harder. Now if somebody actually gives you money—particularly your employer—why refuse it?

Of course, there never is a totally free lunch when it comes to taxes. The big bucks we hope you get to take out of your 401(k) when you ultimately retire finally do get taxed as income based on your tax rate. The rest, however, may continue to grow tax-deferred.

Socking It Away

Why are we discussing 401(k)s in a mutual fund book? Your employer can select a variety of investments for your company's 401(k) plan—including stocks, bonds, insurance, real estate, and virtually anything—provided that there are no special restrictions in your state. Nevertheless, mutual funds are becoming the investment of choice for 401(k)s. The Investment Company Institute says that 39 percent or $334 billion of the $857 billion in all 401(k) plans was invested in mutual funds in 1996.

Depending on your employer's plan, you can agree to put up to 25 percent of your annual compensation (or $10,000, whichever is less) into a choice of the investments. If you're lucky enough to have your employer contributing to your retirement, the total contribution still is subject to these limits. However, the overall maximum—including your employer's contribution—swells to 25 percent of your compensation or $30,000, whichever is less. (The maximum you can contribute to a 401(k) is indexed to inflation as measured by the Consumer Price Index, so that $10,000 limit, effective in 1998, could change.)

Can't afford to put away the maximum? Don't worry. You can contribute less. Say you sock a whopping $4,000 a year into your 401(k) and you're in the 28 percent tax bracket: You can write off $1,120 on your income taxes. Now say you invest the 4 grand in your 401(k) plan's mutual funds, and it grows at an 8 percent annual rate tax-deferred over 25 years. Assume your employer kicks in an extra 50¢ for every buck you contribute to your pension. Your money actually grows to more than $474,000 tax-deferred.

Aside from all the tax advantages to a 401(k), you're signing up for an automatic savings plan. Your company automatically will take money out of your paycheck and invest in the investment of your choice. Plus, you benefit from dollar cost averaging, which is discussed in Chapter 17, "Getting Rich a Little at a Time: Dollar Cost Averaging."

If you invest in a 401(k), it's a good idea to review Chapter 6, "Which Funds Are Right for You?," which discusses how to set up different kinds of mutual funds based on your age, risk level, and expectations.

Different Strokes for Different Folks

There are three different types of 401(k) plans:

1. With the *savings* plan, you kick in all the money, and your salary is reduced for tax purposes. But your company contributes zilch. You can decide how much you want to invest in mutual funds up to the allowable limit.

2. By contrast, with the *cash-only* plan, your employer is the only one who pays. You, as an employee, can decide to invest all or part of the money in the 401(k). If you take the cash, you have to report it on your income taxes as wages. But if you have it all invested, it's not taxed.

3. Many larger companies have *thrift* plans. They match 25¢ to $1 for each dollar of your contribution. What you kick into the plan out of your paycheck reduces taxable income.

> **Technobabble**
> A **pension** is a retirement savings plan you get at work. A **401(k)** or **salary reduction plan** is a type of employer-sponsored pension plan that lets employees make contributions out of their pay so that they needn't pay taxes for the year on that income. A **savings** plan is a type of 401(k) plan in which you kick in money but your employer doesn't. A **cash-only** 401(k) plan is one in which the employer kicks in money, not you, and a **thrift** plan is one in which your employer matches your contributions.

Getting Started

The person at your company who is responsible for the pension plan, known as the plan administrator, will give you a lot of information about your 401(k) plan. We know it's boring, but force yourself to read the following stuff on your coffee break. You might as well do it on company time.

➤ A summary description of the pension plan. This spells out all the rules. You'll learn who's eligible to kick money into the pension plan, your benefits, and your investment options.

➤ Tons of important information about the mutual funds you can pick in your plan. You'll get information on your investment options. A fund prospectus explains the investment objectives, risks, fees, and expenses, as well as transaction fees for buying and selling fund shares. (See Chapter 8, "Secrets of Mutual Fund Shopping," for more information.)

After you've read the material, it's up to you to decide how much money to have taken out of your paycheck and which of the plan's investment options to put it in. Assuming you're dealing with a mutual fund family, you'll probably get a report on the value of your plan every three months. If you don't like how your investments are performing or if you're uncomfortable with your level of risk, you can switch.

News You Can Use

Considering investing in a 401(k) plan? There are two important documents your plan is required to generate. Your employer is required to file a Form 5500 with the Department of Labor and the IRS. You can request a copy from your 401(k) plan administrator. From this document, you can learn such information as how much plan money is invested in your employer's real estate or whether your employer is up to any other funny business. You should also be able to see whether any loans or leases are in default or if any plan consultants have quit or been fired during the year. You'll also want to watch your annual report which shows how much is put into your account and how much is taken out.

To qualify for a 401(k) plan, you must have compensation. The maximum amount of time an employer can keep you out of a 401(k) plan generally is one year. However, there's nothing to prevent your employer from putting you into the plan earlier if he or she wants to.

How Should You Invest Your 401(k)?

If you're among the lucky ducks with a 401(k) pension plan, you probably already know all too well that the newest wave of plans leaves the investment responsibility up to you. Most plans give you a variety of choices so you can split up your investments to get the best return with the least amount of risk.

Chapter 23, "Saving for Important Life Goals," shows how much you can safely invest in stock and bond funds in your retirement account based on your age and when you expect to retire. As a rule of thumb, the younger you are, the more you should invest in stock funds for growth. When you are nearing retirement, you want to preserve what you have, so you invest safely in your 401(k) money funds and bond funds and a tad in stock funds.

First, examine the mutual funds in your 401(k) plan. You'll want to own a mutual fund that invests in stocks, one that invests in bonds, and one that invests in cash or securities of 90 days or less. The younger you are, the more aggressive you'll be in your investments. As you get older and you need money to live on, you don't want to take quite as much risk. Then, it's best to keep more in the bond fund or money fund than the stock fund.

Someone with 10 years or more to invest who doesn't need income from the investments could have 70 percent in stock funds, 20 percent in income funds (which are bond funds or high-yielding stock-funds), and 10 percent in money funds, suggests the American Association of Retired Persons. By contrast, those who are retired and have a 3 to 10 year investment horizon should have about 20 percent in stock funds, 60 percent in income funds, and 20 percent in money funds.

If you pick a stock fund, choose one that has performed as well or better than the average stock fund over the past five or 10 years. If you don't expect your fund to hit a home run, you'll be fine.

If your plan has other investments besides mutual funds, it's important to apply similar principles of diversification to those investments. Make certain you don't have too much in stocks, bonds, or real estate. Avoid having all your plan's holdings in a couple of stocks.

Also, don't put your entire investment into one geographic area. You don't want to own too much of your company stock. Otherwise, if anything happens to your company, both your retirement plan and job can take a pretty heavy hit!

If this strategy all sounds complicated to you, we suspect that's because financial service professionals aggressively are looking for business. There's nothing wrong with getting some help if you need it. (Refer to Chapter 7, "The Cost of Investing.") Just watch what you're paying for it.

Chapters 18 through 22 show you some ways to manage your retirement money so you can limit your losses and let your profits run.

Unfortunately, financial planners say even some of the most knowledgeable people around are failing to respond to their plan administrator about how they want the money invested.

Money Matters

We've already told you about many of the mutual fund fees you can get hit with in Chapter 7. With a 401(k) plan, your company might be paying people and buying supplies to help administer the plan. Although companies frequently pay these costs, an increasing number are financing them with employees' money in 401(k) plans.

The Labor Department requires only that your company's 401(k) fees and commissions be "reasonable." To find how much your plan is shelling out for running it, check out item 32 of Form 5500, add all the expenses, and divide that figure by the plan's total assets. Don't forget to consider loads and fees charged by the investment company you're dealing with.

What happens if you have a 401(k) plan and you fail to determine where to invest your money? It generally goes automatically into a low-yielding money market fund paying around 5 percent. With just a little action, it could be in a stock fund with the potential of growing at a 10 to 12 percent annual rate over the next couple of decades. Say your money stays in the plan for 20 years. Your negligence might cost you a whopping $160,000!

News You Can Use

Many 401(k) pensions offer stable value funds, issued by insurance companies. These funds pay fixed rates of about 6 percent to 7 percent today. They are guaranteed against losses by the insurance companies that issue them. Insurance companies invest in corporate bonds rated A to AAA by Standard & Poor's and other investments that are privately guaranteed. You can switch money out of your stable value funds without penalty into most of your other 401(k)'s mutual funds.

Regardless of which route you take, don't just let your 401(k) money sit there. Do something!

401(k) Fraud

Although most 401(k) plans are great deals, the Department of Labor's Pension and Welfare Benefits Administration (PWBA) anti-fraud department encourages you to keep an eye out for these trouble signs that your 401(k) might not be all it's cracked up to be:

➤ Your 401(k) or individual account statement is consistently late or arrives at irregular intervals.

➤ Your account balance appears inaccurate.

➤ Your employer fails to transmit your contribution to the plan on a timely basis.

➤ You notice a significant drop in the account balance that can't be explained by normal market ups and downs.

➤ Your 401(k) or individual account statement shows that your paycheck contribution wasn't made.

➤ Investments listed on your statement aren't the ones you authorized.

➤ Former employees are having trouble getting their benefits paid on time or in the correct amounts.

➤ You notice unusual transactions, such as a loan to your employer, a corporate officer, or one of the plan trustees.

➤ There are frequent and unexplained changes in the investment managers or consultants.

If you think anyone responsible for investing your money may be violating some rules, call or write the nearest field office of the U.S. Department of Labor's Pension and Welfare Benefits Administration. Cases of embezzlement, stealing pension money, kickbacks, or extortion should be reported to the FBI or Labor Department field office in your area.

If you suspect anyone providing services to the plan has taken advantage of this relationship—through making loans, for example—the Employee Plans Division of the Internal Revenue Service is who you contact. You could be eligible for an IRS "informants' reward" of up to 10 percent of any amount the IRS collects if you also file a written claim with the IRS Intelligence Division. Meanwhile, it's illegal for an employer to fire or retaliate against an employee who provides the government with information about a 401(k)'s investment practices.

Remember: This is your retirement! It's important not to fall asleep at the wheel. Particularly if your employer is contributing to the plan, you want to make certain you get everything you deserve. Monitor all your statements, and make certain all information is correct. Any questions? Contact your plan administrator. Most importantly, make certain your company has the correct personal information about you, including your birthdate and Social Security number.

You also want to ensure that your company keeps its end of the bargain in making contributions. Double-check whether the balance in your account is accurate. Particularly if your company merges, you need to watch that your contributions continue to get credited properly.

> **Hot Tip!**
> For more information on 401(k) plans, pick up *The Complete Idiot's Guide to 401(k) Plans* (Alpha Books). You might also check out the free publications offered by the Pension and Welfare Benefits Administration of the U.S. Department of Labor, 202-219-8776 or online at http://www.dol.gov/dol/pwba/.

Getting Vested

If you work long enough in one place and are fully vested, you can make out like a bandit with your 401(k). You get to keep all the money your company kicked into your plan. That can be a hefty sum over the years. If you fly the coop, you can take the money and run.

You always get to keep any money you contribute to your own 401(k) plan—even if you bid adios to your company. However, if you want to leave and take the dough your employer contributed, it's a different story.

Your employer is required to choose between two rules—known as *vesting schedules*. Of course, a good-hearted employer can always agree to turn over the company's contribution in less time than the rules specify. But here are the worst-case scenarios:

> ➤ A company can require you to work there for at least five years before you're *fully vested*. Those fancy words indicate that at that time, all the money contributed by your employer in the pension belongs to you.

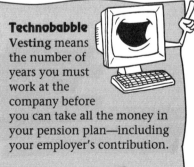

> **Technobabble**
> **Vesting** means the number of years you must work at the company before you can take all the money in your pension plan—including your employer's contribution.

➤ The other option your employer can offer is that after 3 years of service, you're 20 percent vested. Each year, you get to keep a little more, until after 7 years, 100 percent of the money your company contributed to your 401(k) belongs to you.

It works this way: Say you've been working as a hit man for Murder Inc. for three years. You decide you're not cut out for this line of work. Bugsy, your boss, has been kicking in a half a buck for every buck you put in the Murder Inc. pension plan. You have $150,000 salted way in the Smoking Guns Growth Stock Fund, including Bugsy's contribution. Now, you want to leave and take those big bucks with you.

Your own contributions into the plan are worth $25,000. The rest is Bugsy's dough. Because Murder Inc. is on the 7-year vesting plan, you can take 20 percent of Bugsy's $50,000 contributions or $10,000 along with your 100 grand. But say you decide to stick it out at Murder Inc. until you are fully vested. Then, 100 percent of the dough is yours when you get another job in a safer line of work.

News You Can Use

Some 401(k) pension plans let you call a special number 24 hours a day to check on your pension account balance. Others are starting to provide information online. However, unlike most mutual funds, which let you switch funds whenever you want within a family, 401(k) plans often don't let you switch more frequently than quarterly and sometimes twice a year.

Calling It Quits

It takes some fancy footwork to take your pension with you if you change jobs or retire. If you change jobs, you can have your 401(k) pension transferred to your new company's plan. Or you can leave it with your old plan until you retire. (Please don't forget about it!)

If you are leaving your company but you don't immediately have a new job, you should transfer the money in your 401(k) into what's known as a "conduit IRA." This acts as a temporary holding place for your money. If you transfer the money into a regular IRA, it's required to stay there, and you won't be able to transfer the money to your new company's pension plan.

A word to the wise: Don't mix this 401(k) money with your personal IRA. Comingling eliminates your opportunity to:

1. Transfer into your new 401(k)
2. Take advantage of lump sum distribution treatment at retirement

If you're leaving to take a job at a new company, you have the option to move your money to your new company's 401(k) plan or leave it at your old company.

If you decide to move it to your new company's 401(k), don't take possession of the money! You'll be subject to a 20 percent withholding tax, which you won't get back until after you file your income tax. Plus, you'll just have 60 days to open an new account. Miss that 60-day deadline, and you'll owe taxes on the full amount! To avoid this problem, it's best to have your company directly transfer the money to your new account. Then, you have no withholding and no 60-day window to invest.

In Case of Emergency...

The bad part about a 401(k) is that the people who drafted this law don't want you to withdraw from this plan until you're at least 59 1/2 years old. There are some circumstances in which Uncle Sam may cut you a break.

You're allowed to access your money in the event of a hardship, if your company is sold, death, disability, and separation from service. However, you'll pay taxes on the amount withdrawn.

Hardships include paying for educational expenses, medical expenses, or preventing eviction or foreclosure on your home. The 10 percent IRS penalty may be waived if you die, you're disabled, or you use the money to pay tax-deductible medical expenses.

However, a representative at the IRS told us that if you claim a hardship, you had better be prepared to document that you've exhausted all your resources.

Keep in mind that if you do take a hardship withdrawal, 20 percent of the money is withheld for income taxes. You should get this money back when you file your tax return—assuming you remember to file the proper form.

Borrowing from Yourself

Need cash to pay off those holiday debts? Your 401(k) plan could provide a lower-cost option than borrowing from your bank—that is, provided you have a sizable nest egg and you definitely plan to pay back the money.

In fact, "plan loans are a good way to provide for a child's college expenses, a housing downpayment, or any other family need," says Peter Bernstein, author of the *Ernst & Young Tax Savers Guide*, John Wiley & Sons, New York.

Unfortunately, there are downsides to what may otherwise seem like a good deal. If you borrow from your pension plan, you could wind up answering to the IRS if you don't pay back the loan in the time required. Not only could you find yourself stuck paying income taxes on the loan amount, but you also could get stocked with a 10 percent IRS penalty!

Most plans let you borrow up to half of the balance in your pension plan to a limit of $50,000. If you're borrowing less than $10,000, you may borrow more than half of your plan's balance.

With a pension plan loan, you generally pay a variable rate, pegged at one to two percentage points above the prime rate. Prime currently is running 8.50 percent, so your pension loan is apt to cost around 10.50 percent. By contrast, credit cards are charging more than 15 percent. Although the pension loan rate is set by your plan administrator—generally your employer—it typically is slightly less than the collateralized loan rates offered by most banks. You also may be charged up-front fees for the loan as well as an annual fee. (More reasons not to borrow on your retirement plan.)

If you must take a loan on your pension plan, simply talk to your plan administrator and fill out the appropriate forms. In a few days, you should get a check.

Except for a home loan, you're typically required to pay back a loan against a pension plan over five years. You agree to a repayment schedule that requires you make level payments at least every three months.

The good news, Bernstein says, is that depending upon the terms of your plan, the interest you pay probably goes back to your account rather than to the plan administrator or financial institution.

If you're still working, you can have money taken out of your paycheck to pay off your pension plan loan. However, if you are retired and the money is invested with your company, you'll have to make the payments out of your own pocket. Can you deduct the pension fund loan interest on your taxes? Not if you borrow the money for personal reasons or use it to pay off other loans. However, you can deduct the loan interest from your income taxes if you use the money to make investments or to purchase or improve your main or second home. To qualify for this tax deduction, you must put up your home, property, or investments as collateral, warns Dee Lee, a Harvard, Massachusetts certified financial planner.

Pension plan loans have a few other drawbacks. Besides the risk of a 10 percent penalty and additional income tax charges if you fail to pay back the loan as scheduled, you're also in trouble if you lose your job. Once that happens, you have 30 days to pay back your pension plan loan. Otherwise, you guessed it: You get socked with income tax on the loan and the 10 percent IRS fine. Most financial experts will tell you not to borrow from your pension plan at all because you are mortgaging your future. Why take money out of the only nest egg you might have when you grow older?

Time for Retirement

When you reach age 59 1/2 and you retire, you can begin taking your retirement stash penalty-free, but you'll owe taxes on the amount withdrawn. Unlike an IRA, you don't have to begin withdrawing your 401(k) when you hit age 70 1/2—provided that you're still working.

If you retire and you have a 401(k), it's also a good idea to transfer the money into what is called a rollover IRA, which is separate and unaffected by any contribution you might have made to a regular IRA. You open it specifically to transfer your pension account for a couple of tax-smart reasons.

With a rollover IRA, you avoid an automatic 20 percent withholding tax that ordinarily kicks in when you withdraw money from your 401(k) pension. That 20 percent tax is on top of income taxes on your retirement pay. If you're in the 28 percent tax bracket, the tax man taxes 48 percent of your pay. The IRS rules are a weird breed. At the end of the year, you'll get the 20 percent withholding refunded to you—assuming you remember to fill out the right forms on your tax return.

With a rollover IRA, you escape the 20 percent withholding tax. You'll pay taxes on the check you receive from your IRA each month. However, the remaining money in your IRA grows tax-deferred. Once you roll over the money into an IRA, you can start receiving your retirement pay a couple of different ways, based on your life expectancy. (You'll read more about this in Chapter 25, "Making Your Money Last as Long as You Do.")

Financial planners say that if you're at least 50 years old on January 1, 1986, it could pay to take advantage of a rule that lets you cash out your 401(k). This rule is particularly attractive if you have the cash to pay the tax and you're a sophisticated investor that can earn more than 10 percent annually by investing that money. The rule lets you use what's known as 10-year income averaging to pay your taxes. You can pay taxes on the money as if you receive equal amounts of income over 10 years. Nevertheless, few people cash out their pensions and use income averaging. Someone in the 28 percent tax bracket would owe Uncle Sam $28,000 if he cashed out a $100,000 401(k).

To avoid problems with the IRS's convoluted rules, you may have your employer transfer the 401(k) directly to the institution where you want to invest. That way, you avoid the 20 percent withholding tax as well as any other tax problems.

You simply fill out an account application with your bank, mutual fund, or brokerage firm. You also fill out a transfer form. Your financial services company will arrange for your money to be transferred. It usually takes about a week. If you haven't been notified of the transfer after 7 days, call the institution.

Money Matters

Do not accept a distribution check written to you, thinking that you'll deposit the money into the rollover IRA. If you do, that pesky 20 percent withholding-tax rule kicks in. Plus, if you fail to put the money into the IRA within 60 days, you'll pay income taxes on the entire kit and caboodle.

Alphabet Retirement Soup

Talk about choices! Could the people who wrote the tax laws possibly make it more complicated for us working folks? You got your 401(k), IRAs, and Roth IRAs. Which is the best deal? If you have a 401(k), can you invest in any other types of retirement accounts? Think there's a simple answer? Nope! We'll break it down for you.

Before you do anything, it's generally best to sock away as much money as you can in your 401(k) plan. Your wages are reduced by the amount you contribute, so you pay less taxes. Plus, your employer usually kicks in some extra money. You don't want to miss out on that deal.

Next, consider either a traditional IRA or Roth IRA—depending upon which you qualify for and whether you need the deduction now or later in life. (Refer to Chapter 20, "Retirement Savings Strategies for the Faint Hearted.") As you recall, either one lets you contribute a maximum of $2,000 annually. But with a traditional IRA, your tax-deductible contributions start getting cut if you already have a pension plan, such as a 401(k) and you make between $30,000 and $40,000 in 1998. That income cut-off, however, was scheduled to increase in subsequent years. Married folks' IRA deductions are phased out between $50,000 and $60,000 in 1998.

With a Roth IRA, your contribution is not tax-deductible at all. But provided that you're 59 1/2 and you have held it 5 years, you can take out your money and pay zilch to the tax man forever after. Plus, even if you have a company pension plan, including a 401(k), you still can have a Roth IRA.

Money Matters
You can't put money in both a Roth and traditional IRA at the same time and get the full tax benefits.

Some people who make big bucks might not be able to get a full deduction of 2 grand in the Roth IRA. If you file a joint tax return, the contributions are phased out if you have an adjusted gross income of between $150,000 to $160,000 a year. Have you already contributed as much as you possibly can to take advantage of all these tax-advantaged instruments? Annuities, tax-efficient mutual funds, and municipal bond funds are other investments that can help you cut taxes.

The Least You Need to Know

➤ 401(k) pensions let you sock away big bucks.

➤ Your taxable income is reduced by your 401(k) contributions, leading to lower taxes.

➤ Many 401(k)s let you invest in mutual funds.

➤ You can borrow from your 401(k) if you need a loan.

➤ You can stretch out your retirement pay.

Making Your Money Last as Long as You Do

"Where's the chapter on how to win the state lottery?" you ask. Sorry. We're staying away from the subject of lotteries.

Nevertheless, your question is understandable when you consider that one of every four persons at least 65 years old today will live into his or her 90s. By the time Generation Xers retire around 2050, almost everyone in the United States could be living into his or her 90s. With this book, we've tried to help you understand how to make money with mutual funds. But because so many of you could have a retirement that goes into extra innings, we've decided to add a final chapter on how to retire comfortably.

Consider what follows the Saran wrap of our book. Now that we've taught you to make money in mutual funds, this chapter shows you a slew of ways to preserve it!

Yes, there is some hope for us all besides winning the state lottery. It boils down to analyzing exactly how much money you'll need when you finally call a halt to the daily grind. Then, you need to figure out how much you already should have based on your current assets, future earnings, pensions, and Social Security.

How Much Money Will You Need?

The good news about retirement is that you'll be saving a few bucks when you hang up your spikes. You probably won't spend money commuting to work any more. Plus, your entertainment, clothing, and tax expenses may decrease. You've probably paid off your mortgage and life insurance. That's a nice bundle of cash you won't need to shell out any more.

Unfortunately, however, medical expenses may take a growing chunk of your budget. As it currently stands, after you hit age 65, Medicare will take care of many of your bills, including hospital bills, nursing home care, in-patient and outpatient services, and more.

You'll also be spending more on leisure activities, such as travel. In addition, the cost of fuel, food, and clothing probably will continue to rise, due to inflation.

News You Can Use

Many experts predict that as the population ages and Social Security benefits decline, more seniors will opt to work part-time to make ends meet. In fact, a 1997 USA Today/CNN/Gallup poll of 77 million Americans born between 1946 and 1964 indicated that three quarters actually would choose to continue working. How do you feel about working after retirement? It may be worth exploring. After all, if you can generate a little extra income, your investments don't have to work so hard.

It's a good idea to pinpoint exactly where your retirement dollars will go; the following worksheet will help you figure it out.

Your housing costs, including insurance, utilities, taxes, rent, or mortgage, should be 30 percent of your income or less when you retire. Figure that the cost of just about everything will rise about 3.5 percent per year. Each year, multiply your annual expenses by 1.35 to give you an estimate of how much more things will cost you in the future when you retire.

Expenses During Retirement as a Percentage of Your Income

Food: 15%	_____	
Housing: 30%	_____	Health Care: Varies _____
Transportation: 10%	_____	(but may make up a large part of your expenses)
Insurance: Varies	_____	Taxes: Vary _____
Entertainment: Varies	_____	Debts: Vary _____

How Much Money Will You Have?

In the olden days, Americans counted on Social Security to see them through their retirement years. Unfortunately, as we've noted elsewhere in this book, the future of Social Security is questionable. For the purposes of this chapter, we assume that you will collect Social Security when you retire.

The Social Security Administration estimates that Social Security will cover about 25 percent of your income if you averaged $60,000 annually during your working years. Another 20 percent will come from your pension, and a whopping 30 percent will come either from working after you retire or other sources of investment income. Keep in mind that the more money you make, the lower the proportion that Social Security income will replace.

Today, you can collect 80 percent of your Social Security when you're 62 years old. If you wait until age 65, you will collect the full amount. Those born after 1943, however, won't be able to take full Social Security pay until they hit age 66. Those born after 1960 won't tap their full benefits until age 67.

Provided that you've socked away money in your company pension plan, a variable annuity or IRA, and other investments, as we've suggested in earlier chapters, you should have the resources you need to live.

News You Can Use

Obtain an advance estimate of your benefits by calling the Social Security Administration at 800-937-2000 and requesting form SSA-7004. You also can get a copy at your local Social Security office.

Keep in mind that you might have to work longer, and Congress might cut back on Social Security benefits over the next couple of decades.

Once you do that, you can insulate your retirement with a couple other cushions. For one thing, insurance companies are coming out with new longevity investments and insurance policies that guarantee your income for a lifetime. (More about that later in this chapter.) Sure, insurance is expensive, but as we write this, costs are coming down and new, sexier insurance investment options are being introduced.

Plus, once you know the ropes, you can stretch out the length of time over which you withdraw your 401(k) and IRA money. By doing this, not only do you keep your cash out of the tentacles of Uncle Sam for a longer period, but you also keep your money invested during that period. There also are ways to take systematic withdrawals from your taxable accounts so that they continue to grow in value while you get the cash you need to pay your expenses.

You can stock up on life and health insurance coverage to keep doctors, hospitals, and nursing homes from taking all your money.

Now, you've nailed down about how much you should get from Social Security. Total up how much you'll be able to collect from your other retirement savings accounts—including IRAs, company pensions, annuities, and life insurance. Plus, add in the reams of other investment income we hope you'll have by now. Use the following worksheet to help you make these calculations.

Annual Income from Retirement Assets

IRA or Pension	$_____
Annuity	$_____
Other Savings	$_____
Real Estate	$_____
Life Insurance Cash Value	$_____
Trust Assets	$_____
Social Security	$_____
Total	$_____

Retirees Still Need to Invest

Even though retirees should preserve what they have, you still need to keep investing when you retire, or you could run out of bucks pretty fast. The rule of thumb is the longer you have to invest, the more you should have in stocks or stock funds. If you're in your 60s, you still need the growth to help your assets keep pace with inflation.

Earlier in this book, we told you that historically, stocks and bonds perform better than CDs. Stocks have grown at about 7 percent more than the inflation rate over the years. Bonds historically have grown at about a 5 percent annual rate. T-bills, money funds, and short-term bank CDs have grown at about 3 percent. Inflation has logged in at around 3 percent.

Of course, there's no guarantee that this trend will continue, and once you get well into your 80s and 90s, you need to concentrate on keeping what you have. You should have less invested in stocks and more in less-risky income-producing investments such as CDs, Treasury bonds, and utility stocks or annuities. If your need for income is low and you have 10 years to invest, you should keep at least 70 percent in a well-managed stock fund, 20 percent invested for income in a bond fund, and 10 percent in a money fund.

What if you need your principal over the next three years? You might consider keeping 50 percent in a money fund, 50 percent in a bond fund, and zero in stock funds.

Remember: We told you in earlier chapters that you can get some of the growth you need from mutual funds that invest in common stocks. On the other hand, you get the income from bonds, bond funds, annuities, utility stocks, or municipal bond funds.

News You Can Use

It's always a good idea to keep some of your investments in at least a good growth and income fund. Funds we like that carry top ratings from Morningstar Inc., Chicago, and Value Line, New York, include:

➤ Vanguard S&P 500 Fund, which invests in the 500 largest companies traded on the New York Stock Exchange.

➤ AARP Growth and Income Fund, which invests in large company stocks that pay high-dividend yields.

➤ Scudder Growth and Income Fund, which also invests in high-yielding, dividend-paying stocks.

➤ T. Rowe Price Equity Income Fund, which also invests in stocks that pay high dividends.

➤ Invesco Industrial Income, which also invests in rock solid companies.

Whatever you choose to invest in, we can't stress enough how important it is to diversify your mutual funds—particularly when you retire. Also, be sure to have some money in cash.

In late 1994 and early 1995, many retirees who invested only in bonds, bond funds, or income funds saw the market values of their investments decline as much as 10 percent. These people got hit with the dreaded double whammy feared most by most mutual fund investors. Already out of the work force, they were forced to withdraw from their retirement accounts when the poorly performing stock and bond markets drove down the value of their investments. Needless to say, there were a lot of unhappy campers in those years.

If you ever get into this unfortunate situation, do not panic. Historically, the markets have bounced back. If you have cash available, you might consider restructuring your mutual fund holdings so that you don't have too much of your money in one particular type of fund.

Tapping Your Mutual Funds for Monthly Income

Meanwhile, you can do several other things to make your money last as long as you. The first thing is to figure out how much you can take out of all your investments each year and still have cash left over.

Most people don't want to touch their principal when they retire. They want to live off their interest and dividend income. But if you must tap principal, you still can boost your income—as long as your investments are growing at an attractive rate of return.

The following figure shows you how long your money will last, assuming your investments earn a certain rate and you withdraw a certain rate.

Match up your annual withdrawal rate on the left with the rate of return your investment is earning on the right. Where they meet represents the number of years your money will last. For example, if you withdraw 6 percent and your money earns 5 percent, the money should last 36 years. If you don't see a number in the little box, it means the money will last forever. For example, if you withdraw 4 percent and your money earns a 5 percent rate of return, it will last forever!

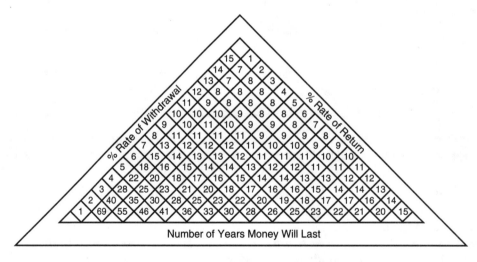

How long your money will last at a given rate of withdrawal.

Look at 80 year-old Aunt Minnie. In addition to her Social Security and pension, she has about $100,000 in investments and savings. She continually worries about the 100 grand, so she invests in a safe place that pays her 6 percent interest. If she withdraws 7 percent of the money each year, she will receive $7,000 a year, or $583 a month. Because the money keeps growing at 6 percent, it will last a whopping 33 years. We hope Aunt Minnie lives that long!

If she took out 8 percent a year, the money would last 30 years. She could safely get $667 a month from this stash.

If Minnie takes out 5 percent of her stash, her money will last indefinitely.

Today, most stock funds sport dividend yields of just 1 to 3 percent. When you retire, you will receive those dividends, plus any capital gains. However, that doesn't go very far.

Another often-overlooked option is to take *systematic withdrawals* from your stock funds. That means you automatically have your mutual fund company sell shares of your fund each month and send you a check. The money comes out of three parts of the fund—your principal, dividends, and capital gains.

You can have the fund send you a check monthly. Or you can have the money automatically deposited into your checking account or your money market mutual fund.

If you have money deposited into your checking account, be sure it pays you interest. Have the money deposited at the beginning of every month. That way, you'll earn interest—although granted, it's not much nowadays—on the deposited money from the very first day of the month.

Because stocks have grown historically at a 10 percent annual rate, most financial planners suggest that you take 5 percent to 6 percent a year in monthly amounts out of your stock funds. But you can always call an investment company and make an adjustment. In bad years, when the fund is doing poorly, you can take less out. In good years, you can take more.

Keep in mind, however, that because your money isn't in a retirement savings account, you'll pay taxes on the trades when you cash out and have the money sent to you.

Hot Tip!
Worried about not leaving enough money for your loved ones when you're not around? You can tap some of your principal and still have plenty left over for your heirs. Enjoy yourself. You can't take it with you!

Technobabble
You make a **systematic withdrawal** when you sell a certain percentage or dollar amount of your mutual fund, typically every month.

We plan to do this with some of our mutual funds that we have invested outside our IRA if we need extra cash when we retire. If we have an extra $100,000, we expect to get an extra $500 a month from this stash. If our fund grows at around 10 percent a year, we figure we should do just fine.

Systematic Withdrawal in Action

Let's see how a systematic withdrawal worked from an actual stock fund based on past performance. We've given the fund an assumed name because we don't want to recommend it over other good funds that can do the same thing. Nevertheless, this example gives you an idea how all this complicated financial stuff works.

Let's assume that Jake retired at the end of 1973 and put a $100,000 lump sum into the Long Life Stock Fund. Also assume he withdrew $500 a month (6 percent annually) from the fund for his retirement.

Jake passed away in 1994, but he was a good family man and lived a long and fruitful life. Over 20 years ending in December 1993, he withdrew $120,000 in total from his stash. He paid himself $6,000 a year from his original $100,000 kitty. But by year-end 1993, the total value of his investment was worth $158,767. Jake's savings still grew because the investment continued to grow at an annually compounded rate of return of 7.55 percent—even though he took money out of the account monthly! Of course, there's no guarantee that the stock market always will do this well. Then again, it also could do better!

News You Can Use

To help you determine how much to withdraw from your savings and investments upon retirement, examine your life expectancy. Use these American Council of Life Insurance guidelines to help you figure out how much longer you're apt to live:

➤ At age 60, a male is expected to live another 18 years. A female should live another 23 years.

➤ At age 65, a male is expected to live 14 years. A female should live 19 years.

➤ At age 70, a male is expected to live 12 years. A female should live 16 years.

➤ At age 75, a male is expected to live 9 years. A female should live 12 years.

Here's an idea of how long your money—regardless of how much you have—should last if you take 6 percent annually out of your investment and the remainder continues to grow at the follow rates of return:

➤ At a 4 percent annual return, your money will last 28 years.

➤ At a 5 percent annual return, your money will last 36 years.

➤ At a 6 percent annual return and above, the money will last infinitely.

Which Funds Are Good for Withdrawals?

What kind of mutual funds make good systematic withdrawal candidates?

You want to take your withdrawals from a well-managed growth fund, growth and income fund, or equity income fund. These funds tend to invest in well-seasoned blue-chip companies that pay high dividend yields.

At the time of this writing, the typical growth and income fund sported a dividend yield of 4 percent. With a growth and income fund, you're likely to see more of your monthly income come from the dividends compared with a growth fund. That's a good deal because it means you won't be withdrawing as much of your principal as you might with other types of funds.

Although you also may be taking out less principal from higher-yielding equity income or income funds, which we talked about in Chapter 4, "Mutual Funds for Everyone," keep in mind that those types of funds may not provide the growth of capital over the years that a growth fund or growth and income fund provides. So your money may not be worth as much over the long haul.

Money Matters
Stay away from lower-yielding bond and money market funds if you use systematic withdrawals. You get less growth from these investments, so you might end up taking out more of your principal than you bargained for.

Take Your Retirement Money and Run

Once you reach your retirement years, you finally get to take out all the pension money you worked so hard to save. Of course, Uncle Sam sure doesn't make this easy! Your objective, assuming you can ever figure out the IRS's strict and convoluted rules, generally is to withdraw as little as possible so that more of your nest egg grows tax-deferred for as long as possible. After all, the less you fork over to Uncle Sam, the more money you have available to grow.

Hot Tip!
It's best to consider systematic withdrawals from your mutual fund only if you expect you'll be able to take them over at least 10 years. A couple of bad years can cause the value of your nest egg to drop like a rock—particularly if you're pulling out another 6 percent annually! You want to make certain you have plenty of time to make back those losses.

As discussed in Chapter 24, "Care and Feeding of Your 401(k)," most people roll their 401(k) pension into an IRA. Otherwise, 20 percent of distributions are withheld for income taxes. So some people may have big bucks in their IRAs. The IRS requires retirees to begin withdrawing money from an IRA or 401(k) by April 1 of the year after they hit age 70 1/2—not age 70, mind you! If your withdrawals or distributions are less than IRS rules permit, Uncle Sam hits you with a 50 percent excise tax on the shortfall.

There are a number of ways to handle these wrinkles. Naming the right beneficiary or person to automatically inherit your IRA is the first step. (See Chapter 26, "Managing Your Estate.") Financial planners warn you not to name your estate, a trust, or charity as the sole IRA beneficiary. The reason: If you die before the date you're required to start withdrawing your stash, all the IRA money must be paid out in one shot. That means, based on the wisdom of the IRS, that all of the income tax is due by the end of the fifth calendar year following the year you die.

There are two basic ways to take your IRA pay. These methods also apply to your 401(k) company pension plan or other profit sharing plans where you make tax-deductible contributions:

➤ **Fixed payment method.** All the money must be withdrawn out of your IRA or retirement plan based on your life expectancy. For example, someone age 71 has a life expectancy of 15 years, according to IRS life expectancy tables. In year one, one-fifteenth of your money is withdrawn. Assuming you have $100,000 in your retirement kitty, you'd have to withdraw $6,536. Ten years later, you would take $18,868 out of your IRA. By the time you hit age 86, you would have deleted most of your account. If you want more retirement income, use this method.

➤ **Recalculation method.** With this technique, you get an extra few years for your money to grow tax-deferred, which can be great! Every year, you get to recalculate your life expectancy based upon the IRS tables. This means less is taken out of your kitty because each year you live, the IRS figures you'll be around an extra few more years. The same 71-year-old would withdraw $6,536 from his or her IRA in the first year. But in year 10, the amount is $11,236. By the time the 71-year-old reaches age 86, she can still rely on a few years of tax-deferred IRA income.

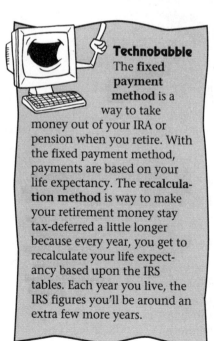

Technobabble
The **fixed payment method** is a way to take money out of your IRA or pension when you retire. With the fixed payment method, payments are based on your life expectancy. The **recalculation method** is way to make your retirement money stay tax-deferred a little longer because every year, you get to recalculate your life expectancy based upon the IRS tables. Each year you live, the IRS figures you'll be around an extra few more years.

Say you name a spouse as beneficiary. Another strange IRS rule kicks in. If you die before you are required to take distribution, your spouse can wait until the date you would have reached 70 1/2 to do it. This way, the payments can be stretched out over your surviving spouse's life expectancy.

A better option if one spouse is significantly younger than the other, say some financial planners, might be for the surviving wife or husband instead to treat the IRA as his or her own. This way, he or she gets to defer taking distributions until age 70 1/2. Example: Jack dies at age 69. His 62-year-old wife, Mary, can claim the IRA as her own and avoid taking distributions for more than 8 years—until age 70 1/2. This way, she also gets to name another person as a beneficiary to the IRA.

Most people leave their retirement savings to their spouses. Widows or widowers typically leave the money to their children or grandchildren. If you are married or have a younger beneficiary, the IRS lets you base payouts on a joint life expectancy using the younger person. Then, you can recalculate the joint life expectancy each year.

Because one person is younger, the joint life expectancy is greater. You get to take less money out of the IRA. Unfortunately, the IRS limits that age difference to 10 years. So if you happen to be 70 3/4 years old, forget the idea of naming your one-year-old grandchild as joint beneficiary. He or she would have to be 60 3/4 under IRS payout rules.

News You Can Use

Most people name their spouses as beneficiaries of their IRAs. Then, they take IRA payments based on the recalculation of their joint life expectancy. This not only extends the number of years for distribution, but also keeps more of your money tax-deferred longer.

However, if your wife or husband is in lousy health, experts say, you might be better off using the fixed payment method. If you're both using the recalculation method on your IRA over a joint life expectancy and your spouse happens to pass away first, your IRA distributions become based on your life expectancy alone. Plus, when you finally die, all of your retirement funds must be distributed to your beneficiary in just one year—zapping that poor heir with a whopping tax bill!

Say you have $200,000 in an IRA and your beneficiary is your daughter who is in the 28 percent tax bracket. She would owe the IRS 28 percent of $200,000 or a staggering $56,000 at tax time.

On the other hand, had you opted for the fixed payment method, you would receive higher annual payments from your IRA. But your beneficiary would be able to take payouts based on his or her life expectancy rather than take it all within a year of your death.

Do as the Romans Did: Annuities

Another way to lock into some guaranteed income for life is through an immediate annuity.

Annuities have been around since Roman times. Yes, even the Romans retired after working to keep the coliseum bright and shiny for the next chariot race. Today, there are contracts with insurance companies that let you get income for a lifetime.

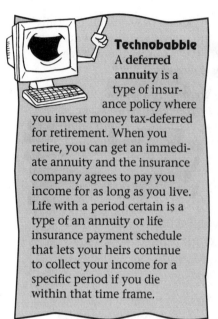

With an immediate annuity, you give the insurance company your money in a lump sum. In return, it pays you income for as long as you live. If you live to be 200, you still collect. The biggest drawback with an immediate annuity is that once you sign the contract, you can't change your mind. Although you can collect for a lifetime, the insurance company pockets your money when you die unless you agree otherwise.

If you want to make certain your heirs get some part of the investment, you can select a life policy with a period certain payout option for a specific term that normally runs 5 or 10 years. This means you continue to get payments for as long as you live, but if you die within the term you select, your heirs collect for the rest of the term. Of course, if you die after the term expires, your heirs get nothing. That's why you might not want to put your entire life savings into one of these things.

Then, you get to choose from a *fixed* or *variable immediate* annuity. With a fixed immediate annuity, the insurance company will pay you a fixed amount for a long as you live. With a variable immediate annuity, you select a mix of mutual funds and your monthly income payments are based upon their return. If the mutual funds perform well, you stand a chance of earning more income from the annuity compared with the fixed annuity. If they tank, you get less each month—although insurance companies generally set a guaranteed minimum return, so you should at least get something.

Immediate annuities haven't been a big hit with consumers. It's no wonder. The whole thing is so darn confusing!

Immediate annuities have one other major benefit. You only pay taxes on that part of the income that represents earnings.

Of course, as with any other investments that sound too good to be true, immediate annuities have their drawbacks:

➤ The greatest problem: Although this insurance instrument promises you income for life, unfortunately (or fortunately), you don't know when you're going to die. If you die before you get back all your principal and earnings in the form of periodic payments, the insurance company pockets the balance of your investment—that is, unless you select a period certain policy that allows you to designate a beneficiary. Even then, the period for which that beneficiary can collect is limited.

➤ You can't get out of most immediate annuity contracts today, although that is changing. Once you make your investment, you're stuck. You can't change the terms either.

News You Can Use

More and more insurance companies are coming out with new annuity plans specifically for people who want to make certain their money will last.

The Equitable's Accumulator variable annuity (800-789-7771), for example, lets you invest in mutual funds until you retire. It guarantees that your investment will grow at a minimum 6 percent annual rate. That's higher than most minimum guaranteed returns.

Hartford Life Insurance Company (800-862-6668) and Keyport Life Insurance Company (800-367-3654) both offer a new breed of immediate annuity. You receive income for a lifetime based on your mutual fund investments. The insurance companies, however, let you withdraw cash from the annuity if you need money, typically in exchange for a lower payout. This is a real help if you need money for medical expenses or if you want to give some of your money to family members before you die.

What if you're seriously ill and you need income? Canada Life (800-905-1959) has an immediate annuity for people who are expected to live five years or less. You must have medical proof from a doctor before you can get this kind of annuity.

Allianz Life Insurance Company (888-810-0881) offers the Family Income Legacy, a reversionary annuity, which is an insurance policy that pays a specific amount of monthly income to the policyholder's loved one for a lifetime when the policyholder dies. It bases your monthly insurance premium on the amount of income you want to replace from your pension or Social Security so your surviving spouse will have extra income to live on.

➤ With a fixed immediate annuity, your payments are fixed based on your life expectancy. As inflation increases over the years, the purchasing power of your annuity payments shrinks. You may or may not have this problem, however, with a variable immediate annuity because payments are based on the performance of the mutual funds you choose. Typically, variable immediate annuities have a rate floor of 3 percent to 5 percent.

➤ You have no federal guarantees with an immediate annuity. If you pick an insurance company that is financially weak today, it could be gone tomorrow. If you consider an immediate annuity, stick only with the safest insurance companies rated at least A+ by A.M. Best or B+ by Weiss Research and double A claims-paying by Standard & Poor's and Moody's.

Technobabble
If you take a **life only payout** from your pension, you get a bigger monthly check. However, when you die, your spouse gets nothing. If you take a **joint and survivor payout** option, you get a lower pension check. But when you die, your spouse continues to receive about 75 percent of your pension.

Hot Tip!
If you selected the joint and survivor payout on a pension and you outlive your spouse, you could find yourself short-changed on benefits. If there's any doubt about the health of your spouse, financial planners advise taking a lump-sum payment from the pension plan and transferring it into an IRA. This way, money can be paid out over your joint life expectancy when you reach age 70 1/2, resulting in higher payouts compared with payments from the pension plan. Plus, unlike with a pension plan, the IRA money goes to beneficiaries when the second spouse dies.

Putting Some Zip in Your Pension Checks

If you have a company pension, checking the right payout option can go a long way toward preserving your cash. Of course, you want both you and your spouse to get the most income possible out of it. The federal Employee Retirement Income Security Act (ERISA) provides two options to most married employees who are entitled to a pension from their employer.

Option A provides a lifetime pension for the retired employee, but if the employee dies before his or her spouse, the spouse gets nothing. This is known as the maximum pension or "life only" payout option.

By contrast, Option B, known as "the joint and survivor option," provides a reduced lifetime pension of about 20 percent for the retired employee. If the employee dies first, 50 to 75 percent of the monthly income is given to the surviving spouse. Most married couples opt for the joint and survivor option.

Financial planners say it could pay to investigate alternatives so that you don't necessarily give yourself a paycut in return for your spouse's continued income. One option to consider while you're still in your 50s is choosing the maximum pension payout and purchasing a cash value life insurance policy to provide death benefits to the surviving spouse. The proceeds from the policy would pay as much as or more than the surviving spouse would receive from the joint pension payout, yet the retired employee winds up with a larger monthly check. This idea can work if the pension has a low payout and insurance can be purchased at a reasonable cost.

A House Is Not a Home: Refinancing Your Mortgage

Still fearful your money won't last?

You can tap your home for cash when you retire through a *reverse mortgage*. With a reverse mortgage, you're actually taking out a loan against the equity in your home and receiving payments. Typically, you don't have to pay it back until you move, sell the home, or die. Depending upon the program you select, you can take out a lump-sum loan, or a credit line, which lets you draw on it only as needed. Most reverse mortgage programs require that you're at least in your 60s and preferably in your 70s.

Technobabble
A reverse mortgage enables you to receive monthly income based on the equity value or the principal you paid off on your home.

Often, with a reverse mortgage, you pay either an insurance fee or higher rate so that you needn't worry about paying back the loan when you die. Generally, the older you are and more equity you have in your home, the more you can borrow. Like any other loan, you need to compare rates and fees before signing on the dotted line.

Typically, the loan is repaid after your house is sold, or the balance comes out of your estate. Some lenders may also take a cut of your home's appreciation.

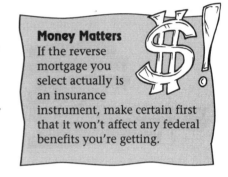

Money Matters
If the reverse mortgage you select actually is an insurance instrument, make certain first that it won't affect any federal benefits you're getting.

For more information, and an updated list of those offering reverse mortgages, send $1 and a self-addressed, stamped envelope to Reverse Mortgage Locator, Suite 115, 7373 147th St., Apple Valley, MN 55124.

Protect the Downside

Although we hope this book taught you a great deal about mutual fund investing, mutual fund investing should never be conducted in a vacuum. Nor are mutual funds the only investment to consider. Some experts, for example, advise that people in unusually high tax brackets consider adding single stocks to their holdings because they can more easily be bought and sold against each other to cut capital gains taxes. Owning real estate also is important. Remember, it's essential to keep some money in cash or the bank for an emergency.

Plus, you always need to make certain you have adequate health and life insurance. Otherwise, if you get sick or injured, you'll have to sell your hard-earned savings in mutual funds to pay your health care bills. You may be able to get health insurance, as well as some group life and disability insurance, as part of your employee benefits at your job. But the group life and disability insurance may be limited. Be sure to talk to an experienced insurance agent or financial planner.

If you're supporting a family, you need to consider disability insurance even if it's not among your employer's benefits. Disability insurance, which provides you with income if you can't do your job, should cover 50 percent to 70 percent of your gross income.

News You Can Use

When comparing disability insurance policies, it's important first to make certain the policy is non-cancelable and guaranteed renewable. This means the policy can't be changed or canceled without the policyholder's consent. Also, check for these features:

➤ Compare policy premiums.

➤ You should be able to collect benefits to at least age 65.

➤ Obtain a policy with a cost-of-living adjustment. This way, disability benefits should rise as inflation increases, but your premium stays the same.

➤ The policy should pay off if you can only return to work part-time.

➤ Make certain it pays if you can't perform in your particular line of work.

➤ You also should have the option to increase your coverage as your income rises—despite any medical problems you may have.

It's also important to consider long-term care insurance, which pays the bills if you need health care at home or have to go into a nursing home. Many companies are beginning to offer long-term care policies as part of an employee benefits package.

Almost one of four senior citizens end up in a nursing home for an average of 3 years at the cost of more than $40,000 a year.

Experts recommend that you start this type of insurance when you're between the ages of 50 and 60. If you're in your 40s and 50s, you can get coverage for as little as $50 to $80 a month that will pay for $150 a day in coverage either by a home health care aide or a nursing home. Once you're in your 60s and 70s, however, the cost can zoom to $200 monthly for coverage!

For up-to-date quotes on long-term care insurance prices, call Long Term Care Quote at 800-587-3279. As of this writing, the consensus among financial planners was that American Express Life Insurance Co., Fortis, John Hancock Mutual Life Insurance Co., CNA, and The Travelers Insurance have the best overall long-term care policies. But they also are the most expensive and may not necessarily fit everyone's needs.

On the life insurance side: If you have a family, you should consider getting 5 to 8 times your current wages in insurance coverage. If you make $50,000 a year, you should have about $250,000 in coverage.

Term insurance is the lowest cost coverage because you get insurance protection for a specific period of time, ranging from 1 year to 20 years.

Those who want more permanent coverage should consider *universal variable life insurance* (UVL), which covers you for as long as you live. Because the policy has a cash value or savings component, you can invest your cash value in a choice of stock, bond, and money market mutual funds for growth. Your life insurance protection will increase along with the growth of your mutual fund investments in the cash value account. In addition, you can borrow up to 90 percent of the cash value tax-free if you need cash, for example, to pay for your child's college education or to supplement your retirement.

The Least You Need to Know

➤ When you plan for retirement, be sure to calculate how much income you will get from Social Security.

➤ Consider withdrawals 5 to 6 percent from your non-retirement mutual funds annually.

➤ Evaluate ways to stretch out your pension and IRA paychecks.

➤ Be sure you have adequate insurance coverage. Otherwise. the doctors, hospitals. and nursing homes will take your lifesavings.

Managing Your Estate

If you think estate planning is only for the rich, think again. Anyone who has a family or business responsibilities needs some type of plan for his or her surviving loved ones. Besides, once you start applying the principles in this book, you'll be amazed at how your money will grow over the years!

You might already own a house, a car, some jewelry, and at least one collectible. (What about those marbles or the Monopoly game you used to play when you were a child? Those items still lodged in your attic all are starting to add up in value.)

A complete guide to estate planning may be beyond the scope of this book, but you certainly want your loved ones to reap the maximum benefits of your newly acquired investment prowess. This chapter reviews what to do so that your loved ones have the income and property they need when you're not around. Just think how much further ahead they'll be if you take the time to plan.

Where There's a Will...

The most common estate planning tool is a will. A will is a legal document that determines who will manage your estate, who will get your property and belongings, and who will become guardian of your minor children when you die.

If you die without a will, which is called dying *intestate*, the state determines who gets what and who takes care of your children when you are not around. You don't want the state making those decisions for you, do you? That's why it's important to register the ownership of your property, valuables, bank accounts, mutual funds, and other investments the right way with the help of a lawyer or financial planner. In this section, we'll focus on the ownership of your investments.

When you set up the family's mutual funds (as well as other securities), there are several ways to set up the accounts. You must be sure to claim the proper ownership of the investment. If you do it the wrong way, your heirs will end up paying income taxes that could have been avoided. (Later in the chapter, you'll learn about estate taxes.)

There are three ways to own property whether it's a mutual fund or a piece of real estate:

➤ **Outright ownership.** In this method, you own all of the property. Suppose you have $50,000 sitting in a mutual fund in your name. Your will can specify, for example, that you want your daughter to own the mutual fund. After your will is probated, the executor (the person you name to handle your estate) will transfer the fund to the person designated in the will.

Say your daughter, Lorraine, inherits your mutual fund. She does not have to pay income taxes on the inheritance. If she sells the mutual fund later, the cost of the investment for income tax purposes is based on the fair market value at the date of your death. Suppose you left Lorraine a no-load mutual fund worth $50,000. Lorraine's cost for tax purposes is $50,000. If she sells the fund a few years down the road for $55,000, she owes taxes on the $5,000 gain.

➤ **Joint tenancy with right of survivorship.** With this method, you own all the property with someone else. If you own a mutual fund jointly with your wife or husband, for example, the ownership automatically passes to the surviving spouse. You don't have to go through probate court as you do with a will. The ownership automatically transfers to the joint owner of the mutual fund.

When you die, the surviving owner does not pay income taxes on the inheritance. When he or she sells the mutual fund, however, he or she owes taxes on the sale of the mutual fund at a profit. Capital gains taxes are based on half the fund's value at the time of your death, plus the surviving owner's share of the investment, including reinvested dividends and interest.

➤ **Tenancy in common.** With the third method, you own part of the property, and you can give, sell, or leave your portion to others when you die. If you own a mutual fund under this form of ownership, you can designate in the will who gets that portion of the investment. Say you designate your best friend, Sam. Sam pays no income taxes on the inheritance. But if he sells those shares, the cost of the investment for income tax purposes is based on the fair market value at the date of your death.

It's a good idea to have your lawyer prepare a *durable power of attorney* and a *living will*.

The durable power of attorney delegates the power to handle your business and financial affairs should you become disabled or incapacitated. By selecting a trusted person to exercise this power, you may avoid interruptions in your business and financial matters. Without it, no one will be able to access your bank account, securities, or any other property in your name without resorting to lengthy legal proceedings.

A *living will* is a legal document prepared in advance of a serious illness that details your wishes about future health care.

Technobabble

Probate is the procedure by which state courts validate a will's authenticity. Once the will is approved, the property can be given to the heirs. An **executor** is the person named in the will to handle the estate and carry out other duties stated in the will.

By giving someone you trust **durable power of attorney**, you're legally giving that person authority to manage your affairs if you become ill or incapacitated. A **living will** is a legal document prepared in advance of a serious illness that details your wishes about future health care.

News You Can Use

Please note that accountants refer to the *basis* of an investment. Basis is the original cost of the investment, which is its purchase price less out-of-pocket expenses that must be reported to the Internal Revenue Service when an investment is sold. If a no-load mutual fund was purchased for $2,000 and it is sold today for $3,000, the basis is $2,000.

The basis is used when calculating the taxes due on long- and short-term capital gains. Long-term capital gains or losses are based on investments that are held for 18 months. Short-term capital gains or losses are investments that are held for less than 18 months.

A Matter of Trust

Trusts, which attorneys say are a bit more flexible than wills, have been gaining popularity as estate planning tools. A trust, like a will, is a written legal document. You have your money and other assets managed by a trustee so that your heirs get your assets when you die.

Some types of trusts enable you to save money by foregoing probate and letting you leave money directly to your heirs. You can transfer your existing mutual funds into a trust once it is set up. The *trustee*, the individual responsible for managing the trust, may also invest in new mutual funds. When you go to the great beyond, your estate will pass to your beneficiaries, based on the terms of the trust agreement.

Technobabble
A **trust** is a legal document similar to a will that does not have to be approved by probate court before your loved ones can inherit your wealth.

Other kinds of trusts can reduce your estate taxes and provide income to your spouse or children. However, these goals also might be accomplished by a will, and a trust is not always the right answer. A trust, like a will, is a written legal document. You have your money and other assets managed by a trustee so that your heirs get your assets when you die.

Trust and estate tax laws are complex, so before you act, seek the advice of an experienced attorney who specializes in trusts and estates.

Types of Trusts

Technobabble
There are two kinds of trusts. A **testamentary trust** is created within a will and takes effect when you die. A **living trust** or **inter vivos trust** operates when you are alive.

A trust can be set up as either revocable or irrevocable. Here's how the more popular trusts work:

> ➤ **Revocable living trust.** With a revocable living trust, you can avoid the costly process of probate, which, depending on the size of the estate, can cost several thousand dollars. You control a revocable living trust and can change the terms of the trust at any time. You can manage the assets or hire someone to manage the money based on the trust's instructions. In addition, you can distribute the assets in the trust to your loved ones, or you can keep the money in the trust for as long as you want.

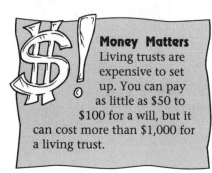

Money Matters
Living trusts are expensive to set up. You can pay as little as $50 to $100 for a will, but it can cost more than $1,000 for a living trust.

Living trusts have drawbacks. You cannot put all of your assets in a living trust. You might need a will for other property such as cars, household items, and jewelry. You can't get a mortgage from some lenders if the home is included in a family or living trust. Plus, although you avoid probate cost with a revocable living trust, the assets in the trust are considered part of your taxable estate. Your heirs might face a large tax bill if your estate is sizable.

➤ **Irrevocable trust.** You can reduce the tax bite in addition to avoiding probate with an irrevocable trust, but the terms of an irrevocable trust can't be changed. A trustee manages and distributes the assets of the trust based on the trust document. You give up ownership of any asset you place in this type of trust. That's why you save on taxes. Legally, the assets are considered gifts to your beneficiaries.

Irrevocable trusts also have drawbacks. They are expensive to set up. It might cost a few thousand dollars in legal fees. Once you establish an irrevocable trust, you can't change the terms of the trust. You're stuck.

➤ **Testamentary trust.** Testamentary trusts are used for special situations. For example, say you want to establish a fund to pay for your grand-children's education but believe they might squander the money. With a testamentary trust, you can see to it that they're taken care of. The will, containing instructions, goes to probate, and the trust is set up. A trustee then takes control of the assets. Assets in a testamentary trust are considered part of your taxable estate because you've had control of the money during your lifetime.

> **Money Matters**
> Be careful setting up a trust, warns Peter Strauss, New York attorney and author of the *Elder Law Handbook for Caregivers and Seniors*. You'd be surprised how many people spend $4,000 to draw up a trust but never retitle assets, Strauss says. As a result, you might have an operational trust without your assets in it!

Tax Planning for Naysayers

You could be very wrong if you think you'll never have enough money to worry about estate taxes. The number of taxpayers subject to estate taxes was expected to grow to almost 45 percent by the close of this century—from 80 tax filings per thousand taxpayers to 115 per thousand in 1999.

When you factor in your home and personal belongings, chances are you're worth a lot more than you think—or at least, you could be worth a bundle sooner than you think.

Starting in 1998, taxes must be paid on estates worth more than $625,000. The Taxpayer Relief Act of 1997 gradually increases this until it reaches $1 million in 2006. The inheritance tax ranges from 37 percent to 55 percent on estates worth more than $3 million. On top of that, you might also face state inheritance taxes.

Could you and your loved ones ultimately get socked with a big estate tax bill? Yes! The value of your assets could increase substantially, particularly if you have a good 10 years to retirement. Sit down with your accountant or financial advisor and look at the numbers now.

Ten Steps to Estate Planning

You need a game plan. Here are a few suggestions to help you and your loved ones handle the transition:

1. Take your financial inventory. Review your net worth, which is your total assets less your total liabilities.

2. Meet with an experienced CPA, financial planner, and attorney to help you set up an estate game plan.

3. Review your financial goals. Make sure you're saving for retirement and you have adequate life insurance and disability insurance coverage.

4. Decide who should inherit your money and property when you die. Ask yourself how much you want to leave your spouse, children, relatives, or friends.

5. Determine the cost of probating a will versus establishing a revocable or irrevocable living trust.

6. Review the tax ramifications. Estimate how much your estate will be worth by the time you die.

7. Look into ways you can cut the size of your taxable estate.

8. Make provisions to pay any estate taxes due. You might not think your heirs will owe the estate tax man, but over time, your assets could grow to more than $625,000.

9. Evaluate the cost of life insurance, which can be used to pay estate taxes.

10. If you set up a trust, make sure that it is valid. A trust agreement should include the following items: how the trust is managed and how the assets should be distributed, identification of the property in the trust, names of beneficiaries (those who will receive your assets), name of a trustee to manage the trust assets, and the terms of when the trust will end.

Our Guide to Living Happily Ever After

All this estate planning stuff isn't worth a hill of beans if you don't keep good records. Whether you are paying the bills or the tax man or hiring a lawyer to draw up a will, you need a lot of important information at your fingertips. Here are a few steps you can take to make life a little simpler:

➤ File all investments and bank statements you get in a drawer or filing cabinet. Make certain all members of your family know where to find them. Most recent statements should be readily available in a folder up front, where you can refer to them quickly if needed.

➤ Place your important lifelong documents in an unlocked, fireproof safe-deposit box. Lifelong documents include marriage certificates, copies of your will, passports, birth certificates, powers of attorney, living wills, deeds to your home, and so on. If these documents are removed for any reason whatsoever, they must immediately be replaced. Don't leave them sitting in a briefcase somewhere. Don't leave them in a purse.

Take some time to plan what will happen to your estate while you're alive. This way, you'll be sure your loved ones get exactly what you want them to have.

We congratulate you. You've learned about an awful lot of financial stuff. We've armed you not only with ways to make money in mutual funds, but also with ideas on how to preserve your cash. Now, it's time to take your cash to the freezer. (Just checking to see if you're still awake!)

Actually, the earlier you get to work on many of the principles we've outlined, the better. But don't give up the ship—even if you happen to be starting out late as an investor. After all, by reading this book and knowing the ins and outs of investing in mutual funds, you're further along than most.

We wish you good markets, happy investing and—particularly now that you're well-armed with ways to prolong your cash—a long and healthy life!

The Least You Need to Know

➤ You must have a will to make sure that the ones you love inherit what you want them to have.

➤ Give someone you trust durable power of attorney. Then, you know someone is available to manage your financial and medical affairs in the event you are seriously incapacitated.

➤ If you and your family are worth a few hundred thousand dollars, a living trust may serve you better than a will. Living trusts avoid probate.

➤ Use irrevocable trusts to reduce your estate tax bill.

Technobabble Glossary

m the earnings of your mutual fund to cover a fund's sales

expense Charge for maintaining your mutual fund ac-

ADV form Form on file with the Securities and Exchange Commission that contains important financial information about a Registered Investment Advisor.

Advisor **1.** Person or company responsible for making mutual fund investments. **2.** Organization employed by a mutual fund to give professional advice on the fund's investments and asset management practices. Also known as investment advisor.

Aggressive growth funds Mutual funds that strive for maximum growth as the primary objective.

Annual report Updates that detail performance for the year.

Annual return The percentage of change in a mutual fund's net asset value over a year's time, factoring in income dividend payments, capital gains, and reinvestment of these distributions.

Asset-allocation fund Balanced fund in which changes are made in the stock and bond percentage mix, based on the outlook for each market.

Automatic investment plan Program that allows you to have as little as $50 a month electronically deducted from your checking account and invested in the mutual fund of your choice.

Average price per share Most popular method of paying taxes on mutual fund sales, in which you calculate gains or losses by first figuring an average cost per share. You calculate the total cost of all the fund shares you own and divide that by the number of shares you own.

Balanced funds   Mutual funds that invest in both stocks and bonds, typically in relatively equal proportions.

Bankers Acceptance (BA)   Short-term loan to companies that export worldwide. It is secured by goods that are to be sold.

Bear market   Period during which the stock market loses more than 15 percent of its value.

Beta value   Measure of a fund's volatility. The lower the beta value, the less risky the fund.

Blue-chip stocks   Stocks issued by well-established companies that pay dividends.

Bond   A debt instrument issued by a company, city, or state, or the U.S. government or its agencies, with a promise to pay regular interest and return the principal on a specified date.

Bull market   Period during which the stock market moves higher for 12 months or longer.

Callable   Debt that may be redeemed before it matures.

Capital appreciation funds   Mutual funds that strive for maximum growth. Although these funds can earn the greatest gains, they also can rack up the heaviest losses. Also known as aggressive growth funds.

Capital gains   Profits on the sale of securities.

Certificates of Deposit (CDs)   Debt instruments issued by banks and thrifts.

Certified Financial Planner (CFP)   Financial planner who obtains a license issued by the College of Financial Planning. The designation shows that the financial planner has had training in budgeting, taxes, savings, and insurance.

Charitable lead trust   Legal document used to avoid estate taxes, in which the charity receives the investment income and the principal goes to the trust beneficiaries when you die.

Charitable remainder trust   Legal document set up with a charity, in which the charity pays you income for life. When you die, the money goes to the charity, tax-free.

Chartered Financial Consultant (ChFC)   Designation issued indicating completion of a program in financial, estate, and tax planning, in addition to investment management.

Chartered Life Underwriter (CLU)   Designation issued indicating training in life insurance and personal insurance planning.

Check-a-month plan   Program through which money is automatically taken out of your checking account and invested in your mutual fund.

Closed-end funds   Funds whose shares are traded on an exchange, similar to stocks. The price per share doesn't typically equal the net asset value of a share.

Commercial paper   Short-term loans to corporations.

Common stock   Unit of ownership in a public corporation with voting rights but with lower priority than either preferred stock or bonds if the company is ever liquidated.

Constant dollar investing   Investment strategy that preserves profits by periodic evaluation and adjustment of a portfolio. You maintain the same amount in your stock fund each year by channeling funds from and to a bond or money market fund.

Convertible bond funds   Mutual funds that invest in bonds that can be converted into stocks.

Corporate bonds   Debt instruments issued by corporations.

CPA Personal Financial Specialist (CPA, PFS)   Financial planning designation indicating that a Certified Public Accountant (CPA) has passed a tough financial planning exam administered by the American Institute of Certified Public Accountants.

Custodian   Bank or other financial institution that safeguards mutual fund securities and may respond to transactions only by designated fund officers.

Distributions   Dividends income and capital gains generally paid by mutual fund companies to their shareholders.

Diversification   Act of investing in different kinds of investments to lessen risk.

Diversified   Spread out, as among a variety of investments that perform differently.

Dividends   Profits that a corporation or mutual fund distributes to shareholders.

Dollar cost averaging   Strategy of making regular investments into a mutual fund and having earnings automatically reinvested. This way, when the share price drops, more shares are bought at lower prices.

Dow Jones Industrial Average   Model for the overall stock market that tracks the performance of 30 U.S. blue-chip stocks.

Equities   Investments in stocks.

Equity income funds   Mutual funds that favor investments in stocks that generate income over growth. As a result, they can be less risky than other types of stock funds.

Eurodollar CDs   CDs issued by U.S. banks that have branches in other countries. These tend to have higher yields than domestic CDs.

Ex-dividend date   Date on which the value of the income or capital gains distribution is deducted from the price of a fund's shares.

Face value   Value of a bond or note as given on the certificate. Corporate bonds are usually issued with $1,000 face values, municipal bonds with $5,000 face values, and government bonds, $1,000 to $10,000 face values. Also known as the principal.

Financial planner   Individual who helps establish a financial game plan. Although a financial planner may have certain licenses or designations indicating the extent of his or her training, there is no requirement that a financial planner have a license. Financial planners carry professional designations, such as CFP and ChFC.

First In, First Out (FIFO)   Basis for calculating the tax impact of mutual fund profits and losses that assumes shares sold are the oldest shares owned.

Fixed-income fund   Another term for a mutual bond fund.

Front-end loads   Sales commission paid to purchase shares of mutual funds.

General purpose money funds   Mutual funds that invest largely in bank CDs and short-term corporation IOUs called commercial paper.

Global funds   Mutual funds that invest in both the U.S. and foreign countries. Also known as world funds.

Government-only money funds   Mutual funds that invest in Treasury bills and short-term loans to the U.S. government. These are the least risky money funds because their investments are backed by Uncle Sam.

Growth and income funds   Mutual funds that own primarily blue-chip stocks of well-established companies that pay out a lot of dividends to their shareholders. These funds generally develop stock portfolios that balance the potential for appreciation with the potential for dividend income.

Growth funds   Mutual funds that invest in the stocks of well-established firms that are expected to be profitable and grow for years to come.

Hedging   Strategy of investing in one or more securities to protect yourself from potential losses in other investments.

High-quality corporate bond funds   Mutual funds that buy bonds issued by the nation's financially strongest companies.

High-yield bond funds   Risky bond mutual funds that invest in high-yield bonds of companies with poor credit ratings. The bonds are rated below triple B by Standard & Poor's and Moody's. Also known as junk bond funds.

Income   Periodic interest or dividend distributions obtained from a fund.

Income funds   Mutual funds that invest in higher-yielding stocks but may own some bonds. You get income first along with some growth. These funds usually invest in utility, telephone, and blue-chip stocks.

Inflation   Rise in prices of goods and services.

Inflation hedge   Term describing an investment that performs well when inflation heats up.

Installment investment strategy   Investment strategy in which you divide your investment among several mutual funds and make any new investments into the fund that performs the worst.

Insurance agent   Individual licensed to sell insurance.

Insured municipal bond funds   Mutual funds that invest in insured bonds issued by cities, towns, states, toll roads, schools, water projects, and hospitals. The interest income is tax-free, and the bonds are insured against default by large private insurance companies, such as American Municipal Bond Assurance Corp. (AMBAC) and Municipal Bond Insurance Association (MBIA).

Interest income   Earnings received, often from bonds.

Intermediate-term bond funds   Mutual funds that invest in bonds that mature in about 5 to 10 years.

International bonds   Debt instruments issued by foreign governments or corporations.

International funds   Mutual funds that invest in stocks or bonds of worldwide companies.

Investment banker   Firm that sells stocks or bonds to brokerages which, in turn, sell them to investors on a securities exchange.

Investment company   Firm that, for a management fee, invests pooled funds of small investors in securities appropriate for its stated investment objectives.

Investment objective   Description, included in a fund prospectus, of what a mutual fund hopes to accomplish.

Irrevocable trust   Legal document that allows you to avoid probate and reduce the tax bite. You give up ownership of any asset you place in this type of trust, and it can't be changed.

Junk bond funds   Mutual funds that invest in bonds issued by companies or governments that are rated below triple B by Standard and Poor's or Moody's. Also know as high-yield bond funds.

Long-term bond funds   Mutual funds that invest in bonds that mature in more than 10 years.

Management fee   Charge for running the fund.

Market timing   Strategy by which investors attempt to buy low and sell high by buying when the market is turning bearish and selling at the end of a bull market.

Maturity date   Date that a bond is due for payoff.

Money market mutual fund   Mutual fund that invests typically in short-term government and company loans and CDs. These tend to be lower yielding but less risky than most other types of funds. Also known as money market funds or money funds.

Municipal bond funds   Mutual funds that invest in tax-exempt bonds issued by states and local governments.

Net asset value (NAV)   Per-share value of your fund's investments. Also known as share price.

No-load mutual fund   Mutual fund that is sold without sales commission.

No-transaction fee account   Brokerage firm account that allows customers to purchase a selection of mutual funds with no charge or a limited charge.

Note   Another word for short-term bond.

Open-end funds   Funds that permit ongoing purchase and redemption of fund shares (mutual funds are open-end funds).

Over-the-counter market   Market that uses a network of brokers rather than an exchange to buy and sell securities.

Portfolio manager   Person responsible for making mutual fund investments.

Precious metals mutual fund   Mutual funds that invest in precious metals and mining stocks.

Preferred stock   Type of stock that takes priority over common stock in the payment of dividends or if the company is liquidated.

Principal   Original investment.

Prospectus   Legal disclosure document that spells out information you need to know to make an investment decision on a mutual fund or other security.

Rebalancing   Investment strategy in which you adjust your mix of investments periodically to keep the proper percentages of money in each fund, based on your tolerance for risk.

Regional funds   Mutual funds that invest in one specific region of the globe.

Registered Investment Advisor   Person registered with state or federal securities regulators to manage money.

Registered representative   Person licensed to sell stocks, bonds, mutual funds, and other types of securities.

Repurchase agreements   Generally, overnight loans secured by U.S. Treasury securities.

Risk   In relation to a mutual fund, chances of losing money.

Risk tolerance   Amount of money you can stomach losing in a given year.

S&P 500 index   Measure of the performance of a large group of blue-chip stocks in the U.S.

Salary reduction plan or 401(k) plan   Retirement plan that allows employees to have a percentage of their salaries withheld and invested prior to the payment of federal taxes. Often, the employer might match the contribution, and earnings are tax-deferred until retirement.

Secondary market   Market wherein bonds, stocks, or other securities are bought and sold after they're already issued.

Securities   Stocks, bonds, or rights to ownership, such as options, typically sold by a broker.

Securities and Exchange Commission (SEC)   U.S. government agency in charge of regulating mutual funds and other securities.

Securities exchange   Tightly regulated marketplace where stocks, bonds, and cash are traded.

Share   Unit of ownership.

Shareholder   One who owns shares. In a mutual fund, this person has voting rights.

Short-term bond funds   Mutual funds that generally invest in bonds that mature in less than three years.

Simplified Employee Pension Plan (SEP)   Retirement plan that permits tax-deferred investments for self-employed individuals.

Single-country funds   Mutual funds or closed-end funds that invest in one country.

Single-estate municipal bond funds   Mutual funds that invest in the bonds of a single state so that investors avoid paying both state and federal taxes on their interest income.

Small company stock funds   Volatile mutual funds that invest in younger companies whose stocks are frequently traded on the over-the-counter stock market.

Socially responsible funds   Mutual funds that invest in companies that don't pollute the environment or sell arms. They will not own tobacco or alcohol stocks, nor invest in companies with poor employee relations.

Specialty funds   Funds that invest in one specific industry or industry sector.

Speculation   Gambling on a risky investment in hopes of a high payoff down the road.

Stock   Investment that buys ownership in a corporation in exchange for a portion of that company's earnings and assets.

Stock fund builder   Investment strategy in which you invest your bond fund's interest income into a stock fund to build your wealth.

Stockbroker   Person licensed to sell stocks and other types of securities. Also known as a registered representative.

Swap   Switch, as in what bond fund managers do to obtain higher-yielding bonds that have credit ratings similar or equal to their existing bonds.

Tax-deferred investment   An investment that is not taxed until money is withdrawn, usually at retirement.

Tax-free bond funds   Tax-free mutual funds that invest in municipal bonds issued by states, cities, and towns.

Taxable bond funds   Bond mutual fund in which interest income is taxed by Uncle Sam.

Testamentary trust   Legal document set up by a will when a person dies that is used for special situations, such as to establish a fund to pay for a child's education.

Total return   The rate of return on an investment, including reinvestment of distributions.

Transfer agent   Entity that maintains shareholder records, including purchases, sales, and account balances.

Treasury bills   Short-term IOUs to the U.S. Treasury.

Trust   Legal document that does not have to be approved by probate court before your loved ones can inherit your wealth.

Uniform Gift to Minors Act (UGMA)   Law adopted in most states that sets rules for distribution of an investment to a child.

Uniform Transfer to Minors Act (UTMA)   Law in some states that governs how a child takes custody of an asset.

Uninsured high-quality municipal bond funds   Mutual funds that invest in the least risky municipal bonds. These bonds are rated single A to triple A, but they are not insured.

Uninsured high-yield municipal bond funds   Mutual funds that pay the highest tax-free yields but invest in states or municipalities with lower credit ratings.

U.S. government agency bonds   Debt instruments issued by federally sponsored agencies of the U.S. government.

U.S. Treasury bond funds   Mutual funds that invest in U.S. Treasury bonds and notes.

U.S. Treasury bonds   Debt instruments directly backed by the U.S. Treasury.

U.S. Treasury-only money funds   Funds that invest in Treasury bills, or T-bills, which are short-term IOUs to the U.S. Treasury. These funds typically pay the lowest yields but are considered the least risky money funds.

U.S. Treasury securities   Generally, Treasury notes, bills, or bonds issued and guaranteed by the U.S. government.

Value averaging investing   Investment strategy in which you always make sure that the value of your fund increases by a specific amount over a specific time period.

Variable annuities   Insurance program that allows you to direct your investment in a choice of mutual funds. Meanwhile, you get tax deferment of your earnings and a death benefit guarantee, and you are able to obtain periodic checks for life.

Wash sale   Strategy in which a security is bought back within 31 days after it is sold, washing out any capability of writing off losses on income taxes.

World funds   Mutual funds that invest in both the U.S. and foreign countries. Also known as global funds.

Yankee dollar CDs   Debt instruments issued by some of the largest foreign banks in the world that have offices in the United States. They often yield slightly more than U.S. bank CDs.

Yield   Interest or market earnings on a bond or other investment.

Zero coupon Treasury bond funds   Mutual funds that invest in a certain type of Treasury securities that provide no monthly income, but, instead pay the investor accumulated income and principal at the bond's maturity.

Resources

Mutual Fund Newsletters

Dow Theory Forecasts
7412 Calumet Ave.
Hammond, IN 46324

Fabians Investment Resource
P.O. Box 2538
Huntington Beach, CA 92647

Fidelity Insight
Mutual Fund Investors Association
P.O. Box 9135
Wellesley Hills, MA 02181

Fund Exchange
1200 Westlake Ave. N.
Suite 700
Seattle, WA 98109

Growth Fund Guide
Growth Fund Research Building
Box 6600
Rapid City, SD 57709

Income Fund Outlook
The Institute for Econometric Research
2200 SW 10th St.
Deerfield Beach, FL 33442

InvesTech Mutual Fund Advisor
2472 Birch Glen
Whitefish, MT 59937

Jay Schabacker's Mutual Fund Investing
7811 Montrose Rd.
Potomac, MD 20854

Moneyletter and Income Investing
290 Eliot St.
P.O. Box 9104
Ashland, MA 01721

Mutual Fund Forecaster
The Institute for Econometric Research
2200 SW 10th St.
Deerfield Beach, FL 33442

Mutual Fund Letter
Investment Information Services, Inc.
12514 Starkey Rd
Largo, FL 34643

Mutual Fund Performance Reports
CDA/Wiesenberger
1355 Piccard Drive
Rockville, MD 20850

No Load Fund Analyst
300 Montgomery St.
Suite 621
San Francisco, CA 94104

No Load Fund Investor
P.O. Box 318
Irvington-on-Hudson, NY 10533

No Load Fund X
235 Montgomery St.
Suite 662
San Francisco, CA 94104

The Sagami Report
4176 Burns Road
Palm Beach Gardens, FL 33410

Sector Funds Newsletter
P.O. Box 270048
San Diego, CA 92198

Stockmarket Cycles
P.O. Box 6873
Santa Rosa, CA 95406

Investment Regulatory Agencies

State Securities Agencies

Alabama Securities Commission
334-242-2984

Alaska Department of Commerce &
Economic Development
Division of Banking, Securities &
Corporations
907-465-4242

Arizona Corporation Commission
Securities Division
602-542-4242

California Department of Corporations
213-736-2495

Colorado Division of Securities
303-894-2320

Connecticut Department of Banking
203-240-8230
800-831-7225

Delaware Department of Justice
Division of Securities
302-577-2515

District of Columbia Services Commission
Securities Division
202-626-5105

Florida Office of the Comptroller
Division of Securities
904-488-9805
800-848-3792

Georgia Office of the Secretary of State
Securities Division
Information: 404-656-2695
Complaints: 404-656-3920

Hawaii Department of Commerce &
Consumer Affairs Securities Commission
808-589-2730

Idaho Department of Finance
Securities Bureau
208-334-3684

Illinois Office of the Secretary of State
Securities Department
217-782-2256
800-628-7937

Indiana Office of the Secretary of State
Securities Division
317-232-6681
800-223-8791

Iowa Department of Commerce
Insurance Division
Iowa Securities Bureau
515-281-4441

Kansas Securities Commission
913-296-3307

Kentucky Department of Financial
Institutions
Division of Securities
502-573-3390
Requests for information must be in writing:
Department of Financial Institutions
477 Versailles Rd.
Frankton, KY 40401
Attn: David Ashley

Louisiana Securities Commission
504-568-5515
Requests for information must be in writing:
Louisiana Securities Commission
Energy Centre
1100 Poydras St. Suite 2250
New Orleans, LA 70163

Maine Department of Professional &
Financial Regulation
Bureau of Banking
Securities Division
207-582-8760

Maryland Attorney General's Office
Division of Securities
410-576-6360

Massachusetts Secretary of the
Commonwealth
Securities Division
617-727-3548

Michigan Department of Commerce
Corporation and Securities Bureau
517-334-6200

Minnesota Department of Commerce
Information: 612-296-2283
Complaints: 612-296-2488

Mississippi Office of the Secretary of State
Securities Division
601-359-6364
800-804-6364

Missouri Office of the Secretary of State
Securities Division
314-751-4136
800-721-7996

Montana Office of the State Auditor
Securities Department
406-444-2040
800-332-6148

Nebraska Department of Banking &
Finance
Bureau of Securities
402-471-3445

Nevada Office of the Secretary of State
Securities Division
702-486-2440
800-758-6440

New Hampshire Bureau of Securities
Regulation
603-271-1463
800-994-4200

New Jersey Department of Law and
Public Safety
Bureau of Securities
201-504-3600

New Mexico Regulation & Licensing
Department
Securities Division
505-827-7140
800-704-5533

New York Department of Law
Bureau of Investor Protection and Securities
212-416-8200
Requests for information must be in writing:
New York State Department of Law
Bureau of Investor Protection and Securities
120 Broadway, 23rd Floor
New York, NY 10271
Attn: Alice McInerney

North Carolina Office of the Secretary of State
Securities Division
919-733-3924
Complaints: 800-668-4507

North Dakota Office of the Securities
Commissioner
701-328-2910
800-297-5124

Ohio Division of Securities
614-644-7381

Oklahoma Department of Securities
405-235-0230

Oregon Department of Consumer &
Business Services
Division of Finance & Corporate Securities
503-378-4387

Pennsylvania Securities Commission
717-787-8061
800-600-0077

Rhode Island Department of Business
Regulation
Securities Division
401-277-3048

South Carolina Securities Division
803-734-1087

South Dakota Division of Securities
605-773-4823

Tennessee Department of Commerce
& Insurance
Securities Division
Information: 615-741-3187
Complaints: 615-741-5900

Texas State Securities Board
512-305-8332

Utah Department of Commerce
Division of Securities
801-530-6600
800-721-3233

Vermont Department of Banking,
Insurance & Securities
Securities Division
802-828-3420

Virginia State Corporation Commission
Division of Securities & Retail Franchising
804-371-9051

Washington Department of Financial
Institutions
Securities Division
360-902-8760

West Virginia's State Auditor's Office
Securities Division
304-558-2257

Wisconsin Office of the Commissioner
of Securities
800-472-4325

Wyoming Secretary of State
Securities Division
State Capitol Bldg.
Cheyenne, Wyoming 82002
307-777-7370

National Regulators

Commodity Futures Trading Commission
202-254-3067 (Enforcement Division)

National Association of Securities Dealers
202-728-8000 (Main)
800-289-9999 (Information about brokers and firms)

National Futures Association
Disciplinary Information Access Line (DIAL)
200 W. Madison St.
Suite. 1600
Chicago, Illinois 50505
800-621-3570 (National)
800-572-9400 (in Illinois)

U.S. Securities and Exchange Commission
202-942-7040 (Main)
800-SEC-0330 (Complaints/consumer information)

Authors' Picks: Mutual Funds That Have Withstood the Test of Time

Although past performance is no guarantee of future results, there is something to be said for mutual funds that have withstood the test of time. What follows is a list of load and no-load growth and income funds and balanced funds that have done well for more than five decades ending in mid-year 1995, according to CDA/Wiesenberger. These funds are also rated as above average for return and below average for risk by Morningstar.

Stock Funds

➤ **Investment Company of America.** Over the 54 years ending in 1994, this growth and income fund grew at an annual average total return of 12.31 percent. Over the past three years ending in 1997, the fund grew at a 26.4 percent annual average total return. The fund is rated above average for return and below average for risk by Morningstar, Inc. It invests in large company stocks for the long term. The fund has a 5.75 percent front-end load.

➤ **Fidelity Fund.** Over the past 54 years ending in 1994, this growth and income fund grew at an annual average total return of 11.78 percent. Over the past three years ending in 1997, the fund's annual average total return gained 28.1 percent. It is also rated above average for return and below average for risk by Morningstar. Stocks held by the fund include IBM, Scott Paper, Tyco International, and Viacom. The fund is no-load.

➤ **Safeco Equity Fund.** Over the past 54 years ending in 1994, this growth and income fund grew at an annual average total return of 11.43 percent. Over the past three years, the fund grew at an annual average total return of 24.8. This fund rates high for return and average for risk.

Presently, the fund is invested primarily in mid-sized companies that are either undervalued or have strong earnings growth. Stocks in the portfolio include GTE, US West, Motorola, and Salomon Brothers. The fund is no-load.

➤ **Fundamental Investors.** Over the past 54 years ending in 1994, this growth and income fund grew at an annual average total return of 10.93. Over the past three years ending in 1997, the fund has grown at a 26.8 percent annual average total return. Its return is rated above average. Its risk is rated below average. The fund focuses on companies that should benefit from changing economic conditions. Holdings include Capital Cities/ABC, Intel, Federal Express, and Walt Disney. The fund has a 5.75 percent load.

➤ **Lexington Corporate Leaders.** This growth and income fund grew at a 10.3 percent annual average total return over the past 54 years ending in 1994. Over the past three years, the fund's annual average total return was 28 percent. The fund is rated above average for return and below average for risk. The fund has invested in the same 30 blue chip stocks for over five decades. Holdings include Eastman Kodak, Mobil, Exxon, Sears Roebuck, General Electric, and AT&T. The fund is no-load.

Balanced Funds

➤ **Delaware Fund.** This balanced fund has grown at an annual average total return of 10.8 over the past 54 years ending in 1994. Over the past three years, it has grown at an annual average total return of 21.31 percent. The fund invests in larger companies that are expected to increase their dividends. The fund invests about 40 percent in intermediate-term bonds rated A or above by Standard & Poor's and Moody's. For these reasons, this fund typically pays a higher dividend yield than similar funds. There is a 5.75 load.

➤ **American Balanced Fund.** This balanced fund has grown at an annual average total return of 9.65 percent since 1940 ending in 1994. Over the past three years, the fund has grown at an annual average total return of 16.2 percent. The fund buys undervalued blue chip stocks and intermediate-term investment grade bonds. There is a 5.75 percent load.

➤ **CGM Mutual.** This balanced fund has grown at an annual average total return of 9.44 percent since 1940 ending in 1994. Over the past three years, it has grown at an annual average total return of 18.5 percent. This is an aggressive balanced fund that can invest up to 75 percent in stocks. The fund looks for undervalued blue chip or smaller company stocks. The fund is no-load.

➤ **George Putnam Fund.** This balanced fund has grown at an annual average total return of 9.38 percent since 1940 ending in 1994. Over the past three years, it has grown at an annual average total return of 22.3 percent. The fund can invest up to 75 percent of its assets in stocks. The fund wants to own undervalued stock in large companies that should show improved earnings. On the bond side, it invests in higher-yielding corporate bonds. The fund has a 5.75 percent load.

➤ **Dodge & Cox Balanced.** This balanced fund has grown at an annual average total return of 9.2 percent since 1940 ending in 1994. Over the past three years, it has grown at an annual average total return of 21.2 percent. The fund may invest up to 75 percent of assets in stocks. It also invests in longer-term government and investment grade corporate bonds. The fund buys undervalued stocks with the potential of registering strong earnings growth. This is a no-load mutual fund.

➤ **Vanguard Wellington.** This balanced fund has grown at an annual average total return of 9.02 percent since 1940 ending in 1994. Over the past three years, the fund has grown at an annual average total return of 23.9 percent. The fund can invest 60 to 70 percent in stocks. The fund invests in undervalued large company stocks that pay high dividends and should appreciate in value. On the bond side, the fund sticks with government securities and high-grade corporate bonds. The fund is no-load.

The 10 Most Popular Funds: How Have They Done?

You can see why people like these funds. In recent years, they've all had double-digit returns. In addition, they all have performed well historically. The following table summarizes the performance of the 10 most popular funds. (Source: Lipper Analytical Services.)

Fund Name	Assets (Billions)	Objective	Annual Return, 3 Years Ending December 31, 1997
Fidelity Magellan	$64	Growth	26.6%
Investment Company of America	$38	Growth and income	26.5%
Washington Mutual Investors	$38	Growth and Income	31.7%
Fidelity Puritan	$23	Balanced	19.6%
Vanguard Windsor	$21	Growth and income	26.1%
Income Fund of America	$19	Income	22.0%
American Century Ultra	$22	Aggressive growth	24.5%
Janus Fund	$19	Growth	23.9%
Fidelity Growth & Income	$37	Growth and income	28.4%
Vanguard Index 500 Portfolio	$49	Growth and income	31.3%
Other Indexes			
S&P 500			31.3%
Treasury bills			5.45%
Lehman Brothers Aggregate Bond Index			10.4%

Mutual Fund Problem Solver

You know the old saying, "If things can go wrong, they will." When it comes to your hard-earned cash, any mistakes can wind up being more expensive than you'd like.

Fortunately, some of the most common mutual fund problems can be nipped in the bud by taking a few simple steps up front. Here's how to handle some of the most common headaches you might experience with your mutual fund:

➤ *Problem:* You need to sell your mutual fund, and the fund group's toll-free numbers are tied up.

Avoid this situation by taking these steps when you first open your account. Always get a non-toll-free number for the mutual fund. Also get the fund's street address where fund transactions are handled (not a post office box number). Then, have an overnight express-mail letter ready to send the fund group in the event you want to sell. Before you send express mail, however, call the fund's non-toll-free phone number. It may cost you a few dollars, but it's cheaper than express mail.

➤ *Problem:* The fund service representative made a mistake on your order.

Again, take some advance action while you're conducting the transaction. Make it a practice to keep a record of the time, date, and name of the person who handled your order. Most mutual fund groups record your transactions. Next, find the name of the service representative's supervisor. Speak to the supervisor and put your request in writing. If you have access to a fax machine, zip him or her a letter with your problem. Your problem should be resolved.

➤ *Problem:* You are supposed to receive a check from your fund, and it gets lost in the mail.

Call the toll-free number listed on your mutual fund statement. This will put you in touch with a service representative, who, upon hearing your problem, should be able to stop payment on the check and issue a new one. Be sure to verify that they have your correct address.

➤ *Problem:* You change your mind about a trade.

You can revoke an order if you call the fund before 4 p.m. E.S.T. the same day. That's the time the fund group settles its transactions.

➤ *Problem:* You've transferred your IRA or retirement plan to a mutual fund family from another financial institution. It's delayed.

This happens frequently. Sometimes, it can take a few weeks for a transfer to be completed due to misplaced instructions or computer foul-ups. If it's been more than five business days and you haven't heard from your new fund group confirming completion of the transaction, call and ask what the problem is. Your new fund group should call the other institution and then call you back.

What if nothing happens? Call your old fund group and talk to the supervisor of the department that handles transfers. Explain your problem. Then, follow up with a letter. It may take some time, but paperwork problems should be solved.

➤ *Problem:* You've lost some of the mutual fund statements, and you need the information on shares you bought in the past for tax purposes.

Call your fund. Most groups have at least 10 years' worth of data about your investments. It may take time to fish it out of the computer or other records, so be patient and don't wait until the last minute to do your taxes.

➤ *Problem:* You need to stop payment on a money fund or bond fund check.

Just call the fund. Be sure you have the date, check number, and amount of the check. The fund family either will do it for you or give you the toll-free number of the mutual fund's custodian bank. Some funds charge $10 to stop payment on a money fund or bond fund check. Others will stop payment free of charge.

➤ *Problem:* You've got a beef with your broker or financial planner. Perhaps the financial advisor put you in unsuitable mutual funds, funds that don't fit your investment objective or tolerance for risk. Maybe an advisor keeps switching you from one fund to another to make fat commissions.

Again, avoid this problem from the beginning by conducting all your transactions in writing. Note dates and times of your trades. Keep copies. Complain to your broker or financial planner briefly in writing, documenting the precise trades and times, and solicit a written response. If you get no relief, try the person's supervisor. Explain the situation. Still no satisfaction? File a complaint with your state's securities division (listed in Appendix B, "Resources").

If you're still not satisfied and your dispute is with an individual licensed by the National Association of Securities Dealers (NASD), there's more hope. You can arbitrate with the NASD. Call 212-480-4881 to obtain an arbitration kit. This material shows you how to file a legal complaint with a securities arbitration committee, which will hear your case and determine whether you should be compensated. The cost of arbitration depends on the amount of your claim. It's also a good idea to consult with an attorney before you act.

Index

J

K

N

O

353

X-Z